Inside
City Parks

Peter Harnik

**Urban Land
Institute**

THE
TRUST
FOR
PUBLIC
LAND

About ULI–the Urban Land Institute

ULI–the Urban Land Institute is a nonprofit education and research institute that is supported and directed by its members. Its mission is to provide responsible leadership in the use of land in order to enhance the total environment.

ULI sponsors education programs and forums to encourage an open international exchange of ideas and sharing of experiences; initiates research that anticipates emerging land use trends and issues and proposes creative solutions based on that research; provides advisory services; and publishes a wide variety of materials to disseminate information on land use and development. Established in 1936, the Institute today has more than 15,000 members and associates from more than 50 countries representing the entire spectrum of the land use and development disciplines.

Richard M. Rosan
President

ULI Project Staff

Rachelle L. Levitt
Senior Vice President, Policy and Practice
Publisher

Gayle Berens
Vice President, Real Estate Development Practice
Project Director

Oliver Jerschow
Research Associate

Nancy H. Stewart
Director, Book Program
Managing Editor

Bita Lanys
Manuscript Editor

Helene Y. Redmond
HYR Graphics
Book Design/Layout

Kim Rusch
Map Design

Meg Batdorff
Graphic Designer
Cover Design

Diann Stanley-Austin
Director, Publishing Operations

Maria Rose Cain
Word Processor

About the Trust for Public Land

The Trust for Public Land (TPL) is a private, nonprofit land conservation organization that works nationwide to conserve land for people. Founded in 1972, TPL specializes in real estate, applying its expertise in planning, negotiation, public finance, and law to protect land for public use. Working with private landowners, communities, and government agencies, TPL has helped protect more than 1 million acres nationwide for people to enjoy as parks, playgrounds, community gardens, recreation areas, historic landmarks, and wilderness lands.

In 1999 TPL launched its Greenprint for Growth campaign to conserve land as a way to guide growth, protect air and water, and ensure a high quality of life in communities nationwide. Through its work in almost 30 cities, TPL is increasing awareness of the vital role of parks and open space in the quality of urban life; generating funding to create, improve, and maintain urban parks; and protecting public open spaces that preserve and celebrate a city's unique heritage. TPL seeks to bring the best techniques of American business to bear on the unique problems of conserving open space, lending creativity and citizen involvement to the process.

William B. Rogers
President

Recommended bibliographic listing:
Harnik, Peter. *Inside City Parks.* Washington, D.C.: ULI–the Urban Land Institute, 2000.

ULI Catalog Number: I12
International Standard Book Number: 0-87420-832-7
Library of Congress Catalog Card Number: 00-105574

Cover photo: ©Pat Powers and Cherryl Schafer/Photodisc

Acknowledgments

THIS BOOK began back in 1996, with a remarkably simple question: What is the largest city park in the United States?

The rather astonishing difficulty of answering that query opened my eyes to the dearth of data about urban parks. Numbers that are available about national parks in every schoolchild's almanac cannot be found anywhere for city parks—not in an almanac, not in a technical directory, not even in the Library of Congress. I realized that this lack of basic data is one reason for the underfunding and undervaluing of city parks. In modern life, things that are important are counted, things that aren't are not. If we are to improve our cities' parks, I believed, we need to start with better numbers.

The person who enabled this idle speculation to become a full-fledged two-year research project and who also expanded the scope of the book from mere number crunching to a much higher level of inquiry and analysis is Kathy Blaha, vice president for national programs at the Trust for Public Land (TPL). Kathy's commitment to urban parks, her ability to synthesize disparate facts into a truly understandable message, and her unfailing willingness to talk through (and solve) every conceivable hurdle carried me past the many pitfalls that threatened the completion of this book.

The other person who was instrumental in turning the idea into reality is Gayle Berens, vice president of real estate development practice at ULI–the Urban Land Institute. Gayle, who in 1997 was also project director and coauthor of the first joint ULI–TPL book, *Urban Parks and Open Space*, not only is ULI's leading exponent of city parks but also is a true professional when it comes to creating books that are attractive, readable, and marketable.

Special thanks are also due the Wallace–Reader's Digest Funds for support of research and database development; the Graham Foundation for support of historical research and interviews; and EDAW, Inc., for helping with costs of publishing.

I owe a large debt of gratitude to the wisdom and the ideas of the 25 able members of my advisory board, who generously gave of their time and experience and played a key role in scoping the purposes and style of the book. (The full list of advisers is on page vi.) I also benefited from the writings and impressive research on city parks done by amateur historian Richard Amero, who literally blazed a trail for me to follow.

This book would never have been possible without the long hours of research, telephoning, and computer entry by my three hardworking interns, Jonah Zern, Lynda Frost, and Mark Jafar. And it would not have looked as good graphically without the skilled mapping assistance of Betsy Van Buskirk and photo-finding assistance of Oliver Jerschow.

I want to specially thank the people who generously gave of their time and knowledge in showing me around the park systems of the cities I visited in person: John Anderson in St. Louis, Darryl Baker in Dallas, Carol Drummond in San Diego, Ray Irvin and Joe Wynns in Indianapolis, Tom Jenretta in Baltimore, Larry Kaplan and Patrick Kennedy in Los Angeles, Steve Lampone in Kansas City, T. J. Newman in Phoenix, Jess Parrett and Jack Wilson in Cincinnati, Walt Stankas in Philadelphia, Lynn Tyler in Denver, and Bill Walker in Portland.

And finally, my thanks to the more than 200 other people who helped with information, photographs, maps, statistics, analysis, insight, and everything else that went into this book.

iv

All errors of fact or interpretation are, of course, mine, but none of this fact-gathering would have been possible if it weren't for the following individuals:

Joe Abrahams
Kent Anderson
Brenda Andrews
Stephanie Bell Andrews
Larry Annett
Myrna Antonio-Hall
Jerry Arbes
Julia Bachrach
Wayne Bain
Amy Baker
Mike Baker
Becky Ballenger
Marcia Bansley
Glenda Barrett
David Beach
Jeanie Beal
Gary Bess
Joan Blaustein
Peter Bocher
Matt Bohan
Tiffany Bohee
Donna Boley
Kenneth Bounds
Mary Bourguignon
Frank Bracken
Mike Bradshaw
John Brennan
B. J. Brooks
Carol Brown
Margaret Brown
Stephanie Parham Brown
Tom Bruns
Jim Burke
Tim Burke
Ernest Burkeen
Valerie Burns
Greg Bush
Kyle Campbell
Alonzo Carmichael
Jackie Carrera
Pauline Chan
Meg Cheever
Dennis Choquette
Jane Christyson
Barb Clint
Jim Cloare
Laura Cohen
James Colley
Ernest Cook
Elizabeth Cooke
Robin Corathers
Darla Cravotta
Ted Curtis

Mary Dahl
Dave Dahlstrom
Dan Dailey
Marsha Davis
Eddie Dengg
Sushma Dersch
Jim Desmond
Jerry Dettore
Rick Dewees
Kathie Dickhut
Dave Dionne
Lisa Dix
Ira Domsky
Terry Dopson
Mignette Dorsey
Steve Durant
Blake Early
Lee Echols
Bob Elliott
Bruce Engler
Leon Eplan
Donna Ernstson
Ann Fanton
Carey Feierabend
Esther Feldman
Ross Ferlita
Ron Fitzpatrick
Pete Fowler
Yvette Freeman
Stan Fye
Mike Gable
Patti Gallagher
Dave Gamstetter
Charlotte Gillis
Stephen Glazer
Gail Goldberg
Marta Goldsmith
Tony Gomez
Roberto Gonzales
Anita Gorman
Curt Green
Carol Grimaldi
Heidi Grunman
Tom Hahn
Bob Hall
Ann Hamilton
Barry Hannigan
Carrie Hansen
Bill Harvey
Wink Hastings
Sam Hays
Richard Heath
John Henderson

Peg Henderson
Teri Hershey
Heidi Hickman
Eloise Hirsch
John Hoal
Kevin Hobbs
Jenny Hoffner
Anne Howell
Warren Huang
Charles Hudson
Jean Hunt
Eric Iffrig
Vicky Israel
Patti Jencks
Jon Jensen
Gail Johnson
Charles Jordan
Charlotte Kahn
John Karel
Bill Keller
Patrick Kennedy
Ann Kerman
Don Kinney
Bob Kipp
Chris Knopf
Kurt Kocher
Richard Konisiewicz
Ron Kraus
Paul Labovitz
Walt Ladwig
Joshua Laird
Henry Lee
Nancy Lee
Ann Lennart
John Leshy
Katherine Lewis
Justine Liff
Marian Lindberg
Jack Linn
Ben Long
Dave Lutz
Maude Lyon
Beryl Magilevy
Melinda Malloy
Joanne Mangano
James Mann
Robert Marans
Brenda Marshall
Ernie Martin
Jose Matas
Ed McBreyer
Bob McCabe
Barbara McCann

Debbie McCown
Dan McGuire
Marcia McLatchy
Joyce Mendez
Ron Merlo
Blanca Mesa
Sheila Metcalf
Carolyn Williams Meza
Sally Michel
Bill Mifflin
Ari Millas
Julie Moffat
Kevin Mooney
Chuck Moore
James Moore
Gary Mormino
Tom Murphy
Janet Neal
Rex Nelson
Randy Neufeld
Paul Nice
Lee Nichols
Mike Nicoson
Arlene Nordin
Julia O'Brien
Roksan Okan-Vic
Tom Overton
Jim Parham
Tom Perchalski
Frank Perrelli
Laura Perry
Paula Peters
Cordelia Pierson
Pat Plocek
Eldon Pon
Dave Prather
Darrell Pray
Chuck Preston
George Price

George Puzak
Genevieve Ray
Bob Reeds
Marcia Reiss
Julie Riley
Joel Robinson
Mary Roby
Chris Rogers
Tony Rogers
Maytrei Roy
Al Ruder
Chris Ryer
Henry Saavedra
Margine Sako
Helen Sandalls
Harriet Saperstein
Tim Schmand
Steve Schuckman
Randy Sederquist
Rick Sessinghaus
V. C. Seth
Jane Shivers
Jeff Shoemaker
Kathryn Shreves
Cynthia Silveri
Al Singer
Chris Slattery
Rick Smith
Dave Snyder
Steve Soboroff
Laura Solano
Sandy Sparks
Oliver Spellman
Fran Spero
Terry Speth
Gary Stromberg
Beth Strommen
Jim Summerville
Nancy Supik

Jackie Tatum
Patrice Todisco
Tim Tompkins
Steve Turner
Ed Uhlir
Karrie Underwood
Diane Van Buren-Jones
Holly Van Houten
Sherry Van Winkle
Karlyn Voss
Isabel Wade
Bill Walker
Tim Walker
Mary Beth Wallace
Gerry Wang
David Warm
Frank Weddle
Bob Weinberg
Bob Weinreb
Fred Weiss
Rand Wentworth
Joshua Whetzel
Alyson Whiddon
Dana White
Cynthia Whiteford
Karen Whitman
Bruce Williams
Dan Williams
Al Wittman
Amy Wolf
David Wolff
Carol Wood
Bill Woods
Pamela Woolford
Martha Wycoff-Byrne
David Yamashita
Tom Zarfoss

Board of Advisers for *Inside City Parks*

For

Edith B. Harnik, *who taught me about conservation,*

Carol A. Parker, *who taught me about parks, and*

Jane Jacobs, *who taught me about cities.*

About the Author

Born and raised in New York City, Peter Harnik moved to Washington, D.C., where he began a 30-year career in conservation advocacy and environmental protection. A cofounder of the Rails-to-Trails Conservancy and a longtime board member of the Washington Area Bicyclist Association, Harnik has worked to create parks and trails at both the national and local levels.

In 1995, he became a consultant on urban park issues to the Trust for Public Land. A 1970 graduate of The Johns Hopkins University in Baltimore, he now lives with his wife and two children in Arlington, Virginia.

Contents

List of Figures and Tables

Figures

Tables

Foreword

THIS IS AN EXCITING and remarkable time to be designing parks for American cities. In our work as landscape architects, EDAW has witnessed the ascent of the urban park as a powerful tool for civic identity. Throughout the United States, urban parks are being recognized, at long last, as a critical part of any revitalization strategy, an impressive stimulus to development. Enlightened, savvy business people are now proponents of new parks that generate real value and civic signature. Park administrators are restoring forgotten historic parks in order to reclaim their city's grandeur. Energetic citizens are becoming park sponsors, forging new alliances between government agencies and private organizations to forward their cause. We are seeing a greater commitment to America's urban parks than we have seen for decades. New places—and new ways—for people to gather as communities are proving to be an essential foundation for stronger, more vibrant cities.

In fact, what we have seen in the last five years seems like another City Beautiful movement: in the number of parks constructed or revamped, in the substantial amount of money invested in them, and, notably, in the public's stake in the park's success as a city emblem. In the early 20th century, a similar awareness of design transformed the civic landscape of American cities. Following the World Columbian Exposition in Chicago in 1893, visitors—dazzled by the white neoclassical buildings and the orderly arrangement of public space and promenades—went home clamoring for parks, monuments, and boulevards that would be beautiful to behold and a credit to their towns. Are we experiencing something similar now? The statistics are convincing. In 1998, Americans passed $4 billion worth of park bonds

and tax referenda. Recently, voters have been approving an incredible 70 percent of park bonds and referenda; no other ballot issue achieves even 50 percent of the vote.

Inside City Parks is not only an important marker of this phenomenon; it is certain to be instrumental in securing a better future for our parks and cities. Peter Harnik establishes the centrality of parks in what he calls the City Revival movement. *Inside City Parks* documents the current thinking, the prominent accomplishments, and the latest statistics; the author examines the status of American urban parks as no one has done before. In engaging form, Harnik recounts the story of contemporary park development in 25 American cities, emphasizing "the most innovative programs and initiatives." He then groups the cities by density for statistical analysis so that fair comparisons can be drawn. The 30-plus charts in this book provide much needed data that until now have been almost impossible to gather or come by—data on budgets, resource distribution, facility counts, open space, and employment. The Trust for Public Land supported Harnik's research, knowing that a shortage of quantitative analysis limits general understanding of parks and is therefore detrimental to their funding. The Trust for Public Land should be encouraged to continue to measure the economic benefits of strategic works of landscape architecture.

People often do not recognize the fact that parks are political. Parks must rank high on the political agenda in order to get the backing required. "If parks are not one of your mayor's top three issues, and they rarely are," cautions my colleague Barbara Faga, chair of the EDAW board, "then parks aren't likely to get funded." But she is quick to advise us that, "economic development tops every mayor's list. If you can link parks and economic development in the mayor's mind, you've got it made." This is not a ruse or an angle; this can be done in good faith. Good examples abound: parks are being used as an engine of redevelopment in Boston, Seattle, San Francisco, Chicago, and Houston, as well as in Paris, Barcelona, Manchester (England), and Sydney.

Possibly the best example—certainly EDAW's favorite example—is Centennial Olympic Park in Atlanta. Conceived as the grand central space for the 1996 Summer Olympics, Centennial Olympic Park is a dynamic, interactive plaza, laced with local character and sparked by vibrant visual excitement. When the international games concluded, the park was intended to become the legacy of the Olympics for the people of Atlanta. In the early 1980s, the property value in the immediate area was $2 per square foot; it is now $150 per square foot. Executives want their corporate address at Centennial Olympic Park, which has generated a billion dollars in real estate value in Atlanta. No one expected that much. Fortunately, EDAW had established development sites and made sure that surrounding properties would have views into the park.

New and restored parks attract private sector investment by transforming neglected real estate along park boundaries into valuable property. In Louisville, Kentucky, $100 million in reinvestment followed a half-dozen park and streetscape projects, including the centerpiece Riverfront Plaza and Belvedere, designed by EDAW as a jubilant tribute to the Ohio River. In Fort Worth, Texas, to prompt commercial revitalization, EDAW is reviving the grand old street of the 1930s, Lancaster Avenue, by building on the imagery of its "Zig-Zag Moderne" and "Cowboy Moderne" architecture. In Miami Beach, the firm is glamorizing Collins Avenue by introducing a procession of shade structures designed by fashionable architects. By thus depicting Miami's chic ethos in a linear park, the city encourages developers to respond with sophisticated upgrades to the resort hotels that flank the boulevard. In Washington, D.C., the National Capital Planning Commission has produced a far-reaching plan that calls for expanding McMillan's monumental green core to provide the next urban framework, including reconnecting the city to the rivers, which were largely ignored in the 1901 plan.

We have observed that today's park proponents are alert to another economic reality: how to fund park construction and ongoing maintenance. As never before, parks must pay their own way. We have been asked to design for affordable upkeep; to create retail opportunities for revenue flow; and to help initiate tax incentive districts, business improvement districts, and other innovative strategies to get parks built and to keep them running. *Inside City Parks* will be valuable in these efforts, because it gives parks a higher profile among decision makers, the populace, and even park administrators themselves. Many park departments underdocument the systems in their care, which inadvertently suppresses financial support. It took 15 months of research (and thousands of phone calls) for Harnik and his team to collect these numbers and present them in usable form.

Our clients routinely compare their hometowns with others, but in a generic way. They want a marketplace like Boston's Faneuil Hall, a festival waterfront like Baltimore's Inner Harbor, or a civic icon like St. Louis's arch. But clients do not have the information that would empower them to seek true equity with competing or more prosperous cities. The citizen leader or park professional can now seize the figures in this book, go to the city council, and say, "Look at this. Look at other cities our size. Look at our rival city. Look at these affluent cities. Look what they have achieved by funding parks. If we want to get where they are—if we want to be great—we must invest in well-designed parks!"

IT HAS TAKEN almost 50 years to invent a new kind of park. We have been fixated on the Olmsted model—the "green lung" approach —underpinned with social theory, preserving nature in the city while redressing societal ills. We are now ushering in the "smart park," a more intensive and less pastoral park, an entertainment venue, and a magnet for activity that still abides by ecological ideals. Americans are asking their parks to be more than domesticated woodlands and meadows; people get enough isolation at the computer. They want programmed events that draw people together for stimulation; they want diversion and change, such as a farmers' market one weekend, a jazz festival the next, and a concourse of vintage cars the week after that.

What makes a park succeed? Attendance, activity, and a sense of shared ownership are what make a park effective in upgrading its surroundings. How does a park become popular? The design must have strong aesthetic appeal, and it must be flexible, accommodating the diverse programs that sustain a multiple constituency. At Atlanta's Centennial Olympic Park, the dancing waters—the theatrical, participatory landscape—draws everyone into the fountains, and draws them back to the park again; the park has helped Atlantans to see urban parks as a positive force rather than a repository of social problems.

Preoccupied as we are with virtual realities, real place making becomes all the more pressing. The park must be right there in the roiling center of energy. One must select a significant site to begin with, then extract its meaning into physical form. Harnik's profiles bring out the individuality of each city. EDAW can attest to the enormous importance of this approach. With the homogenization of America's cityscapes and the advent of a global culture, it takes determination to maintain the distinctions that confer identity and preserve meaning. In cities like Dayton, Denver, Omaha, and Cincinnati, the desire for local identity has been voiced loudly and clearly. At design workshops and open houses, we hear from residents that they want to embrace the singular features, the particular lore, that set their city apart from the rest. We try to convey that heritage with their "narrative landscape," a way of literally or poetically expressing local history in landscape form. City dwellers want interpretation; they have chosen a hometown in part for its history, and they want to see it come alive.

A few examples can elucidate this approach. Because Chattanooga, Tennessee, is an exuberant town, Ross's Landing Park and Plaza is an exuberant tapestry: bold bands of paving and planting rarely encountered anywhere else. Within these bands are elements of local culture: a swath of green erupts into a 20-foot-high band shell, covered in trees and trailing plants to resemble the Smoky Mountains; steel rails from a train track form a musical staff with oversized notes that play the irresistible song "Chattanooga Choo-Choo" as people hop from note to note. In Louisville, Kentucky, at Riverfront Plaza and Belvedere, a statue of the city's founder, George Rogers Clark, had been shunted off in a corner of the old site; now Clark stands on the river's edge, the focus of a visual axis and a herald to park visitors. The plan gave meaning to the statue, and the statue gave meaning to the park. More popular still is the way the Ohio River and the cities along it are mapped to scale in the pavement of this dramatic overlook; as your feet follow the swath of blue, it takes you down to the Ohio River itself.

We see in narrative landscape an entrée to local ownership. There is a burgeoning repopulation of American cities. New housing types have emerged: factories, department stores, and office buildings have been converted to condominiums, live/work lofts, and cohousing facilities. Parks must advance in concert with residential growth; there will be increasing demand for what parks provide.

Finally, I join Peter Harnik in affirming the importance of strong leadership in bringing well-designed parks to fruition. EDAW's experience has shown that it usually takes two key players: a politician and the person who makes the construction happen.

We feel very fortunate to be a part of the City Revival movement, to have a hand in reestablishing the primacy of parks. My partners at EDAW tell me over and over again that they derive tremendous satisfaction from working on urban parks. They take a personal interest in the success of the project, the usefulness and pleasure the park brings to a city and its residents. They want to see the community benefit, and this is a very emotional experience.

I expect Inside City Parks to be instrumental in securing a better future for American parks. I envision the readers of this book recognizing similar challenges in other cities and seeing the potential of working together to create a national constituency. Today, federal funding for the restoration and construction of major urban parks is limited. Yet there is no organized group to promote urban parks as instruments of change, community loci, and hallmarks of cosmopolitan cities. This book can be the genesis of a network that brings national attention and political strength to the cause of urban parks.

I congratulate the Trust for Public Land and the Urban Land Institute for their vision in publishing Inside City Parks. I urge policy makers, park advocates, and forward-thinking members of the business community to read and utilize this intelligent, practical work. Readers can make the most of the best models and the hard data to inspire and guide the improvement of their cities. As they do so, they will also be building our national heritage of great urban parks.

Joe Brown, FASLA, President/CEO, EDAW, Inc.
EDAW *is an international landscape, architecture, and planning practice with offices on four continents.*

How to Use This Book

Inside City Parks reports on the central cities of the largest metropolitan areas in the United States. All numbers and most of the narrative in the book refer only to the core cities, not to surrounding suburban towns and counties. In other words, the chapter on Seattle does not include King County, Miami does not include Miami Beach (a separate city), and Detroit does not include the regional Huron–Clinton Metroparks Authority. The purpose of this book is to provide data and information specifically on the park systems and parklands of the political jurisdictions at the heart of our biggest metropolitan areas.

In order to give a complete picture of each city's park resources, *Inside City Parks* examines both the municipal park agency holdings and all the parkland located within each city—that is, parks owned or operated by county, metropolitan, or state agencies; by the National Park Service; or by specialized agencies like a convention center, a water district, or a business improvement district, if the facility is run as a public park. To get a complete picture of Los Angeles's park resources, for instance, one must realize that the city has over 15,000 acres of open space operated by state, federal, county, and water management agencies—more land than the Los Angeles Department of Recreation and Parks itself operates.

It is important to note that, for all agencies profiled in this book, the amount of parkland shown is only the land within the city boundaries. Several agencies, such as Denver's Department of Parks and Recreation, have landholdings outside the city limits, but neither these nor their expenses are counted in *Inside City Parks*.

To make comparisons more useful, the 25 cities have been divided into three levels of population density—high, medium, and low—based on 1990 city acreages and 1996 city population estimates. This breakdown helps compensate for the fact that a greater number of residents in low-density cities have backyards, while more residents of high-density cities have rail transit and other ways to gain access to their parks. The divisions are relative rather than absolute, and the density difference between Los Angeles (high) and Detroit (medium), for example, is minimal (although it will probably increase because Los Angeles is becoming more dense and Detroit is becoming less so). Density, of course, is a factor of both the population and the physical size of a city; if a city annexes land faster than it gains people, it will lose density even as its population increases.

Most cities have a single agency in charge of both parks and recreation. However, several cities have multiple agencies. Therefore, when individual agencies are being compared, it is important to take into account sister-agency situations found in Cincinnati (the Park Board and the Recreation Commission); Philadelphia (the Department of Recreation and the Fairmount Park Commission); Tampa (the Parks Department, the Recreation Department, and the Sports Authority); Boston (the Parks and Recreation Department and the Department of Community Centers); and Baltimore and Pittsburgh (both of which have transferred aspects of their parks program to the Department of Public Works). In addition, many of the cities have a significant amount of state, regional, county, or national parkland within the city boundaries—all of which is included in charts depicting total parkland in the city. Where possible, financial information on parklands operated by outside agencies is also included.

Not every acre classified as parkland or open space is an area with grass and trees. Every park agency owns auto storage areas, equipment garages, mulch piles, and other utilitarian facilities. Most also have buildings such as museums, planetariums, aquariums, and even stadiums. The acreage also generally includes surface water that is under the park agency's jurisdiction (or specialized situations, such as water department reservoirs within parks). City parkland and open-space acreage also include public golf courses (even where they are operated under contract by a private entity), zoos, arboretums, and botanical gardens. All this acreage (even the land underneath park buildings) has been included; it is assumed that every city has similar constraints on usable open space and that they generally cancel each other out.

Every effort was made to bring each city agency's financial numbers into conformity so that comparisons can be accurate and meaningful. Therefore, all extraneous nonpark and recreation activities—including the operation of zoos, museums, aquariums, stadiums, and cemeteries—have been deleted from agency budgets, because these big-ticket items can significantly skew the numbers. On the other hand, because virtually every agency operates golf courses, these have been left in the calculations.

The financial bottom line reached in this book is often significantly different from the agency's published bottom line. This disparity is attributable to the deletion of nonpark items in many agencies' budgets and also to the fact that *Inside City Parks* combines each agency's yearly operating budget and its capital budget, which most agencies report separately. For this reason, the book uses the phrase "Adjusted Park Budget." Every agency's adjusted park budget refers to actual numbers from one particular year (usually 1998–1999). Thus, the numbers are specific snapshots (not averaged over time) and may be subject to some unusual fluctuation (for example, if an extraordinary capital campaign took place that year). Because of the low inflation rate and the short time span that varies by only two or three years, it was not deemed necessary to convert dollar figures into constant dollars.

Each agency's adjusted budget is broken into two categories, revenue and expenditure. These items generally (but not always) balance each other; when they do not balance, the figure used is from the expenditure column. Revenue includes six different sources of money coming into the agency's coffers:

1. General funds: all monies that are appropriated by the city on a discretionary, year-to-year basis;
2. Dedicated taxes: all monies provided through public, city-based revenue but not voted on annually (for example, funds from the gas tax, hotel tax, or property assessment);
3. Fees retained by the agency: revenue generated by the park and recreation facilities themselves, but not counting money that reverts to the citywide general fund;
4. Grants and donations: philanthropic revenue from individuals, foundations, and corporations;
5. State and federal support: funds from contracts, grants, and appropriations received from state and federal agencies; and
6. Capital income: monies specifically earmarked for construction, acquisition, or other capital activities for that particular fiscal year (including from bonds).

Expenditure includes three categories:
1. Grounds and facilities maintenance and repair: staff time and equipment, plus a prorated share of the agency's administrative overhead, that are assigned to the agency's physical plant (including any work contracted to private organizations);
2. Recreational programming and activities: staff time and equipment, plus a prorated share of the agency's administrative overhead, that are assigned to the agency's human services tasks (including such items as summer lunch; after-school, day-care, and senior citizen programs; and any work contracted to private organizations); and
3. Capital expenditure: monies spent on construction, acquisition, or other capital activities in that fiscal year.

The statistic of dollars per acre is a hypothetical calculation of the adjusted annual budget divided by total park acreage and does not indicate the actual amount of money spent on each acre of parkland. Because of overhead, recreational programming, and other factors, the actual expenditure per acre is considerably lower.

The words "park," "preserve," "green space," and "open space" are, by necessity, used somewhat loosely in this book and may sometimes refer to such diverse facilities as

Urban parks must be considered in the context of a city's population density. Tompkins Square Park has a different meaning to the apartment dwellers of lower Manhattan than Hermann Park has to Houstonians, with their backyards and trees.

passive parks, sports fields, natural reserves, formal brick squares, and even undeveloped, future parkland. Ideally, in the future, more consistent city-to-city nomenclature and record keeping will make it possible to use more precise terminology. It should also be pointed out that "green," "greenway," and "green space" are generic terms that are not always literally accurate; in parts of the arid West, for example, parks and open spaces are brown, golden, and other colors much of the year.

Numerical information in this book was compiled from information provided by the surveyed agencies. In some cases, such as "regional parks," "neighborhood parks," and "playing fields," there is no precise definition to guarantee that all the numbers are parallel.

There is no accepted difference between the definitions of "recreation center" and "community center," with different cities using one phrase or the other. Therefore, the words are used interchangeably in this book. Generally, centers are counted only if they include a gymnasium; smaller centers used primarily for meeting rooms are not.

All city and metropolitan area acreage figures are from the 1990 U.S. Census. All population figures are from the 1996 U.S. Census estimate. Metropolitan area population figures are from Census Bureau definitions. In the case of cities that adjoin other large cities in a Consolidated Metropolitan Statistical Area (such as New York and San Francisco), the book uses the smaller Primary Metropolitan Statistical Area to define the immediate surrounding metropolitan population.

"Publicly Owned Vacant Lots" refers to properties, generally in old, low-income neighborhoods, that have no structures still standing and whose owners have ceased paying property taxes. It does not refer to undeveloped land on the edge of still-expanding cities that is awaiting first-time development.

"N.A." signifies "Not Available."

"Developer Impact Fees" refers to a payment imposed by the city government on a developer and used to purchase open space for parkland. Although from city to city there is no standard form or amount for these fees, and their complexity is beyond the scope of this book, it is useful for park watchers to know which cities have such fees in their arsenal of financial resources for parks.

Where Are Washington, D.C., and Milwaukee?

Of the 27 largest metropolitan areas in the United States, every core city is profiled in this book, except Washington, D.C., and Milwaukee. The former is not included because the National Park Service owns and operates virtually its entire park system. Even though the District of Columbia has its own Recreation Department, the fact that almost every acre of open space in the city is a national park makes a comparison with other cities misleading. Milwaukee is not included because the city does not have its own park agency. The park departments of Milwaukee City and Milwaukee County were merged in 1937, and the Milwaukee County Park Commission cannot break out its acreage and budgetary numbers by political jurisdiction, thus making comparison with other cities impossible.

Introduction

ONCE UPON A TIME, America had compact cities surrounded by vast, pastoral areas of fields, streams, and forests. Today, America has enormous cities surrounded by even more colossal metropolitan regions. As a result, most city dwellers now principally experience nature—or even simple open spaces—through their city's park systems.

Most of us have memories about a city park—a romantic stroll, an athletic triumph, a family gathering, a clamber in a playground, a bike ride, a hike through the snow, an autumnal drive—yet the literature on these evocative places is slim. Thousands of books have been written about cities (few of them mentioning parks) and thousands have been written about natural areas and national parks (almost none of them mentioning cities), but precious little has been published about that complex amalgam, the city park. City parks are not as famous as national parks, and most of them are not kept up as well. They don't have geysers, or underground caverns, or snowcapped mountaintops but, acre for

Jake Wyman, Grand Central Partnership

New York's Bryant Park is owned by the city but managed by a private business improvement district. A key to the success of a city's park system is the relationship between the park department and the many private forces at work in the urban core.

acre and hour for hour, city parks are the places where Americans most often enjoy open space and outdoor recreation.

At the same time, there is not a city in the nation whose space, layout, real estate value, traffic flow, public events, and even civic culture are not significantly defined by its urban parks, plazas, squares, circles, waterfront promenades, linear greenways, civic centers, and public gardens. Instead of encircling residents as in the past, natural areas must be threaded among and between the structures and streets where urban creatures live, work, and play. For this reason, it is imperative for Americans to understand city parks—not only how much land they encompass and what they cost to operate, but also how they should be preserved and improved.

Yet very little information exists about our city parks: their locations and sizes, their geology and ecology, their histories, and the politics of their creation and utilization. Little has been written about what city parks contain, how they are used, how much is spent on them, and how many visitors they get. Even less is known about the larger issues—how much total parkland each city has, how many acres of open space per 1,000 residents, and how many dollars are spent per person or per acre.

Finally, all that information has been brought together in a book about big city parks. Parks with evocative names like Golden Gate, Mission Bay, Belle Isle, Druid Hill, Eden, and Encanto. Parks with topographical names like Piedmont, Prospect, Forest, Fairmount, and Bayfront. Parks with workaday names like City, Memorial, and Central. Parks honoring the great, such as Lincoln, Grant, Washington, Jackson, and Franklin; the rich, such as Rockefeller, Schenley, Griffith, Swope, and Hermann; and the uplifting, like Freedom, Volunteer, Friendship, and Pioneer. The book also profiles city parks that are right around the corner and down the street, as comfortable as well-worn shoes but also as special, at times, as a top hat and tails.

The urban parks partnership between the Trust for Public Land and the Urban Land Institute began in 1997, with the publication of *Urban Parks and Open Space*, a detailed look at 16 innovative and influential new city green spaces in the United States today. Each project was analyzed from the standpoint of both design and politics, showing the great opportunities in our metropolises as well as some of the harsh realities that urban open-space proponents face at every turn.

This book takes the investigation a step further. Instead of looking at single parks, the book contemplates how entire city park systems function, highlighting innovative programs and initiatives. It analyzes the link between park departments and other public agencies, and it explores the relationship of the government to the many private forces at work in the urban core. The discussion shows the public's enthusiasm for park conservancies (like the pioneering Central Park Conservancy), for business improvement districts (like New York's Bryant Park Restoration Corporation), for greenway networks (as in Houston, Indianapolis, and elsewhere), for waterfront parks (as in Pittsburgh and Portland, Oregon), for conversion of old, used brownfields into brand new parks (as in Denver and Minneapolis), and for conversion of former federal facilities into new city oases (as in Phoenix and San Francisco). The profiles demonstrate that park systems not only can be improved during economic boom times but also can be expanded during economic downturns. Best of all, the discussion confirms that the wonderful old city parks of the 19th century still have an enormous emotional grip on countless urban dwellers (and even former urban dwellers), so much so that restoration campaigns are able to generate enthusiasm, millions of dollars, and thousands of hours of volunteer effort.

Which comes first, the healthy city or the healthy park? Not long ago the question itself would have been laughable, since both cities and parks seemed in terminally failing health. Today, both are recovering and the question has real relevance. Attractive, safe, and usable parks bolster their neighborhoods, but cities need a strong economic base to fix (or create) those parks in the first place. That economic base is hard to attain without middle-class taxpayers, who often will not live somewhere that lacks decent parks.

Olmsted National Historic Site

Frederick Law Olmsted (1822–1895) created parks in dozens of cities and is credited with being the father of landscape architecture. Together with his son and stepson, Olmsted exerted a profound and lasting impact on the design of green spaces in almost every major city into the 1950s.

More than a century ago, Frederick Law Olmsted, the great park designer and city planner known as the father of landscape architecture, found this very issue to be central to his work when he pointed out that "a park exercises a very different and much greater influence upon the progress of a city in its general structure than any other ordinary public work." In other words, parks give a city a survival advantage. Every city, after all, is in competition with every other city, not to mention every other suburb and small town. By performing all the miraculous functions that people appreciate—cleaning the air, giving cooling shade, providing space for recreation and play, offering attractive vistas, and furnishing outdoor environmental classrooms—parks improve the quality of life in a city. Each amenity, from the job market to the housing stock to cultural opportunities to even the weather, is part of the equation people use to decide where to live. A great park system can positively tip the balance. Although not every park system is great yet, there is a growing appreciation of this goal, as evidenced by the fact that almost every city described in this book has parkland that has recently opened, is under construction, or is in the planning stages.

And what a diversity of approaches! Are you interested in seeing how parks can help shape the growth of a city? Look at Chicago, Denver, and Kansas City. Intrigued by public/private partnerships? Consider Atlanta, Houston, New York, and St. Louis. Seeking excellent neighborhood-based planning? Study Minneapolis and Seattle. Turning run-down riverfronts into cultural and recreational promenades? Read about Cincinnati, Cleveland, and Pittsburgh. Converting ugly highways into parkland and using the amenity to redevelop neighborhoods? Boston, Portland, and San Francisco. Ecologically based planning? Phoenix.

Boston's Neponset River once provided water-power for the Walter Baker Chocolate Company. Today, the river greenway provides beauty, recreation, and community value for residents of the converted factory—and for the rest of the city.

Community gardens? Philadelphia. Greenways and rail trails? Baltimore, Dallas, and Indianapolis. Parks as stimulators of tourism? San Diego. The list goes on and on. Cities face similar overarching problems yet tackle and solve them in unique and instructive ways.

Moreover, as we're learning, design alone is not enough; parks must also be properly managed and programmed. In fact, it turns out that things are not much different today than they were in Olmsted's day: creating public places and keeping them in excellent condition is and has always been extraordinarily difficult. What it took in 1859 (with Central Park) and 1870 (with Golden Gate Park) is the same thing it took in 1983 (with Cullen Park in Houston), 1991 (Post Office Square in Boston), and 1999 (Friendship Trail in Tampa)—leadership and commitment. The effort requires public or private leadership that has a *vision* of how healthy parks can make healthy cities.

Fortunately, this book reveals that many of our biggest cities now have that leadership, from either the mayor's office, the citizen sector, or the corporate community, and sometimes from all three. There is a "followership" as well. Most big cities have hundreds or thousands of volunteers, who are demonstrating their deep commitment to parks by doing physical labor, donating money or other goods, or giving their time and personal skills to beautify and improve one park or the entire system. As a result of this rejuvenation, parks in some cities are taking on the physical, spiritual, and economic roles that they have been unable to assume since before World War II.

The new urban vision is also playing a role on the other side of the equation—far out in the suburbs. There, some residents are beginning to recognize that large-lot, auto-dependent living has its own set of drawbacks, and as higher-income families with a variety of lifestyle choices realize that there is more than one American dream, the attraction of "green cities" is helping to provide an alternative to urban sprawl and lack of investment in city centers.

Almost exactly 100 years ago, the United States was in the midst of the City Beautiful movement, a great emotional outpouring of enthusiasm for architectural and urban planning that shaped and reshaped many of our cities—clearing tenements, opening up broad avenues and vistas, generating huge increases in parkland, and yielding monumental signature buildings. After centuries of ever more cramped and unhealthy conditions in urban agglomerations, the awesome economic power of cities had finally produced enough personal wealth to allow some people to dream of a life—a city life—that was both beautiful and urbane. The movement was potentially transforming, but it was nipped in the bud by the growth of the automobile culture and by suburbs, which dominated most of what happened for the rest of the century.

Now, 100 years later, we are in the midst of a new movement, a City Revival movement. As one indicator, the park departments themselves are trying to revive and revitalize what they have. Collectively, the 25 cities surveyed in this book spend about $1.2 billion a year on their day-to-day operations and programs. These days they are also spending just under half of that amount—a bit over $500 million in the average year—on capital construction and reconstruction. For Americans, who are generally reluctant to spend money fixing old things when they would prefer to throw them out and buy new ones, that's an impressive development.

The suburbs are by no means passé, but the pendulum is swinging back. With this trend comes a renewed appreciation of the physical location, shape, and design of our big cities—and of the parks that are so instrumental to that design. To understand where each of our big cities is going, we must know where each has come from.

Some of the facts are impressive, some are bleak. Some of the stories are heartwarming, some infuriating. Taken together, the information should help all Americans—including urban planners, park professionals, park advocates, and just plain park users—to gain new insights into the workings of the devilishly complicated public spaces called urban parks.

Part I
High-Density Cities

New York

LIKE EVERYTHING ELSE in New York City, "larger than life" describes its park system and "clamorous" describes its park politics. When the forces align, the results are sublime; more often, dueling interests stymie each other, putting projects on hold for years or even decades.

With an astonishing 28,000 acres, the New York City Department of Parks and Recreation has as much parkland as the Los Angeles Recreation and Park Department, the Chicago Park District, and the Denver Parks and Recreation Department combined; and New York has more parks and playgrounds than any other locality. In fact, if the city's considerable state and national parkland is added in, New York is actually the "greenest" big city in the country,

with fully 26.6 percent of its area blanketed by parks. (To be fair, though, much of that land is hard to reach and some is under water.) All in all, it is not an exaggeration to say that, over the past 150 years, American park policy has been consistently molded by innovations from New York.

Innovation number one is Central Park, the first major work designed by Frederick Law Olmsted and Calvert Vaux and arguably the most successful city park on earth. Even though it is not the biggest park (at 840 acres it is not even the biggest one in New York), and even though Olmsted himself considered his masterpiece to be Brooklyn's Prospect Park, Central Park is the standard against which all other parks are measured.

Paula Hewitt

Central Park, Manhattan's 840-acre oasis, set the standard for the pastoral urban park and still serves as a model. In the distance are the Hudson River and the Upper West Side; in the foreground is the Metropolitan Museum of Art, and the park's right boundary is Fifth Avenue.

New York's network of
parks and open space.

From its very inception in 1857, Central Park's magical design created real estate value for the surrounding environs and tax value for the city. Today the billion-dollar frontage along Fifth Avenue, Central Park South, Central Park West, and even Central Park North in Harlem is proof of the park's ability to attract.

For many Manhattanites, Central Park is what makes the city livable, and it is part of the reason that many wealthy New Yorkers still live in the heart of the city. In Central Park, riches are heaped upon riches. Besides two museums and a planetarium, it has the Wollman Ice Rink, a rowboat concession, a special pond for model sailboats, a romantic restaurant, and a bridle path. Shakespeare's plays and operas are regularly presented in Central Park, and superstars like Paul Simon, Aretha Franklin, and Garth Brooks periodically give concerts attended by up

to three-quarters of a million people. To promote cycling and running on a massive scale, Central Park has become largely car-free (with no autos permitted between January 1 and Thanksgiving, except during weekday rush hours). The park has proven to be a financial powerhouse for the city, with promoters willing to pay for association with its ambience. In 1995, for example, the Disney Company paid $1 million for the right to premier *Pocahontas* on the park's Great Lawn. Even the pretzel and hot dog vendor in front of the Metropolitan Museum of Art is notable: with a permit costing almost $200,000 a year, the concession for that single pushcart is the highest-priced in the United States.

Ironically, it was the rocky and swampy terrain of central Manhattan that stymied mid-19th-century developers and left a large hole in the rectilinear development pattern of the city.

Although millions of parents have said to millions of children, "This is what New York looked like before all the buildings were here," Central Park is, in fact, almost as artificial as Disneyland. Olmsted and Vaux employed 20,000 laborers, engineers, stonecutters, and gardeners to move 3 million cubic yards of dirt, plant 270,000 trees and shrubs, and dig six lakes.

Less than ten years later, Olmsted and Vaux were hired by the then independent city of Brooklyn to create Prospect Park, a similar tour de force so well designed that the surrounding city is not visible even from the center of the park's vast Long Meadow. In one section, the Woodlands, a tumbling Adirondack mountain stream is re-created over the compressed distance of a quarter-mile; a tranquil lowland lake lies a few steps away. Perhaps even more breathtaking is an Olmsted idea that never came to fruition: a stately tree-lined parkway connecting Central Park and Prospect Park. (Olmsted had to settle for creating the nation's first bicycle path, alongside Ocean Parkway.)

The impact of Central and Prospect Parks on the nation was electrifying, and Olmsted (and later his sons) was commissioned to design parks and parkways in Boston; Buffalo; Chicago; Detroit; Montreal; Seattle; Washington, D.C.; and dozens of other cities. But even heavenly creations can crumble when not maintained, and by the 1960s, both parks were in sorry physical shape and were considered dangerous. When New York plunged into a fiscal crisis in the mid-1970s, park maintenance and recreation programs were slashed (and, in fact, still have not fully returned to pre-1970 levels).

City Profile for New York, New York

City Population (1996)	7,381,000
City Area in Acres (1990)	197,696
City Population Density Level	37.3
Counties in Which City Is Located	Bronx, Kings, New York, Queens, Richmond
Counties' Population (1996)	7,381,000
Metropolitan Area Population (1996)	8,643,000
City Relative Cost of Living (base = 100) (Manhattan)	232.1
Number of Publicly Owned Vacant Lots	12,000 (est.)
Does the City Have a Developer Impact Fee for Parks?	No
Municipal Park Acres in City	28,126
National Park Acres in City	24,478
State Park Acres in City	334
County Park Acres in City	0
Total Park Acres in City	52,938

Out of the crisis arose another New York innovation: the private organization formed to support parks. Under the leadership of a dynamic landscape architect, Olmsted scholar, and well-connected park neighbor named Elizabeth Barlow Rogers, the Central Park Conservancy was formed in 1980 and quickly tapped into the commitment of the city's park lovers. By 1999, the Conservancy was a powerhouse with a staff of 250, 1,200 volunteers, and a $65 million endowment. The group was so success-

Prospect Park Archive

Prospect Park, considered by Frederick Law Olmsted to be his masterpiece, is so well designed that the surrounding city is not visible, even from the center of the park's vast Long Meadow.

New York City Department of Parks and Recreation

Address	The Arsenal, 830 Fifth Avenue, Room 401
Zip Code	10021
Telephone	(212) 360-8111
Fax	(212) 360-1329
Web Site	www.nycparks.org
Agency Acreage in City	28,126
Acreage as Percent of City	14.2%
Acres per 1,000 Residents	3.8
Number of Regional Parks	N.A.
Number of Neighborhood Parks	864
Number of Recreation Centers	35
Number of Pools	54
Number of Golf Courses	16
Number of Tennis Courts	584
Number of Sports Fields	860
Number of Marina Slips	5
Number of Beaches	6
Miles of Bikeways/Greenways	N.A.
Number of Skating Rinks	6
Number of Full-Time Employees	2,160
Number of Seasonal Employees	3,000
Number of Volunteers	17,500

Adjusted Budget for Fiscal Year 1999–2000

Revenue

General Funds	$160,217,000
Dedicated Taxes	0
Fees Retained by the Agency	0
Private Grants and Donations	3,200,000
State and Federal Support	7,088,000
Capital Income	165,000,000
Total	$335,505,000

Expenditure

Grounds and Facilities Maintenance and Repair	$140,685,000
Recreational Programming and Activities	26,070,000
Capital Construction and Acquisition	139,057,000
Total	$305,812,000

Expenditure per Resident	$41

ful in upgrading and promoting Central Park that, in 1998, the city signed a contract to pay the Conservancy to take over most of the day-to-day maintenance of the park; the Conservancy supplements the payment with privately raised funds. Soon thereafter, other city park supporters followed suit, forming a number of single-park entities—the Prospect Park Alliance, the Riverside Park Fund, Friends of Van Cortland Park, the Greenbelt Conservancy—as well as the overarching City Parks Foundation, a $6-million-a-year operation that generates and nurtures partnerships with 250 "park friends" groups and 1,800 civic and neighborhood associations.

All that activism led to another innovation: the downtown business-funded park, such as Bryant Park. Located in the heart of downtown, between Times Square and Grand Central Station, surrounded by skyscrapers, and adjacent to the New York Public Library, Bryant Park was once a fashionable place to walk, sit, watch, and be seen. By the 1960s, however, it had become a shunned, crime-ridden space well known for drug dealing. Not only was Bryant Park a depressing place for tourists and residents, but also it was depressing property values and office rents. In 1980, at the behest of the New York Public Library's board, a young MBA named Dan Biederman created the Bryant Park Restoration Corporation—a nonprofit company funded in part by assessments on surrounding property owners—whose mission was to rebuild the park and reinvigorate the neighborhood. Ten years and many bruising battles later, Bryant Park was reopened, complete with a restaurant, food kiosks, spotless public restrooms, spectacular floral displays, nonstop events, and entertainment. The drug trade disappeared, and office rents in the vicinity rose 40 percent.[1]

If New Yorkers learned about park charm from Frederick Law Olmsted and about park funding from Betsy Rogers and Dan Biederman, they learned about park politics from Robert Moses. The city's park commissioner from 1934 to 1960, Moses was never elected to public office, but he did more than any mayor before or since to create the physical look of New York. Early in his tenure, during the depth of the Great Depression, Moses amassed the greatest army of relief workers ever in the United States—1,800 designers and engineers, 3,900 supervisors, and 70,000 laborers—all of whom worked on parks. During his tenure, New York City added 20,000 acres of parkland, 84 miles of parkways, 658 playgrounds, 17 miles of beaches, three zoos, ten golf courses, 53 recreation centers, and 15 huge outdoor swimming pools (the first 11 of which opened on a dazzling one-per-week schedule during the oppressively hot summer of 1936). Moses decked Riverside Park over the railroad tracks and built the Henry

Hudson Parkway. He built the Belt Parkway and opened up the Brooklyn shoreline to promenaders and bicyclists. He converted a swamp and ash dump into the site of two world's fairs and ensured that the land became Flushing Meadow Park afterward.

Moses was feared more than he was loved, however, and his strong opinions and disdain for public participation brought out as many enemies as admirers. His roadways displaced thousands, and the incessant din from automobiles ruined the park experience for others. He tried to run a highway through the middle of venerable Washington Square Park (raising the ire of Greenwich Village homemaker Jane Jacobs and motivating her to write the classic *The Death and Life of Great American Cities*). Finally, with the construction of the Cross–Bronx Expressway and the demolition of 5,000 homes and apartments, Moses overstepped his bounds. Today, the power broker who strode over Gotham's parks like a colossus is memorialized only by a small playground next to an expressway.

The director of the New York City Parks and Recreation Department today is Commissioner Henry J. Stern, a mercurial, quick-witted, shoot-from-the-hip boss, whose 12-year tenure under two different mayors is unusual in this high-turnover city. A former city council member with a gut feeling about New Yorkers and a flair for publicity, Stern is deeply committed to parks and particularly to nature in the city (even starting a program to reintroduce dozens of species of plants and animals that had become extinct in the city). Operating within a bureaucracy famous for instilling alienation, he promotes the human touch, providing his personal E-mail address on the agency's Web site and requiring that every park have a sign that lists the name of its manager. He launched a "Greenstreets" program to convert 2,001 paved, unused street properties, such as medians and traffic triangles, into gardenlike spaces filled with trees, shrubs, and hardy ground cover, which local residents maintain. In 1999, he took that a step further and promised that the city would plant a free tree outside the house of every New York homeowner who requested one. Perhaps Stern's ultimate triumph is his ability to work with his sometimes prickly boss, Mayor Rudolph Giuliani.

Mayor Giuliani, one of a growing number of white Republicans governing multiethnic, overwhelmingly Democratic cities, has staked his reputation on reducing crime, improving the schools, and generally returning civility to New York. Because he lacks sufficient tax money to do the job publicly, Giuliani seeks private assis-

Gateway National Recreation Area

Address	Floyd Bennett Field, Building 69
Zip Code	11234
Telephone	(718) 338-3338
Fax	(718) 338-3560
Agency Acreage in City[a]	24,478
Acreage as Percent of City	12.4%
Acres per 1,000 Residents	3.3
Number of Full-Time Employees	200
Number of Seasonal Employees	450
Number of Volunteers	N.A.

Adjusted Budget for Fiscal Year 1999

Revenue[b]	$16,878,000
Expenditure[b]	$16,878,000
Expenditure per Resident	$2

[a]Acreage includes only that portion of Gateway National Recreation Area located within the city of New York.
[b]Breakdown not available.

tance, and it turns out that the city's green space and recreation programs provide plenty of opportunity for help. In 1998, the city amassed $36 million from park department fees, charges, events, and corporate promotional payments (more than the entire park budgets of six cities profiled in this book). The idea of commercializing the parks has raised the ire of purists and park advocacy groups, but most New Yorkers seem willing to accept more corporate logos in return for cleaner fields, new backboards, state-of-the-art skateboard facilities, and free concerts under the stars. Even the advocates might not mind a bit more commercialism in the mercantile capital of the United States, but they are angry that most of the proceeds flow to the city's general treasury, not to the park department itself. One group, the Parks Council, calculated that only five cents of every dollar generated by the park department goes back to parks. (In fact, New York's policy is no different from that of most U.S. cities, and Stern did better than most of his colleagues. In 1995, he persuaded Mayor Giuliani to let the agency keep all the new revenue it raised; however, the deal was in effect for only one year.)

This is the tightrope that Stern walks every day: between citizens who want public land and services for their high tax payments and a mayor who is willing to sell, lease, or privatize almost anything for which he can find a buyer. A few examples will suffice: the charge for running the food concession in Battery Park where the tourists wait for the Statue of Liberty ferry is $733,000; the fee for operating 13 golf courses is $2.6 million; the charge for unveiling the "James Bond" model of the BMW in Central Park was $500,000; the price for creating a fancy, new, fenced-in, Jack Nicklaus–designed golf course on the site of an old garbage dump is $2 million a year for 35 years.

Counting the fees, leases, private grants, and taxpayer revenue, New York City's Parks and Recreation Department is the largest city park agency in the country; its adjusted budget for fiscal year 2000 is more than $305 million. But with per-capita expenditures of only $42 (19th highest among the municipal agencies described in this book), the New York park system is underfunded. Worse than that, according to the city's watchdog Independent Budget Office, inflation-adjusted public spending on parks dropped by 31 percent between 1987 and 1996. Even though private spending has increased, it has not filled the gap; moreover, the private spending has been concentrated in only a small number of parks. The recreation program has been hit particularly hard. Over ten years, its budget dropped 65 percent, from $20 million (inflation-adjusted) in 1987 to a paltry $7 million in 1996. And the dollar decline has translated

into a precipitous cut in full-time staffing—from 4,161 employees in 1987 to 2,216 in 1996. (This hemorrhage has been partially mitigated by the use of more than 5,000 Work Experience Program [WEP] workers—unemployed persons who are required to work part-time in order to receive their welfare checks. It is estimated that, in 1996, WEP workers put in the same number of hours as 2,900 full-time park employees, although WEP jobs are limited to cleaning, litter and graffiti removal, and other nonreconstruction tasks.) Over the long term, the cut that hurt the most was the shortfall in the capital construction budget, which plummeted well below the $100 million mark for several years after the city's minirecession in 1991. The budget has bounced back, but New York's comptroller has projected that, from 1999 to 2008, only $963 million will be spent on reconstructing the parks and playgrounds, which need $2.7 billion worth of work.

Interestingly, it is not the large parks but the small ones that spur neighborhood residents to action. Community groups and block associations have rescued tiny 50-by-100-foot lots from the rubble and litter that had been burying them and converted them to community gardens and playgrounds. As in Philadelphia and elsewhere, these nuggets of green provide open space, flowers, vegetables, a social gathering place, a venue for artistic expression, and

Community gardens are just as important to New Yorkers as their big, famous parks. This one, on the Lower East Side of Manhattan, provides flowers, vegetables, a social gathering place, a venue for ethnic artistic expression, and a seedlot for political organizing.

a seed for political organizing. But unlike declining cities like Philadelphia, New York is currently experiencing an economic revival (it is one of the few Rustbelt cities gaining in population), and it is actually *losing* community gardens to development.

Of New York's approximately 12,000 city-owned vacant lots, about 700 have been transformed into gardens, primarily in the Bronx, Brooklyn, and Manhattan's Lower East Side. With a growing recognition that the gardens share some of the attributes of traditional parks, 36 of the best—those with stable management that are also kept unlocked for the public at least ten hours a week—have been officially placed under the purview of the park department. The others, however, after operating for years in a laissez-faire atmosphere, have suddenly become vulnerable. In 1996, the Giuliani administration began to make the gardens available for development, and during the next two years about 50 were reclaimed for low-income housing. Then, in 1998, advocates of open space learned that the city was accelerating its sale of vacant parcels, including at least 125 gardens, regardless of the intended use. Garden lovers reacted angrily, and Commissioner Stern found himself caught in the cross fire. On the one hand, some of the well-established gardens had become pillars of their communities; on the other, if temporary gardens could not be reclaimed for housing, the mayor threatened to ban any and all future gardens. In May 1999, the day before a scheduled public auction and with two lawsuits pending, the city negotiated the sale of 112 of the gardens to the Trust for Public Land and actress Bette Midler's New York Restoration Project for $4.2 million. Although those gardens were saved, many others remained threatened (and some were bulldozed a few months later).

Historically, the biggest problem for New York's parks has been the irresistible power that developers have over park planners. As far back as the early 1800s, builders thwarted numerous park proposals on land they wanted and, conversely, assigned park locations because the land could not be developed. Even the famous "vest-pocket park" program pioneered in New York in the 1960s was a compromise with developers: a builder would put in a small park among the skyscrapers in return for permission to add extra height to the new tower.

The paucity of parkland along the city's 578 miles of waterfront is particularly striking. The shoreline includes several beaches, some large riparian areas, and a few notable parks, but

When Mayor Rudy Giuliani sought to sell 125 of the community gardens in 1999, residents reacted angrily with protests and emergency fundraising campaigns.

docks, piers, industry, and highways generally diminish or block public enjoyment of the water. Now, finally, that situation is starting to change. On the west side of Manhattan, as a result of the physical collapse of the old West Side elevated highway (after a cement truck crashed through it) and the political collapse of its proposed Westway replacement, a 6.5-mile stretch of riverfront has become available for creating the 550-acre, $300 million Hudson River Park, a public/private venture that will transform the way Manhattanites think of their island. With a wide range of activities and facilities—including golf driving, ice skating, dog runs, boat launches, ecological preserves, and beaches—the park has something for everyone. In fact, some critics claim it has too much, but creating the park is a financial juggling act that depends on leases from such money-making ventures as restaurants, health clubs, entertainment, and much more—intrusions that purists oppose and pragmatists support. In fact, it is so far from being a "normal" park that Hudson River Park (like the already-created Battery Park City parks nearby) will not be owned by the New York City Department of Parks and Recreation but rather by a special authority chartered by the state.[2]

Other waterside park efforts are underway in conjunction with an ambitious bikeway and greenway system that will link and encircle the city with recreation and commuting trails. The 350-mile route is being planned jointly with the city's transportation department and is funded mostly with transportation dollars. Perhaps the most notable effort is going on along the long-neglected Bronx River, where an enthusiastic combination of city, state, and federal agencies, plus dozens of neighborhood groups, is bootstrapping a greenway in one of the city's most depressed communities. The Bronx actually has a higher proportion of parkland than any other borough in New York, but little of it is found in the impoverished South Bronx, which was famously visited—to little avail—by President Jimmy Carter as well as President Ronald Reagan. Local residents are now beginning to fix what the White House could not solve, not only with a cleaned-up river and a bike trail, but also, nearby, with one of the city's biggest and most vibrant community gardens.

The message from all these endeavors is that entrepreneurship can bring results. Using the vast swirling tides of money, development politics, shifting fashions, and advertising to eke out more land and money for parks has helped the park system in New York. Whether from penthouses overlooking Central Park or from modest homes in the South Bronx, park lovers have challenged the "it's-all-built-up" naysayers to do the seemingly impossible. For example, when megadeveloper Donald Trump horrified New Yorkers by announcing that he wanted to build a 150-story building in a former west side rail yard, the community negotiated not only a scaled-back development but also the creation of a state-of-the-art, 13-block park along the Hudson River. When the state mandated

a new sewage treatment plant, the citizens of Harlem demanded a quid pro quo and got Riverbank State Park—28 acres of high-quality recreation facilities plus a view of New Jersey—on top of the plant. When Prospect Park needed money, Brooklynites turned to the Lila Wallace–Reader's Digest Funds. When a tangle of dead-end roads and industrial plants blocked access to the Bronx River, activists found trail money at the state's Department of Transportation (even though the greenway will cost $1 million per block in some stretches).

Of course, it would be better to have an official New York City parks plan—there is none, and the entire agency has only one long-range planner—but that is not the way New York operates. In a city built by investors and financiers, even conservationists are forced to play the market aggressively.

Notes

1. For a detailed analysis of the renewal of Bryant Park, see Alexander Garvin et al., *Urban Parks and Open Space* (Washington, D.C.: ULI–the Urban Land Institute, 1997), p. 44.

2. For a detailed description of Hudson River Park, see Garvin, *Urban Parks and Open Space*, p. 116.

San Francisco

TAKE A 30,000-ACRE FAULT ZONE, crumple it into a hilly terrain so steep that it is barely walkable, surround the area on three sides with water, add views of craggy ridges and mighty bridges, throw in some fog rolling in from the sea, and you will get the nation's most memorable city—San Francisco. Packed with gawking tourists and passionately activist residents, San Francisco is the country's second most densely populated big city (after New York). Although the wide expanses of water provide some of the visual relief and cleaner air that other cities get from forests and meadows, in San Francisco open space is extremely valuable, and issues surrounding parks and recreation raise passions like few others do.

The primary park passion for San Franciscans is Golden Gate Park, a 1,017-acre wonderland with nine lakes and ponds, an island hillock with a magnificent view, dazzling flower gardens, an AIDS memorial grove, a Japanese tea garden, a Spanish colonial beach chalet with murals from the 1930s, a garden featuring only plants mentioned in Shakespearean plays, a herd of buffalo, two replicas of Dutch windmills, a Temple of Music bandshell, and more. Much of the fun comes from simply watching some of the 12 million strollers, runners, roller bladers, bicyclists, boat rowers, sports players, tai chi enthusiasts, mimes, acrobats, stilt walkers, and musicians who come to Golden Gate Park every year.

Golden Gate Park bears so many similarities to New York's Central Park that most people assume that it was also designed by Frederick Law Olmsted. This is almost the case, but not quite. In the 1860s, when progressive Mayor Frank McCoffin decided that San Francisco should have a grand green space, the city approached Olmsted for a concept. He drew up

Originally a barren patch of shifting, windswept sand dunes, Golden Gate Park's unpromising site was hand fertilized with thousands of cartloads of clay, loam, and manure. Today, the lush paradise includes redwood forests, specialized flower gardens, lakes, playing fields, and cultural sites, and attracts 12 million visitors a year.

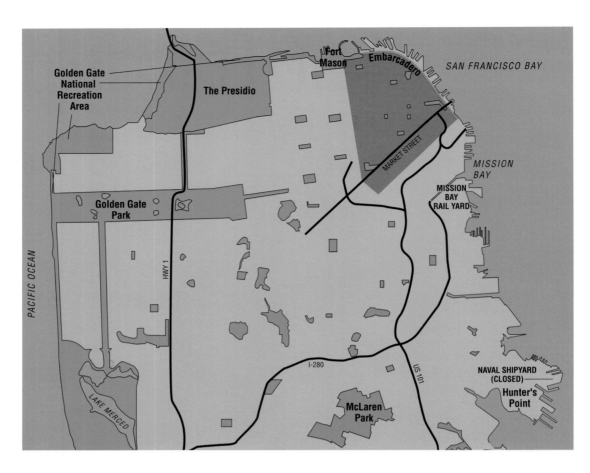

San Francisco's network of parks and open space.

a plan for a large, unique park in the southeastern part of town, but the city rejected the plan as too costly. When the less-expensive land for Golden Gate Park was acquired in 1870, the city turned to a 24-year-old engineer, William

City Profile for San Francisco, California

City Population (1996)	735,000
City Area in Acres (1990)	29,888
City Population Density Level	24.6
County in Which City Is Located	San Francisco
County's Population (1996)	735,000
Metropolitan Area Population (1996)	1,655,000
City Relative Cost of Living (base = 100)	174.2
Number of Publicly Owned Vacant Lots	N.A.
Does the City Have a Developer Impact Fee for Parks?	Yes
Municipal Park Acres in City	3,317
National Park Acres in City	4,106
State Park Acres in City	171
County Park Acres in City	0
Total Park Acres in City	7,594

Hammond Hall, to map out the park and supervise its creation. Golden Gate Park's location on barren, shifting sand dunes on the foggier side of the city provided major landscaping challenges (and a pessimistic site assessment by Olmsted), but Hall responded creatively by constructing serpentine roadways and envisioning planting thousands of cypress and eucalyptus trees (to lessen the impact of the winds) and acres of deep-rooted grasses to hold the sand. (His concept only worked, however, after enough clay, loam, and manure were hauled in to cover all the dunes to a depth of two and one-half feet.) Ultimately, Olmsted wrote enthusiastically of Hall's design, and today the lush park gives no hint of its unprepossessing origins. In the final analysis, though, Olmsted's uncanny foresight does show through: whereas the neighborhood it anchors is perfectly respectable, Golden Gate Park has never equaled Central Park as a mighty engine of growth in real estate value; San Francisco's wealthy residents prefer to hobnob on the sunnier hilltops rather than near the chillier park.

Golden Gate Park's golden years were during the half-century reign (1890 to 1943) of legendary Commissioner Frank McLaren, a Scottish-born horticulturist, who nurtured and defended the park against all possible incursions (once stopping the construction of a trolley line by ordering his gardeners to work all night planting spectacular new beds of flowers and shrubs directly in the path of the rail engineers). McLaren not only raised Golden Gate Park to the level of a national icon but also built and maintained a broad community consensus on parks, enabling him to attract enough funding to create a system that today covers 11.1 percent of the city with green space, a higher percentage than that of all but six of the park agencies in the big cities. (Including the 4,277 acres of federal and state land within San Francisco pushes its "green index" to 25.4 percent, second highest after New York.) McLaren believed in the work ethic (he did not countenance his gardeners wearing jackets in the winter, declaring that if they toiled hard enough they would stay warm), and he died true to his philosophy, in his office in Golden Gate Park, at the age of 96.

Unfortunately, as in most other cities, the post–World War II period saw general park funding and maintenance drop steadily, particularly after the passage of tax-limiting Proposition 13 in 1978 and after the collapse of California's economy in the late 1980s. At the same time, as San Francisco's social problems increased after the late 1960s, more social service tasks were added to the Recreation and Park Department's agenda, including the "School's Out, Rec's In" latchkey and tutoring program, Project Insight for disabled and handicapped persons, and facilities for seniors and community organizations. For more than 50 years, San Franciscans lived off the infrastructure developed by McLaren as it deteriorated around them. Morale at San Francisco's Recreation and Park Department plummeted as its leadership adopted a "circle-the-wagons" mentality; in 1992, former General Manager Mary Burns even abolished the public information office. The department's gardening staff stopped wearing uniforms, making them a less-visible target for public criticism, but prompting complaints that park users could not tell the "workers from the bums."

By 1996, when Willie Brown, the charismatic former state assemblyman, was elected mayor, the park system had hit bottom. Playgrounds were in shambles, virtually every recreation center had a leaky roof, playing fields were pockmarked with ruts and bumps, tree planting had almost ground to a halt, and as many as 1,000 homeless persons had set up semipermanent encampments in various parks, particularly Golden Gate Park. Although many San Franciscans were sympathetic to their plight, the home-

San Francisco Recreation and Park Department

Address	McLaren Lodge, 501 Stanyan Street
Zip Code	94117
Telephone	(415) 831-2704
Fax	(415) 831-2099
Web Site	www.parks.sfgov.org
Agency Acreage in City	3,317
Acreage as Percent of City	11.1%
Acres per 1,000 Residents	4.5
Number of Regional Parks	0
Number of Neighborhood Parks	94
Number of Recreation Centers	17
Number of Pools	9
Number of Golf Courses	6
Number of Tennis Courts	153
Number of Sports Fields	165
Number of Marina Slips	681
Number of Beaches	0
Miles of Bikeways/Greenways	180
Number of Skating Rinks	0
Number of Full-Time Employees	680
Number of Seasonal Employees	355
Number of Volunteers	6,000

Adjusted Budget for Fiscal Year 1998–1999

Revenue

General Funds	$20,757,000
Dedicated Taxes[a]	19,887,000
Fees Retained by the Agency	20,093,000
Private Grants and Donations	0
State and Federal Support	0
Capital Income	9,443,000
Total	$70,180,000

Expenditure

Grounds and Facilities Maintenance and Repair	$40,264,000
Recreational Programming and Activities	20,473,000
Capital Construction and Acquisition	9,443,000
Total	$70,180,000

Expenditure per Resident	**$95**

Note: Adjusted park budget excludes 3Com Park and the San Francisco Zoo.
[a]Includes $3.9 million from city hotel tax and 25-mill ($0.25 per $100) property assessment for the Open Space Program.

less trampled flowers and bushes, left behind trash (including drug paraphernalia), and sometimes intimidated park users; in one hidden vale, police found a "chop shop," where stolen bicycles were brought for stripping. (When the department attempted to enforce the curfew by reprogramming sprinkler systems to turn on in the middle of the night, vagrants countered by vandalizing the nozzles and booby-trapping the hoses with hypodermic needles.)

Mary Burns left, and Mayor Brown elevated her popular recreation director, Joel Robinson, to acting general manager. Mandated to turn the system around, Robinson initiated a major reorganization of the department and began dealing with other image problems (including requiring the staff to wear uniforms), but before he could succeed, the smoldering crisis became a conflagration—literally. In the escalating war between the homeless and the authorities, some of the campers had taken to setting fires in Golden Gate Park. In November 1997, a huge blaze erupted, requiring 70 firefighters and 12 trucks to extinguish it. Realizing that they might actually lose their great park, San Franciscans mobilized, and Mayor Brown ordered the encampments to be shut down.

Meanwhile, the park advocates were ready for action. The city's powerful foundation community moved parks much higher on its priority list and began promoting public/private partnerships based on New York's model. An outspoken community organizer formed a vocal new advocacy group, the Neighborhood Parks Council. Friends of Recreation and Parks, an organization that for 25 years had played a low-key support role for Golden Gate Park, redefined itself, broadened its mission, and increased its budget 30-fold between 1991 and 1999. A children's defense group issued report cards on the quality of playgrounds.

Because the department had no strategic plan, however, the revived activism was almost more than the system could handle. Every group had a different idea of what the department was doing wrong and what it should do differently. The mayor added to the confusion by announcing a nationwide search for a new general manager, then dropping the quest and hiring one of the candidates as his personal assistant to launch an ill-defined, private-sector Park Renaissance Crusade. Citizens' groups, increasingly frustrated, sought more park money from the board of supervisors; when that attempt failed, the groups launched an effort to change the city charter to prohibit a decrease in the Recreation and Park Department's budget for ten years.

In addition to these controversies, the reason for the system's deterioration was unclear. Was the department underfunded or was it operating ineffectively? Compared with other cities, San Francisco's expenditure of $95 per resident placed the funding well above average, and its expenditure of $21,000 per park acre placed it third after Chicago and Cleveland. Pay scales also became an issue; there were reports that the average city gardener and maintenance worker earned three times as much as an equivalent laborer in the private sector. As for procedures, critics pointed out that, because of union and contracting rules and conflicting priorities between city agencies, the renovation of a single playground could take as long as six years. (One union rule seems to explain why few San Francisco street trees are taller than 14 feet, which is the limit under the job classification for most tree pruners; a taller tree requires a differently classified pruner.)

Everyone agreed that a large amount of money—at least $350 million—was needed to deal with deferred maintenance and crumbling facilities, but money was not the only issue. There were also issues of dogs and cars. Leashed dogs are, of course, permitted almost everywhere in San Francisco. But when the National

Golden Gate National Recreation Area

Address	Fort Mason, Building 201
Zip Code	94123
Telephone	(415) 561-4730
Fax	(415) 561-4710
Web Site	www.nps.gov/goga
Agency Acreage in City	4,106
Acreage as Percent of City	13.7%
Acres per 1,000 Residents	5.6
Number of Full-Time Employees	N.A.
Number of Seasonal Employees	N.A.
Number of Volunteers	N.A.
Adjusted Park Budget	N.A.

Note: Acreage includes Golden Gate National Recreation Area land within the city of San Francisco only. The agency is unable to break out any other statistics by geographic region.

Adjusted Budget
(within city of San Francisco only)

Revenue	N.A.
Expenditure	N.A.

Park Service banned free-running, unleashed dogs from some of its expansive beach and bayfront areas (because of the animals' threat to certain endangered birds), some dog lovers began to shift their routines to the city's park system, where unleashed dogs happened to be illegal. Regular park users, particularly mothers of toddlers, complained, but pro-dog militants replied that they, too, were taxpayers and their dogs deserved the same rights in the park as children. The issue became more than just a personal one; with the proliferation of professional dog walkers, it also has commercial ramifications: shepherding ten or more unleashed dogs makes cleaning up their mess almost impossible and increases the potential danger to other park users. The fracas generated outrage on both sides, and Robinson responded by forming an off-leash dog task force. Parks began to be separated into dog and non-dog parks, divided by geography and by time, but the off-leash areas deteriorated through trampling and droppings, and the worst-hit communities have informally renamed some of their parks in honor of canine excrement. By mid-1999, the city had established 17 off-leash areas, some fenced and others not, and agreed to explore the addition of 21 more. Many big-city park systems are struggling with the off-leash dog issue, but San Francisco is at the forefront of the debate.

Cars were another flash point. As in Forest Park in St. Louis, Balboa Park in San Diego, and other parks, the need for parking spaces for the museums in Golden Gate Park conflicted with other park uses, particularly after bicyclists and runners succeeded in getting a one-mile stretch of John F. Kennedy Drive closed to motorized traffic on Sundays and holidays. The lack of easy car access to the DeYoung Art Museum caused the museum's trustees to consider moving to a downtown location, but San Franciscans overwhelmingly preferred to keep the museum in the park. After complex negotiations, the city agreed to let the museum construct a privately financed 1,000-car parking garage under the plaza between the DeYoung Museum and the California Academy of Sciences. In return, 1,000 surface parking spaces in Golden Gate Park will be eliminated. Environmentalists argued that the city would be better served if the $42 million cost of the garage were spent extending a light-rail line to Golden Gate Park, but everyone agrees that the plan will be good for the park itself.

An even more significant replacement of cars for open space took place on the downtown

bayfront between 1991 and 1999, as the city replaced the double-deck Embarcadero Freeway with a handsome 2.5-mile urban promenade, a boulevard, a light-rail line, palm trees, and striking street art. Even though the never-completed Embarcadero had been the bane of antihighway activists since the 1950s, it had not been scheduled for demolition, and city planners struggled for years to design a pedestrian-friendly bayfront under the ugly elevated highway. Then, in 1989, the Loma Prieta earthquake accomplished what politicians had avoided, and the highway's foes rushed to show that repairing the road would be more expensive than tearing it down. Market Street has now been reconnected to the famous Ferry Building and the waterfront, and the city has even constructed the first new pier—for fishing, strolling, and touring—since the 1940s. Although not operated by the Department of Recreation and Parks, the Embarcadero Prom-

A constant stream of cars makes a park seem heavily utilized, but auto-free roadways actually support more users, as shown by Golden Gate Park's Kennedy Drive, which is car-free on Sundays. Like residents of many other cities, San Franciscans are carrying on a lively debate over the proper role of cars in precious urban park space.

enade is an integral part of the Bayshore Trail, a 100-mile-long planned walking and bicycling route around the entire San Francisco Bay.[1]

The Embarcadero project signals a new vision for the San Francisco Bay shoreline. Long consigned to industrial and maritime uses, the bayfront actually has large tracts of unused and underused land ready for conversion to housing, retail establishments, trails, and parks. The first big parcel—a 303-acre abandoned Southern Pacific rail yard in Mission Bay—will be the site of all the uses listed above, plus a new, privately financed baseball stadium for the Giants, a research campus for the University of California, and 49 acres of parks and open space. South of the rail yard, the long-closed Hunter's Point Naval Shipyard has been transferred to the San Francisco Redevelopment Agency, which plans to create some parkland along with other economic uses. On the one hand, redeveloping the bayfront is attractive in many ways, particularly because it is in the sunniest part of town; on the other hand, low-income residents south of Market Street fear that gentrification in already high-priced San Francisco will eliminate the last affordable neighborhoods in the city.

Although San Francisco has picked up almost no new city-owned parkland for more than 30 years, it has steadily gained federal parkland within city boundaries. The Presidio, the famous military base that guarded the entrance to San Francisco Bay for 218 years, has been gradually retired from service and converted to park use. First, in 1972, when the federal government established the Golden Gate National Recreation Area (not to be confused with, and not including, Golden Gate Park), the picturesque shoreline of the Presidio was transferred from the military to the National Park Service under a permanent easement. When the base was decommissioned 22 years later, the entire 1,480-acre Presidio became a national park, albeit under terms that Congress had never before stipulated for a park. The Presidio Trust Act mandates that the Presidio is to be developed as a multiuse facility that must become financially self-sustaining (through rents and leases) by the year 2013. This is the first time that a national park has been designed to include rent-paying residents, shops, and businesses, and the first instance of a park agency—in this case, the Presidio Trust—being challenged to raise money to cover all its costs (an estimated $37 million a year) or face the prospect of having its land sold off to private developers. Regardless of the controversial terms, San Franciscans are getting a park property that is virtually as large and dramatic as Golden Gate Park itself, and the city has thrown itself into planning trails, bikeways, cultural interpretation, forest management, and myriad other tasks with energy and enthusiasm.

With fully one-quarter of the city's surface area covered by parkland, the challenge for San Franciscans is to find the public and private funds—and the shared vision—to retain the beauty of that park system and to ensure that it serves residents' and tourists' needs.

Note

1. For a detailed discussion of the Embarcadero Promenade, see Alexander Garvin et al., *Urban Parks and Open Space* (Washington, D.C.: ULI–the Urban Land Institute, 1997), p. 90.

Chicago

F EW URBAN VISTAS anywhere can compare with the sight of Chicago from Lake Michigan. A massive wall of gleaming apartment buildings, punctuated by even more awesome office towers, meets the unending flat plane of blue water. Between these immutable surfaces lies a splendid skirt of greenery. Whether by car, by bicycle, by skates, or by foot, the unifying element for this tableau of architecture and water is the almost unbroken greenway from Lincoln Park on the north through Grant, Burnham, Jackson, and Rainbow Parks to Calumet Park at the extreme south. With 24 miles and 2,990 acres of shore parks, Chicago has the greenest, most accessible, and most inviting lakefront in the United States.

The many treasures along and near the lake include 31 beaches, almost 5,000 marina slips, the Lincoln Park Zoo, the bicycle and running path through Lincoln Park, Navy Pier with its trademark Ferris wheel, six museums, Jackson Park with a magical Olmstedian landscape that makes the city seem to disappear, scores of sand volleyball courts, and Washington Park, which was also designed by Olmsted with Calvert Vaux and was the first city park to feature playing fields for sports. Even private interests downtown have gotten into the spirit, creating

With 24 miles of shore-line parks totaling 2,990 acres, Chicago has the greenest, most publicly accessible, and most inviting lakefront in the United States.

Chicago Park District

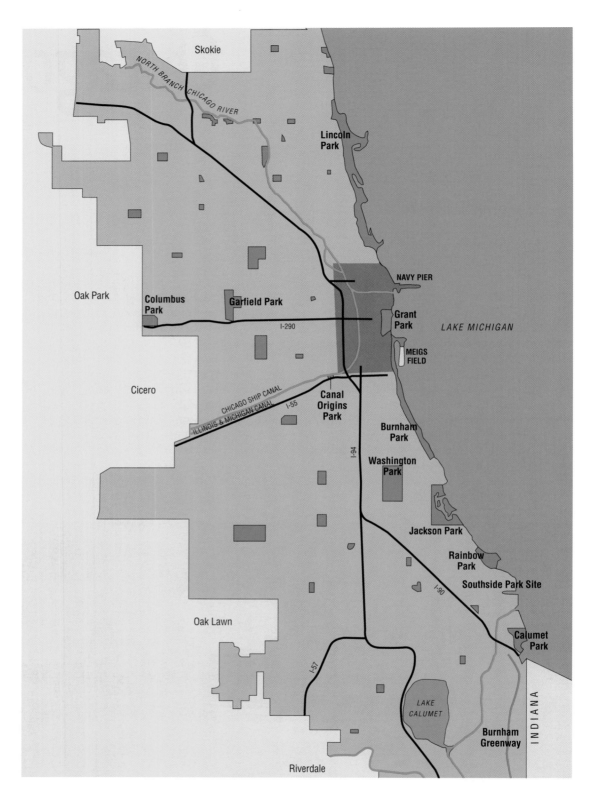

Chicago's network of parks and open space.

a temporary golf driving range and putting green among the skyscrapers until the land can be assembled for another high-rise building.

Back in the 1880s, it was far from a foregone conclusion that Chicago would have either lakeshore parks or a "gold coast" of upscale residences along the shore. (Even today the Chicago model is the exception rather than the rule—it has not been duplicated, for instance, in Cleveland, Detroit, Milwaukee, or Toronto, all of which have relatively modest waterfront park systems.) The concept was first expounded in 1886 by the great city planner and architect, Daniel Burnham, but more than 20 years and much bitter debate ensued before it was formally incorporated in the famous 1909 Plan for Chicago. It then took many more years of relentless lobbying by merchant A. Montgomery Ward and others for it to become a reality. In fact, the waterfront system is still being developed today, with about a half-billion dollars of repairs and improvements currently underway or planned.

Unfortunately, as one moves inland, Chicago's park resources lose their distinction. There are a few great west side spaces like Columbus Park, designed by masterful Jens Jensen, who made use of Illinois native plants and mimicked the original Illinois landscape, as well as Garfield Park, which was designed by Burnham and has the largest plant conservatory in the United States; but if one subtracts the lakefront parks (which constitute 39 percent of the system), the rest of the vast city of Chicago is served by only 4,339 acres of Chicago Park District land, less than the park system of Denver (which has less than one-fifth of the population). All in all, counting city, county, state, and federal parks, Chicago has less parkland per person than every other city profiled in this book except Miami.

Conversely, Chicago makes the most of what it has, intensively managing and using virtually every inch of land, unlike most other cities that have large tracts of undeveloped properties. In fact, with 255 recreation centers, 88 pools, and 11 ice skating rinks, plus thousands of classes, courses, and programs, the Chicago Park District spends more money per capita on its parks and recreational programs—$108 per resident—than all but three of the big cities examined. One reason the district is able to bring in and spend so much—almost $294 million in 1999—is that it is a fully freestanding entity, chartered by the state with the authority to levy taxes and determine its own budget. Although the mayor appoints its board members, the Park District is less subject to political vagaries and fiscal uncertainties than any other big-city park agency in the country (except those in Kansas City and Minneapolis, which have similar structures). For example, the Chicago Park District spends more than twice as much per resident as New York does and more than three times as much as Los Angeles.

When it comes to urban parks and civic beautification, Chicago has been enormously influential, not once but repeatedly. As host of the 1893 World Columbian Exposition, Chicago unveiled "The White City," fairgrounds created by Daniel Burnham and Frederick Law Olmsted,

City Profile for Chicago, Illinois

City Population (1996)	2,722,000
City Area in Acres (1990)	145,408
City Population Density Level	18.7
County in Which City Is Located	Cook
County's Population (1996)	5,097,000
Metropolitan Area Population (1996)	7,734,000
City Relative Cost of Living (base = 100)	N.A.
Number of Publicly Owned Vacant Lots	9,400
Does the City Have a Developer Impact Fee for Parks?	Yes
Municipal Park Acres in City	7,329
National Park Acres in City	0
State Park Acres in City	613
County Park Acres in City	3,687
Total Park Acres in City	11,629

which offered a vision of beautiful, monumental urbanity set among parks and lagoons that instantly electrified and motivated Americans and strongly influenced park and beautification efforts in Denver; Kansas City; San Diego; Seattle; St. Louis; Washington, D.C.; and many other cities.

Sixteen years later, Chicago again attracted planners' and park advocates' attention with Burnham's ambitious comprehensive plan for a green lakefront, a network of inland riverside forest preserves, and a formal boulevard system connecting the elements with civic and commercial areas. Unlike many other cities with great plans, most of this project was implemented.

Chicago's third entry into the national spotlight is occurring now. After a 20-year period of blatant mismanagement, nonperformance, and waste—including six years during which the agency was under an unprecedented court order to reduce race-based inequities—in 1993, Mayor Richard M. Daley targeted the Chicago Park District for a complete overhaul. Despite public skepticism, Daley's top lieutenant, Forrest Claypool, undertook a thorough internal analysis and a massive restructuring of the department, outsourced many of its functions to private contractors, and refocused its mission to the most important core park and recreation activities. Claypool is a lawyer, not a park professional, and his tenure was planned as only a four-year surgical strike, but in that short time the district's turnabout was astonishing. Trees, bushes, and flowers were planted; lighting was upgraded; sports fields were renovated;

ornamental fencing was erected; and projects outside the department's core mission were contracted out, including Soldier Field Stadium, Lincoln Park Zoo, boat mooring rentals, vehicle maintenance, capital construction, and more.

Chicago Park District

Address	425 East McFetridge Drive
Zip Code	60605
Telephone	(312) 747-2657
Fax	(312) 747-6127
Web Site	www.chicagoparkdistrict.com
Agency Acreage in City	7,329
Acreage as Percent of City	5.0%
Acres per 1,000 Residents	2.7
Number of Regional Parks	46
Number of Neighborhood Parks	158
Number of Recreation Centers	260
Number of Pools	89
Number of Golf Courses	6
Number of Tennis Courts	703
Number of Sports Fields	1,019
Number of Marina Slips	4,930
Number of Beaches	32
Miles of Bikeways/Greenways	25
Number of Skating Rinks	12
Number of Full-Time Employees	2,162
Number of Seasonal Employees	568
Number of Volunteers	450

Adjusted Budget for Fiscal Year 1998–1999

Revenue

General Funds	$0
Dedicated Taxes	209,181,000
Fees Retained by the Agency	20,196,000
Private Grants and Donations	4,866,000
State and Federal Support	6,762,000
Capital Income	52,627,000
Total	$293,632,000

Expenditure

Grounds and Facilities Maintenance and Repair	$112,436,000
Recreational Programming and Activities	121,806,000
Capital Construction and Acquisition	59,390,000
Total	$293,632,000

Expenditure per Resident	$108

Staff size was reduced by 33 percent. Current efforts have prevented the threatened demolition of Garfield Park Conservatory—which had deteriorated so much that it was getting fewer than 1,000 visitors a year and $1 million worth of plants froze during the winter of 1993—and it is now being restored through a $20 million public/private renewal.

Despite the improvement, no 2,700-person bureaucracy can be fixed in only four years, and the Chicago Park District is no exception. The agency is still in serious turmoil with regular reorganizations, considerable staff turnover, and a depletion of institutional memory. For instance, after several years of success getting federal transportation grants for bikeways and other projects, the agency appeared to have lost the necessary knowledge base and received no grants at all. Claypool's successor, the Park District's first female, African American general superintendent, Carolyn Williams Meza, was herself a victim of the upheaval and lasted only one and one-half years. Nevertheless, Chicagoans are gradually regaining confidence in their park agency and seem to recognize that improvement is occurring.

The Park District's latest general superintendent, appointed in 1999, is David Doig, a 34-year-old official from the city's Planning Department. Doig's greatest challenge is to increase the gross amount of parkland in the city while maintaining and improving the facilities and programs already in place. Fortunately, he inherited the CitySpace Plan, an award-winning compilation of all Chicago's open space put together over a four-year period by the Chicago Planning Department, the Park District, and the Cook County Forest Preserve (and funded by the Chicago Community Trust). While Chicago is, of course, fully built out, the study found a surprising amount of additional available land and recommended making it usable through joint development, land recycling, and intergovernmental collaboration.

The largest available parcel is an almost one-square-mile brownfield tract on the far south lakeshore that until 1992 was the site of the USX South Works Steel Mill. If pollution and ownership problems can be resolved, the city will formulate a multipurpose development plan that includes a 123-acre park, plus housing, retail establishments, an extension of Lake Shore Drive, and possibly a marina, a museum devoted to labor history and steel making, and more. The park would add two more miles of beach, and the new section of Lake Shore Drive would take a decidedly post–

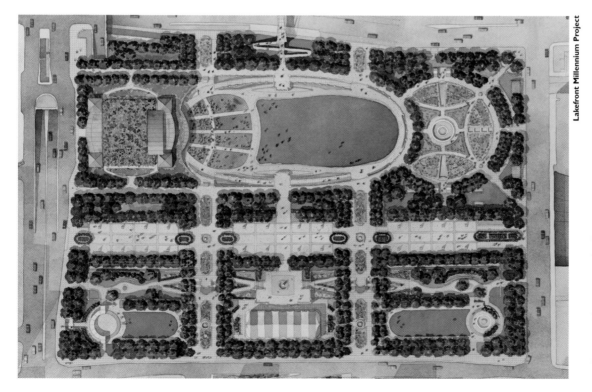

As proof that there is no such thing as a city that's "all built up," Chicago is converting a 16-acre rail yard only blocks from the Loop into Millennium Park, a new visual focus and cultural gathering place for the metropolis.

automobile-age tack. Unlike the rest of the roadway, this section would be located on the west side of the property, far from the shoreline, so as to minimize noise and pollution for nonmotorized lakefront users.

In contrast, the smallest tracts available are house-sized vacant lots scattered throughout

the west, southwest, and northwest sections of Chicago. These parcels were left behind after the demolition of abandoned, tax-derelict buildings in poverty-stricken neighborhoods. Chicago has nearly 10,000 vacant lots but for years failed to take advantage of this potential open space. Finally, through the CitySpace Plan, the logjam

Chicago Park District

The Burnham Greenway, a 7.6-mile trail fashioned from an abandoned Conrail corridor, connects Chicago's south side with neighboring Calumet City. The trail also protects a remnant slice of original prairie that was never disturbed by the railroad. Chicago has hundreds of miles of unused railroad tracks, but the Burnham Greenway is the city's first rail trail.

was broken, and a new public/private enterprise called NeighborSpace was launched in 1996 to provide permanent protection for valuable community gardening sites. Since then, Chicago has been moving into the national forefront of the community gardening movement.

NeighborSpace is technically a private, nonprofit agency, but its $300,000 operating budget is derived from the Park District, the Planning Department, and the County Forest Preserve District, each paying one-third; the first board chair of the agency was the city's planning commissioner. A three-year test project at the outset, NeighborSpace leaped into high gear, permanently protecting 52 green spaces by 1998, and was reauthorized for 20 more years. In addition to community gardens, NeighborSpace promotes small passive parks and green river edges, and it even has three planted railroad embankments. The organization seeks to own most of its properties (and even goes to auctions of tax-delinquent land to bid against private developers), but it takes on a site only if it can sign a maintenance contract with a neighborhood institution. Moreover, for each parcel, the agency requires a $5,000–$7,500 Land Stewardship Fund endowment, money that is frequently acquired from private foundations or local institutions.

The CitySpace Plan also stimulated action on a widely available resource that is severely underused in Chicago (and in virtually every

other city): school yards. For decades the Park District and the Chicago Board of Education had passed each other like ships in the night, but when Mayor Daley took control of the school system in 1994, he was able to begin using the schools' capital construction program as a vehicle to make broader improvements to the city's neighborhoods. Called the School Parks Program, the plan is funded at $12.5 million a year and entails scraping out pavement and replacing it with grass and trees, as well as hammering out joint-use agreements between the schools and the neighborhoods. With a goal of 100 school parks in the first four years, the first significant achievement was in culturally significant Bronzeville, where a grade school, a high school, and some adjacent vacant land were pulled together into a campuslike school and park.

A number of mid-sized park efforts are also underway. Two have been created from classic brownfields, assembled for the Park District by the Trust for Public Land and the Chicago-based Openlands Project. Senka Park, opened in 1998, was a former rail yard; Southside Park, slated to open in 2002, involved the assembly of 169 separate parcels in an economically devastated industrial area near the USX site. Another, the Burnham Greenway, is a 7.6-mile rail trail connecting Chicago's south side with neighboring Calumet City. Even though the nation's very first rail trail—the Illinois Prairie

Path—was created in the Chicago suburbs in 1965, and even though Chicago has hundreds of miles of unused tracks, Burnham is the first rail trail within the city itself. Initiated by the Openlands Project in 1995, the former Conrail corridor will be operated jointly by the Park District and two suburban counties when it opens in 2000.

The most exciting locus of new park activity in Chicago is found along the overworked, underappreciated Chicago River. One highlight is Canal Origins Park, site of the 1836 ground breaking for the Illinois and Michigan (I&M) Canal, the waterway that began Chicago's rise from an obscure lakeside village into the nation's greatest inland metropolis. Only three acres, the canal is extremely significant both historically and culturally, because it marks the city's first effort to join the state of Illinois in creating parkland along the 97-mile I&M Canal. Other river parks have been developed in Chinatown and along the North Branch, where the investment is helping to spur a revitalization of loft buildings in an old neighborhood of brick factories.

Much of the upsurge in Chicago's park efforts is attributable to Mayor Daley, who combines a love of trees, flowers, bicycling, and wrought-iron fences with an impeccable political bloodline (his father was mayor from 1955 to 1976, one of his brothers is currently a Cook County commissioner, and another was the U.S. secretary of commerce). Even though Chicago has long had one of the country's most active and vocal citizens' park advocacy groups, Friends of the Parks, the organization was unable to make much headway until Daley was elected. Established in 1975 to battle against the politicization of the system, Friends of the Parks finally finds itself cheering more often than complaining.

Nevertheless, Chicago has a steep hill to climb to reach its short-term goal of two acres of parkland per 1,000 persons in every neighborhood and its longer-term goal of five acres per person citywide. The first goal requires the development of about 100 acres per year for ten years, which in Chicago could cost as much as $200 million to $300 million on the open market. Because of a cap on its bonding authority, Park District funds will have to be supplemented by other sources—county, state, federal, and private—at much higher levels.

Of course, the city is aggressively pursuing other sources. In 1990, after conservationists protested that a massive expansion of the McCormick Place exposition center would gobble up some parkland, the city came up with an innovative plan to compensate, by relocating several lanes of Lake Shore Drive, with the Metropolitan Pier and Exposition Authority arranging to cover the $90 million cost. The plan resulted in the establishment of 16 acres of new parkland and a beautiful, car-free, museum campus in Burnham Park.

One underused park agency resource for Chicago is the Cook County Forest Preserve District. The Forest Preserve is a gigantic entity with 67,000 acres of mostly natural lands, a $128 million budget, and taxing authority in the second wealthiest county in the nation. Although 55 percent of the Forest Preserve's income stems from Chicago residents, only 5 percent of its land—3,687 acres—is located within city limits, an inequity that has irritated some city residents for years. In reply, the Forest Preserve points out that it also has a cap on its bonding authority and claims that there is virtually no pristine land left in the city, even

Cook County Forest Preserve District (Chicago)

Address	536 N. Harlem Avenue, River Forest, Illinois
Zip Code	60305
Telephone	(312) 261-8400
Agency Acreage in City	3,687
Acreage as Percent of City	2.5%
Acres per 1,000 Residents	1.4

Adjusted Budget for Fiscal Year 1999

Revenue

General Funds	$0
Dedicated Taxes	12,830,000
Fees Retained by the Agency	3,561,000
Private Grants and Donations	689,000
State and Federal Support	0
Capital Income	1,605,000
Total	$18,685,000

Expenditure

Grounds and Facilities Maintenance and Repair	$8,201,000
Recreational Programming and Activities	5,157,000
Capital Construction and Acquisition	4,638,000
Total	$17,996,000

Expenditure per Resident	$7

Note: Adjusted budget is an estimate of expenses solely within the city of Chicago.

Figure 1. Developer Impact Fees

Cities That Have Developer Impact Fees	Cities That Do Not Have Developer Impact Fees
Atlanta	Baltimore
Chicago	Boston
Los Angeles	Cincinnati
Miami	Cleveland
Portland, Oregon	Houston
San Diego	Kansas City, Missouri
San Francisco	Minneapolis
	New York
	Philadelphia
	Pittsburgh
	Seattle
	Tampa

Note: Information on the remaining cities was not available.

though the CitySpace Plan found thousands of acres of relatively undeveloped wetlands teeming with wildlife around Lake Calumet on the city's south side. Although initially resistant because of possible environmental contamination in the area, the Forest Preserve District has been feeling pressure from Mayor Daley and may ultimately increase its holdings in the city.

Daley also succeeded in requiring every new housing development or loft conversion project to include open space or a commensurate payment for the acquisition of open space elsewhere. (This open-space impact fee is expected to generate about $1.5 million a year.) Daley also convinced then Governor Jim Edgar to agree to close tiny Meigs Field Airport so that it can be converted into Northerly Island Park, as Daniel Burnham envisioned nearly a century ago. If the conversion does, in fact, occur, Northerly Island Park will become another lakefront jewel, complementing the decking of unsightly railroad tracks near Grant Park to create the new Millennium Park.

How can a city turn its parks around so dramatically? Perhaps, as Forrest Claypool put it, "It helps to have a crisis." Or perhaps it harks back to the very motto on Chicago's great seal: Urbs in Horto—"City in a Garden."

Boston

IF INNOVATION WERE battery powered, Boston would be the Energizer™ bunny of American cities. Most other early U.S. settlements have, to one extent or another, reached their limits or become resistant to change, while Boston has maintained an energetic trajectory into the future. And nowhere is Boston's inventiveness more apparent than in the way the city deals with parks.

Boston gave America its first park. In fact, it was so long ago—1634—that the word itself wasn't used, and to this day the city's central green space is called the Common. It was in Boston that Frederick Law Olmsted pulled all his ideas together into the park-and-drainage masterpiece known as the Emerald Necklace. Boston began the playground movement in 1891. In addition, Boston took the idea of build-

The Boston Public Garden, dating from 1823, is a key jewel in the Emerald Necklace of parks stretching from Boston Common to Franklin Park. One reason for the Public Garden's lasting luster is the efforts of its private support and advocacy group, the Friends of the Public Garden, the oldest of 60 friends' groups active in Boston.

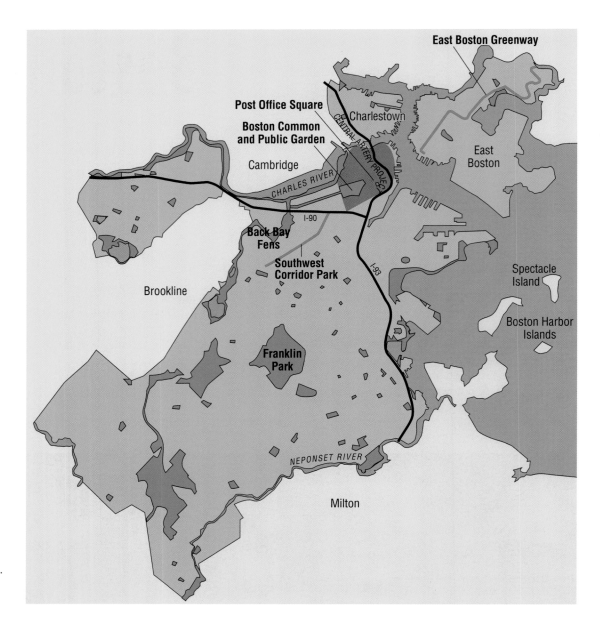

East Boston Greenway

Post Office Square

Charlestown

Boston Common and Public Garden

Cambridge

East Boston

CHARLES RIVER

CENTRAL ARTERY PROJECT

Back Bay Fens

I-90

Southwest Corridor Park

Brookline

I-93

Spectacle Island

Boston Harbor Islands

Franklin Park

NEPONSET RIVER

Milton

Boston's network of parks and open space.

ing a park over an underground parking lot and showed that it could pay for itself. With the city's approaching quadricentennial in 2030, Boston is again innovating, with its plans for a grand new Harbor Islands park and a greenway over the top of the country's most expensive underground highway.

The unending creativity coming out of Boston is not easy to explain. Perhaps it is the result of the unusual combination of old-line preservationism with the constant influx of 130,000 college students in a pressure-cooker space smaller than the island of Martha's Vineyard. Possibly, Boston's location was so challenging that the city could survive only through constant alteration of its environment: first filling in vast areas of shallow marshland, next tackling problems of sluggish river flow and water

pollution, then constructing a tangle of rail lines and roadways, and now seeking to undo the damage of those transportation corridors. Each environmental alteration resulted in different types of green spaces.

Whether or not all these factors have given Boston the country's best park system is hard to determine. Boston's bureaucratic structure is so convoluted that even figuring out the numbers —much less what they mean—is daunting. Despite its diminutive size (the third smallest city covered in this book by land area), Boston has three different agencies handling parks and recreation: Boston Department of Parks and Recreation, Boston Department of Community Centers, and the Metropolitan District Commission. In addition, the city contains land managed by the National Park Service, the state's

Department of Environmental Management, and the city's Conservation Commission, as well as a variety of private institutions, including land trusts and even Harvard University.

Adding it all up yields impressive totals on paper. Of the eight high-density cities described in this book, Boston is second in acres of parkland per resident (after San Francisco), second in park dollars spent per resident (after Chicago), and third in park acreage as a percent of city area (after New York and San Francisco). In reality, however, the friction among so many different entities reduces the efficiency of the systems. Historically, there have been long stretches when one or more of Boston's park agencies strayed from its mission. Through much of the 19th century, the city fell far behind such park leaders as Baltimore, New York, and Philadelphia, until a burst of civic boosterism (buttressed by landscape architects Olmsted and Charles Eliot, son of the famous Harvard president) resulted in the Emerald Necklace as well as the creation of a metropolitan park district that amassed 9,200 acres by 1900. After 1930, the city's system again languished and, in fact, shrank: two of Olmsted's great small jewels were paved over, one for a highway and another for Logan Airport; and 17 acres of Franklin Park were given over for the construction of a state hospital. The situation got worse: in 1954 the Sears and Roebuck Company demanded—and got—a few acres of the Back Bay Fens in return for building a store there. Olmsted's filled-in waterway was used as a parking lot.

Even the post–Earth Day 1970s did not produce a turnabout. At one point when the Boston Parks Department relocated, almost all its records were thrown out, including documents giving the location of underground utility pipes and wires. By the mid-1980s the system was in shambles, with overflowing trash barrels, uncut grass, hoopless basketball boards, unpruned trees, burned-out field houses, glass-strewn tot lots, graffiti-covered walls, and rutted fields. Meanwhile, the city itself was sliding, as disinvestment and arson-for-hire increased the number of vacant lots to 20,000.

Saddest was the condition of 510-acre Franklin Park, generally considered one of Olmsted's three greatest artistic creations (along with Central and Prospect Parks in New York). The park is a grand assemblage of meadows, hills, woods, stone bridges, picturesque gatehouses, rustic shelters, curving roadways and paths, and occasional perfect views to the horizon—in all, a wonderful rural environment in the middle of the city. Unfortunately, in its dilapidated, under-maintained state, the park helped pull down its Roxbury neighborhood, which, in turn, made the park more dangerous and reduced its use. Franklin Park never quite reached its potential, because it was not able to compete with the Common as Bostonians' central park and central love, but the Common also went downhill. Trampled by too many big events and too little upkeep, undermined by a clumsily designed and built underground parking garage, the Common suffered: its band shell was abandoned, the skating pond became unusable, and trees and turf were dying. The other parks, from silt-choked Back Bay Fens to scores of neighborhood playgrounds, were in similar shape.

The tide was about to turn, however. Park activism had been incubating quietly among frustrated but enterprising citizens' groups, beginning with the formation of Friends of the Public Garden in 1971 and the Franklin Park Coalition in 1975. Aware that the city was unwilling or unable to save their parks for them, these groups tackled the task themselves either by raising private money or by undertaking direct physical labor, or both. The idea caught on, and within a few years, 60 or more fledgling friends' groups and community garden land trusts sprang up, as well as an umbrella entity, the Boston GreenSpace Alliance. Because of their agitation, the Boston Foundation convened a year-long series of meetings between

City Profile for Boston, Massachusetts

City Population (1996)	558,000
City Area in Acres (1990)	30,976
City Population Density Level	18.0
County in Which City Is Located	Suffolk
County's Population (1996)	643,000
Metropolitan Area Population (1996)	3,263,000
City Relative Cost of Living (base = 100)	136.6
Number of Publicly Owned Vacant Lots	3,000
Does the City Have a Developer Impact Fee for Parks?	No
Municipal Park Acres in City[a]	2,893
National Park Acres in City	41
State Park Acres in City[b]	1,931
County Park Acres in City	0
Total Park Acres in City	4,865

[a]Includes 200 acres held by the Boston Conservation Commission.
[b]Land held by Metropolitan District Commission.

scores of stakeholders, resulting in an extra-ordinary report, *The Greening of Boston*. Also incubating for several years was an appreciation for greening by populist Mayor Ray Flynn, who saw what a deep emotional response parks and recreation brought out in his South Boston constituents. Working with City Council President (later to become mayor) Tom Menino, Flynn used the impact of *The Greening of Boston* to double the operating budget of the Parks and Recreation Department and to initiate a $75 million capital construction campaign.

At about that time, the Parks Department brought in Justine Liff as its director of planning and development. A dynamic and upbeat manager, who had learned the ropes at the South Street Seaport in New York and Rowes Wharf in Boston, Liff brought to her work a private-sector can-do attitude that, by 1996, had propelled her to the position of commissioner. Although no public agency in Boston ever turns around quickly, Liff has succeeded in raising the profile of the Parks Department, successfully marketing it to both the corporate community (resulting in numerous new public/private partnerships) and the public (increasing usership

Frederick Law Olmsted's Emerald Necklace was a concept, but Donna DePrisco's unique creation was real, complete with 25 karats of emeralds and five karats of diamonds. The necklace was auctioned off at the 1998 Emerald Necklace Ball for $20,000, which helped fund the restoration of Boston's original park system.

Boston Department of Parks and Recreation

Address	1010 Massachusetts Avenue
Zip Code	02118
Telephone	(617) 635-4505
Fax	(617) 635-3173
Web Site	www.ci.boston.ma.us/parks/
Agency Acreage in City	2,693
Acreage as Percent of City	8.7%
Acres per 1,000 Residents	4.9
Number of Regional Parks	9
Number of Neighborhood Parks	215
Number of Recreation Centers	0
Number of Pools	5
Number of Golf Courses	2
Number of Tennis Courts	87
Number of Sports Fields	133
Number of Marina Slips	0
Number of Beaches	1
Miles of Bikeways/Greenways	5
Number of Skating Rinks	1
Number of Full-Time Employees	245
Number of Seasonal Employees	40
Number of Volunteers	997

Adjusted Budget for Fiscal Year 1998–1999

Revenue

General Funds	$9,239,000
Dedicated Taxes	0
Fees Retained by the Agency	0
Private Grants and Donations	1,900,000
State and Federal Support	5,389,000
Capital Income	10,800,000
Total	$27,328,000

Expenditure

Grounds and Facilities Maintenance and Repair	$13,516,000
Recreational Programming and Activities	2,322,000
Capital Construction and Acquisition	10,800,000
Total	$26,638,000

Expenditure per Resident	**$48**

Note: Adjusted park budget excludes the agency's Cemeteries Division.

and awareness). She also knows how to put the fun back in parks: in 1998, she hosted the Emerald Necklace Ball, which included auctioning off a one-of-a-kind necklace (with genuine emeralds) that brought in $20,000.

In the meantime, while park advocates were trying to save what they already had, a number of other forces were coming together to give Boston new parkland. The first was Boston's potent antihighway coalition. Ever since the Massachusetts Turnpike had ripped a gaping gash through Allston, Back Bay, and Chinatown, and Interstate 93 had erected a wall of steel and traffic between downtown Boston and the historic North End, Bostonians had sworn that they would never again allow a gigantic roadway to be built through their colonial-scale downtown streetscape. Therefore, when the next freeway was proposed, they defeated the plan and persuaded the U.S. Congress to give the city the equivalent sum—$1.4 billion—for transit. By excavating underground, the city was able to depress and cover the Amtrak line, a subway, and several commuter tracks. On top, the city constructed the 4.7-mile, 52-acre Southwest Corridor Park, a state-of-the-art walking and biking trail complete with 20 children's play areas, ten community gardens, and scores of ball courts. What had been a dirty, noisy rail line squeezed between low-rent apartment buildings became an unparalleled amenity, adding economic, social, and environmental value to the South End.

A few miles away, Post Office Square in the heart of the financial district had a very different group of visionaries giving that same concept —underground construction—a completely different twist. Led by intrepid developer Norman Leventhal, 20 business leaders gambled private money that they could replace a neighborhood-blighting eyesore with a spectacular park and could make money doing so. Contributing and borrowing $80 million, they bought and demolished a run-down four-story parking garage, excavated an enormous hole and converted it into seven levels of automobile parking, and covered the facility with a $2 million park complete with an outdoor cafe, fountains and sculptures, granite walls, movable chairs, and 125 different species of plants, bushes, flowers, and trees. The Park at Post Office Square added only 1.7 acres to Boston's total green space, but it completely redefined the financial district and has brightened the lives of thousands of downtown workers. The 24-hour underground parking garage not only generates millions of dollars (some of which will be contributed to

Boston Department of Community Centers

Address	1010 Massachusetts Avenue
Zip Code	02118
Telephone	(617) 635-4920
Fax	(617) 635-4524
Web Site	www.ci.boston.ma.us/communitycenters
Agency Acreage in City	0
Number of Recreation Centers	43
Number of Pools	20
Number of Tennis Courts	13
Number of Full-Time Employees	472
Number of Seasonal Employees	1,000
Number of Volunteers	800

Adjusted Budget for Fiscal Year 1998–1999

Revenue

General Funds	$11,750,000
Dedicated Taxes	0
Fees Retained by the Agency	0
Private Grants and Donations	3,000,000
State and Federal Support	2,200,000
Capital Income	1,962,000
Total	$18,912,000

Expenditure

Grounds and Facilities Maintenance and Repair	$540,000
Recreational Programming and Activities	11,210,000
Capital Construction and Acquisition	1,962,000
Total	$13,712,000
Expenditure per Resident	**$25**

neighborhood parks once the loans and dividends are paid off in 2007), but also produces a stream of foot traffic that helps keep the park busy and safe.[1]

But Southwest Corridor Park and the Park at Post Office Square were simply trial runs for the "big dig"—the $13.5 billion Central Artery Project. The largest urban highway project ever undertaken, the Central Artery is Boston's effort to undo the damage of its freeway system by putting most of it underground and decking it with almost $200 million worth of parks, boulevards, walkways, landscaping, and enclosed gardens. The project will result in about 150 acres of new parkland, 23 in the heart of down-

Boston's $13.5 billion Central Artery Project, nicknamed the "Big Dig," involves burying Interstate 93 under the city's central business district and replacing the old elevated highway with a landscaped boulevard and acres of parkland.

town. Among other benefits, Bostonians will finally be able to walk unimpeded to the North End, ride their bicycles along the final "lost half-mile" from the Charles River to Boston Harbor, enjoy open space and spectacular views from park-poor East Boston and Charlestown, and savor the gift of Spectacle Island.

Spectacle Island, one of more than 30 islands scattered throughout Boston Harbor, is slated to become the centerpiece of Boston's next park, the recently approved but not yet developed Boston Harbor National Park Area. Previously used for everything from harbor defenses and wastewater treatment plants to prisons, land-fills, and American Indian internment camps, the islands promise to be a significant conservation, recreation, and visual resource. Every island has a different history of uses and different remains; Spectacle Island, for instance, was the former location of a quarantine hospital, then a summer resort, then a horse-rendering plant, and now the landfill for the Central Artery excavation. When that spoil material is shaped, packed down, and seeded, the island will become the 100-acre hub of the new national park, which will include a visitor's center, a ferry dock, and a marina.

Some of the islands are already parks; others will be used totally or partly as public space after their many nonconforming, nonproductive uses are cleaned up or eliminated. The park thus created will be an archetypal Boston partnership that includes the Boston Parks and Recreation Department, the Metropolitan District Commission, the Department of Environmental Management, the National Park Service, the Massachusetts Water Resources Authority, and 30 other public and private entities.

The Boston park story goes on and on, and the system is as multilayered as any in the nation. The city has a flourishing network of community gardens, many permanently protected by neighborhood land trusts; a fund specifically devoted to the small bits of un-developed, unprotected natural areas sprinkled through the city; and the Boston Schoolyard Initiative. In addition, Boston's "Back to the Beaches" campaign stimulates enjoyment of the city's increasingly less-polluted waterfront areas. Finally, the park system includes the new trail efforts of the Trust for Public Land and the Boston Natural Areas Fund in East Boston and alongside the Neponset River; the Massachusetts Audubon Society's effort to turn an abandoned mental hospital campus into a nature center; and the new Emerald Necklace Conservancy.

Metropolitan District Commission (within Boston)

Address	20 Somerset Street
Zip Code	02108
Telephone	(617) 727-5228
Fax	(617) 727-8301
Web Site	www.state.ma.us/mdc
Agency Acreage in City	1,931
Acreage as Percent of City	6.2
Acres per 1,000 Residents	3.5
Number of Regional Parks	4
Number of Neighborhood Parks	26
Number of Recreation Centers	N.A.
Number of Pools	7
Number of Golf Courses	0
Number of Tennis Courts	N.A.
Number of Sports Fields	15
Number of Marina Slips	N.A.
Number of Beaches	10
Miles of Bikeways/Greenways	14
Number of Skating Rinks	12
Number of Full-Time Employees	N.A.
Number of Seasonal Employees	N.A.
Number of Volunteers	N.A.

Adjusted Budget for Fiscal Year 1998

Revenue

General Funds	$0
Dedicated Taxes	0
Fees Retained by the Agency	0
Private Grants and Donations	0
State and Federal Support	8,543,000
Capital Income	4,724,000
Total	$13,267,000

Expenditure

Grounds and Facilities Maintenance and Repair	$8,543,000
Recreational Programming and Activities	0
Capital Construction and Acquisition	4,724,000
Total	$13,267,000

Expenditure per Resident	**$24**

Note: Statistics refer to Metropolitan District Commission facilities and estimated budget only within the city of Boston.

Can Bostonians keep up this level of effort? Can they deliver on so many projects? Can they cover the cost of daily maintenance and upkeep? Will the money keep flowing if the local economy cools down? There is consensus that Boston's Parks and Recreation Department is doing a better job today than it has in the past 50 years. The city has never witnessed such a cadre of support and advocacy organizations. However, given the city's erratic history with parks—today's burst of activity seems exciting partly because so little happened for so long— there is reason for concern for the future.

Boston's greatest need is more money and a more stable funding base for parks, but the politics of park funding is complicated. With the city's population representing less than 15 percent of the Boston metropolitan area, and with the state deeply involved in virtually every city project, any funding mechanism— such as a real estate transfer tax or property tax add-on—would have to be designed to acquire land regionally, not just in the city. However, the obvious existing entity authorized to acquire land—the Metropolitan District Commission— has too many political liabilities to be given more money by the legislature. Added to this is Massachusetts's almost nonexistent county system, which forces citizens to make all local decisions town by town. Finding a fair, practicable, and profitable income source is a particularly tough challenge.

Ultimately, Boston will have to negotiate a metropolitan service district with its 40–50 neighboring jurisdictions, an entity modeled on the one in Minnesota's Twin Cities, so that the region can plan, implement, and maintain big projects, such as park systems. Until that happens, Boston will have to continue to rely on the radical innovations of its young visionaries, coupled with the preservationist bent of the guardians of the city's Olmstedian heritage.

Note

1. For a detailed description of the creation and design of the Park at Post Office Square, see Alexander Garvin et al., *Urban Parks and Open Space* (Washington, D.C.: ULI–the Urban Land Institute, 1997), p. 146.

Philadelphia

"I'D RATHER BE HERE than in Philadelphia" reads the epitaph on W. C. Fields's tombstone, which only proves that the comedian never set foot in Fairmount Park. No one who has bicycled along Philadelphia's car-free West Park Drive on a crisp weekend day, relaxed for tea in the Japanese Garden, delighted at the lightbulb-outlined boathouses perched beside the Schuylkill River, or attended an outdoor concert in the natural bowl of Robin Hood Dell can forget Fairmount Park. The park has myriad other pleasures as well, including horseback riding on Forbidden Drive, whisking down the 12-foot-wide, polished wooden slide at Smith Playground, gazing at azaleas behind the art museum, and marveling at the mechanical ingenuity of the 19th-century Fairmount Water Works.

W. C. Fields apparently also never set foot in Rittenhouse Square, arguably the most successful six acres of urban green space in the country. In *The Death and Life of Great American Cities*, Jane Jacobs called this elegant oasis amid high rises "one of Philadelphia's greatest assets today, the center of a fashionable neighborhood —indeed the only old neighborhood in Philadelphia which is spontaneously rehabilitating its edges and extending its real estate values."[1]

When William Penn laid out Philadelphia in 1682, he decreed his village a "greene countrie

Alexander Garvin

One of five squares laid out in 1682 by William Penn himself, Rittenhouse Square continues to be one of the most successful urban parks in the United States, anchoring and adding value to its mixed residential and commercial neighborhood in downtown Philadelphia.

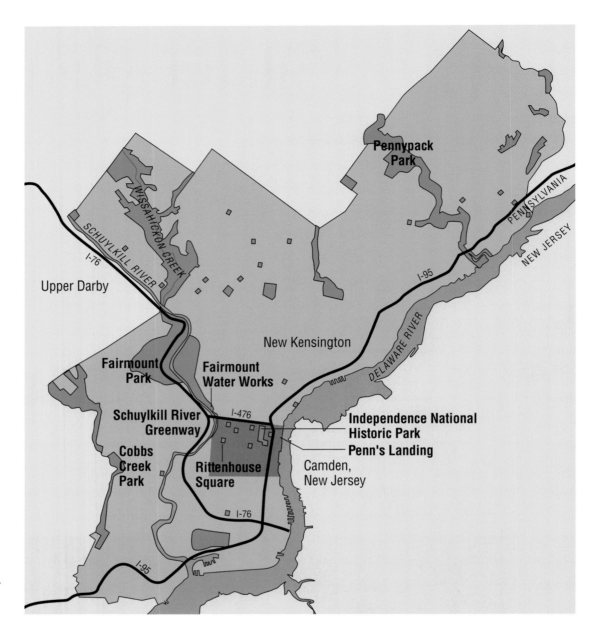

Philadelphia's network of parks and open space.

towne" and instructed his surveyor to provide one acre of open space for every five acres of development. Surprisingly, despite some stretches of dismal, gray rowhouses on almost treeless streets, Philadelphia remains a greener city than most people realize, with fully 12.4 percent of its area devoted to parkland, more than the other densely populated cities covered in this book, with the exception of Boston, New York, and San Francisco. Moreover, the city boasts an astonishingly extensive recreation program, which has more recreation centers (158) and more swimming pools (85) than any city but Chicago. In addition, the city hires 1,700 seasonal employees every summer and runs a sports league program that involves 10,000 young people.

Nevertheless, Philadelphians are facing critical challenges with the city's park and recreation system. Natural vegetation is being choked out by invasive species like knotweed, ponds are filling up with cattails and sediment, an explosion of deer is eating away the undergrowth, recreation centers have deteriorated to the point of uselessness, roadways are crumbling, some tennis courts are "BYON" (bring your own net), and staffing levels have been slashed. In addition, trees on streets are dying faster than they are being replaced, bicyclists are wrangling with motorists for more time and space on park roadways, ballfields are overbooked and overused, and commuter traffic frequently clogs West Park Drive. The easiest way to spot the distress is to look at the budget: ranked by dollars per resident, Philadelphia spends less on parks and recreation than all but six of the cities profiled in this book.

Part of the explanation is that Philadelphia's economy has been *in extremis*. The city has lost more than one-quarter of its population since the 1950s, and it is overwhelmed by one of the nation's highest rates of abandoned buildings. This is a city that has been under the watchful eye of a financial control board since 1991. Although things are looking up, there is still a long way to go, and—unlike in Pittsburgh—city hall does not have a strategic plan that ties parks into the city's overall marketing and economic development picture.

Economics do not tell the whole story, however. Unlike every other municipality except Boston, Cincinnati, and Tampa, Philadelphia does not have a unified parks and recreation department. It has two unrelated agencies: the Fairmount Park Commission, an independent entity that manages 8,900 acres of parks and forests and has a mission that focuses mainly on land protection; and the Philadelphia Department of Recreation, a city agency that operates scores of recreation centers and whose mission is to serve people. To complicate matters, the Park Commission also runs some recreation centers, while the Recreation Department owns about 100 squares and parcels of parkland. Moreover, while the head of the Recreation Department is appointed by the mayor and serves on the mayoral cabinet, the Fairmount Park Commission is governed by a 17-member board of directors. (By statute, the mayor is one of the directors but not the chair, and most of the directors are appointed by a group of judges, none of whom is directly responsible to anyone in Philadelphia.)

The gulf between the two agencies is wide. Whereas most Americans automatically assume that parks and recreation go hand in hand, Philadelphians have come to believe that the same bureau cannot administer both trees and people. In fact, in the early 1990s, when the president of the city council proposed combining the agencies as part of a larger revision of the city's charter, the ensuing outcry from Fairmount's extensive support network quashed not only that idea but brought down the entire charter proposal as well. As a fallback, the two agencies agreed in principle to exchange parkland for recreation programs, but even that plan fell victim to bickering.

Understanding the split requires knowing some history. The seeds of Philadelphia's park system were sown in the 1790s, when a cata-

City Profile for Philadelphia, Pennsylvania

City Population (1996)	1,478,000
City Area in Acres (1990)	86,464
City Population Density Level	17.1
County in Which City Is Located	Philadelphia
County's Population (1996)	1,478,000
Metropolitan Area Population (1996)	4,953,000
City Relative Cost of Living (base = 100)	120.5
Number of Publicly Owned Vacant Lots	15,800
Does the City Have a Developer Impact Fee for Parks?	No
Municipal Park Acres in City	10,364
National Park Acres in City	46
State Park Acres in City	275
County Park Acres in City	0
Total Park Acres in City	10,685

strophic epidemic of yellow fever, attributed to infested drinking supplies, killed 10,000 persons and led to a civic outcry for clean municipal water. With the town's primary waterway—the Delaware River—already polluted by commerce and industry, city leaders turned to the more pristine Schuylkill River for construction of a waterworks and a reservoir. In 1844, as growing pollution threatened the Schuylkill, the city purchased a 43-acre estate just above the water intake pipe. The land became the first parcel of Fairmount Park, which was then steadily expanded through public and private fundraising efforts. In 1867, the Fairmount Park Commission was created to care for the growing property, which soon included watershed lands on both sides of the Schuylkill as well as along sparkling Wissahickon Creek. Eventually, industry made water from the lower Schuylkill unfit to drink, but today, while the Delaware River waterfront is still almost devoid of parkland, the Schuylkill is the city's premier recreational artery, bolstered by parks along other stream valleys like Cobbs Creek and Pennypack Creek.

It is noteworthy that the Fairmount Park Commission was chartered by the state rather than by the city. Once the nation's preeminent city, by 1830 Philadelphia had fallen behind New York in population, commerce, and national leadership. Although the city continued to grow tremendously (and today is the nation's fifth most populous city), the flame of civic vitality seems to have flickered, and for more than a century Philadelphia settled into a pattern of complacency tinged with governmental corruption. Progress in Philadelphia, when it came, was attributable mostly to private individuals or to the state of Pennsylvania, not to the city government's leadership. (Even under exceptionally dynamic mayors, parks sometimes suffered: near the end of his life Mayor Richardson Dilworth, the most respected of them, admitted that the worst decision he had made was giving up 450 acres of pristine Fairmount Park forest to allow construction of the Schuylkill Expressway.)

The Fairmount Park Commission gets 80 percent of its budget from the city council but has a structure largely divorced from all other city agencies (and, fittingly, is housed far from City Hall in a gargantuan edifice left over from the 1876 Centennial Exposition). The commission's director is 30-year veteran William Mifflin, a native Philadelphian, who worked his way up through the ranks, starting as a groundskeeper in 1968. Though woefully underfunded, with millions of dollars' worth of deferred maintenance, the commission has one matchless asset: the support of 75 private friends' organizations, which, in 1998, collectively raised well over $2 million and provided more than 21,000 volunteers. In addition, over the years, lovers of

Fairmount have established perpetual park trust funds with total assets of about $4 million. In 1996, in reputedly the nation's largest city park grant ever, the William Penn Foundation celebrated its 50th anniversary by awarding the commission $26.6 million to improve facilities and develop environmental education programs.

Meanwhile, the Philadelphia Recreation Department, headquartered in a center-city office building, could hardly have a more different heritage or culture. Established initially as a small program within the Welfare Department around the turn of the century, the agency was spun off as a full-fledged department only in 1952. Under the 24-year leadership of Robert Crawford, the department ballooned swiftly in staffing and in physical plant, so that by the mid-1980s it employed more staff members and operated more recreation facilities per capita than any other comparable agency in the nation. The Recreation Department was a glowing showpiece on paper, but its output and performance did not always measure up to its description. Too many centers were created as political favors to city council members, and more than a few employees landed jobs as a result of cronyism rather than merit. When

Philadelphia Department of Recreation

Address	1515 Arch Street, 10th Floor
Zip Code	19102
Telephone	(215) 683-3600
Fax	(215) 683-3599
Web Site	www.phila.gov/departments/recreation
Agency Acreage in City	1,464
Acreage as Percent of City	1.7%
Acres per 1,000 Residents	1.0
Number of Recreation Centers	150
Number of Pools	82
Number of Golf Courses	0
Number of Tennis Courts	100
Number of Sports Fields	N.A.
Number of Marina Slips	0
Number of Beaches	0
Miles of Bikeways/Greenways	0
Number of Skating Rinks	5
Number of Full-Time Employees	550
Number of Seasonal Employees	1,700
Number of Volunteers	N.A.

Adjusted Budget for Fiscal Year 1998

Revenue

General Funds	$29,379,000
Dedicated Taxes	0
Fees Retained by the Agency	0
Private Grants and Donations	627,000
State and Federal Support	5,961,000
Capital Income	12,317,000
Total	$48,284,000

Expenditure

Grounds and Facilities Maintenance and Repair	$8,744,000
Recreational Programming and Activities	27,223,000
Capital Construction and Acquisition	14,288,000
Total	$50,255,000

Expenditure per Resident	**$34**

Note: Adjusted park budget excludes Veterans Stadium, the Mummers Museum, and the Afro-American Museum. Acreage owned does not include Camp William Penn, located in the Pocono Mountains.

Fairmount Park Commission

Land along the Schuylkill River was first purchased in the 1840s to protect the purity of Philadelphia's drinking water. Today, 4,167-acre Fairmount Park–Wissahickon Valley is the city's recreation and conservation centerpiece, the second largest municipal park in the East and the home of famed Boathouse Row, shown here.

the city collapsed into near-bankruptcy, the Recreation Department's bubble burst and the staffing level plunged from 1,200 to 489.

A phoenix is slowly rising out of the ashes, however, thanks to former Mayor Ed Rendell's choice in 1992 of Mike DiBerardinis, a dynamic and charismatic former community organizer, as commissioner of recreation, and thanks to the work of an exceptional private group, the Pennsylvania Horticultural Society. Recreation commissioner until Mayor John Street took office in January 2000, DiBerardinis was a graduate first of the rough-and-tumble politics of the near-north neighborhood of New Kensington, and then of the staff of U.S. Representative John Foglietta. The commissioner was well suited to his mission: in his younger days as a community organizer DiBerardinis once took a sledgehammer, called the press, and threatened to personally tear down a dilapidated shed that was encouraging criminal activity in his neighborhood park. (The city agreed to improve the park.) "For a city recreation department to survive today's tough political and financial realities, it's got to prove its value to the whole community," DiBerardinis said. "Sports and crafts in and of themselves are not enough— the vision has to include youth intervention and crime prevention."

To give his message reality, the department started symbolically, scrapping its old motto, "Life—Enjoy It!" for the more relevant, "Building Youth, Building Neighborhoods." It then launched a huge after-school program, which now provides activities at 150 locations three

hours a day, five days a week. Situated at recreation centers, churches, and other community facilities, the program is funded jointly by private foundations and the city, and it employs local staff members chosen by local leaders. "Starting at zero, after two years we were the biggest after-school provider in the city," reported DiBerardinis.

Tapped by Mayor Rendell to chair a multiagency Violence Prevention Committee, DiBerardinis landed a $10 million grant from the

Philadelphia Recreation Department

Because Philadelphia has two different agencies for parks and recreation, the Recreation Department can focus all its efforts on a wide array of cultural, sports, arts, after-school, and violence prevention programs. Despite this strength, coordination with the Fairmount Park Commission can sometimes pose a challenge.

Fairmount Park Commission (Philadelphia)

Address	42nd Street and Parkside Avenue
Zip Code	19131
Telephone	(215) 685-0000
Fax	(215) 878-9859
Web Site	www.phila.gov/departments/ fairpark
Agency Acreage in City	8,900
Acreage as Percent of City	10.3%
Acres per 1,000 Residents	5.8
Number of Regional Parks	8
Number of Neighborhood Parks	56
Number of Recreation Centers	8
Number of Pools	3
Number of Golf Courses	6
Number of Tennis Courts	100
Number of Sports Fields	125
Number of Marina Slips	0
Number of Beaches	0
Miles of Bikeways/Greenways	45
Number of Skating Rinks	1
Number of Full-Time Employees	215
Number of Seasonal Employees	100
Number of Volunteers	21,000

Adjusted Budget for Fiscal Year 1997–1998

Revenue

General Funds	$12,609,000
Dedicated Taxes	0
Fees Retained by the Agency	107,000
Private Grants and Donations	3,793,000
State and Federal Support	202,000
Capital Income	4,039,000
Total	$20,750,000

Expenditure

Grounds and Facilities Maintenance and Repair	$9,665,000
Recreational Programming and Activities	906,000
Capital Construction and Acquisition	8,181,000
Total	$18,752,000

Expenditure per Resident	$13

Robert Wood Johnson Foundation to identify neighborhood leaders in low-income areas and to help forge a common youth agenda that would unite all segments of the community. His second goal was to develop better communication between the Recreation Department and the Police Department's Police Athletic League program. Unfortunately, differing cultures and expectations have hampered the success of that affiliation.

Meanwhile, a marriage that *is* working is the one between the Recreation Department and the Pennsylvania Horticultural Society. Growing out of a modest effort 30 years ago to encourage flower boxes and street trees in the inner city, the Society has built its Philadelphia Green program into the nation's most ambitious and successful private program to revitalize hard-hit neighborhoods through community gardening, greening, side-lot acquisition, and creation of jobs in horticulture.[2] In communities that also contain a park (scores of which are owned but rarely tended by the Recreation Department), Philadelphia Green works to bring those spaces back to life, too. Since 1993, thanks to grants from the ubiquitous William Penn Foundation and the Pew Charitable Trust, Philadelphia Green has adopted nine parks; if more funding comes through, the group will take on all 100.

Almost everything that goes on in neighborhood-based Philadelphia plays out against a backdrop of abandoned housing. According to a 1992 study, except for northeast Philadelphia, the swank Chestnut Hill area, and Society Hill downtown, virtually every neighborhood is awash in abandoned residential buildings, deserted factories, relinquished shops, and 15,800 parcels of vacant land. The greatest challenge faced by advocates of parks and open spaces is what to do with this land. They must find a way to work with housing advocates and community development interests to turn the abandonment crisis into a sustainable city opportunity that will provide the next generation of Philadelphia residents—which the city hopes will include returnees—with a more livable city the second time around. No one anywhere in the country has found a common language between community developers and nature conservationists. But if a modern inner-city unity is possible, it is likely to be in Philadelphia, where Philadelphia Green and community groups in New Kensington and elsewhere are on the leading edge of meeting the challenge.

Because the neighborhood groups concentrate on local parks, the Fairmount Park Commission can pursue a larger-scale, if more tradi-

Figure 2. Number of Publicly Owned, Abandoned Vacant Lots (Selected Cities)

City	Number
Baltimore	14,000
Boston	3,000
Chicago	9,400
Cleveland	20,000
Detroit	36,800
Indianapolis	1,000
Philadelphia	15,800
St. Louis	17,000
Tampa	9,300

Source: Telephone interviews and newspaper articles, 1999. Data for other cities not available.

tional, vision: turning the downtown Schuylkill River waterfront into both a showpiece for the city and a more successful entryway into Fairmount Park. Currently the Fairmount Water Works is undergoing a $22 million renovation, transforming it into a promenade, museum, restaurant, and site for concerts, public festivals, and private parties. The commission is also cooperating with two private groups to bring to fruition a project that has been on the books for 30 years: the Schuylkill River Greenway, a trail that would safely carry pedestrians and bicyclists from the park to the historic downtown area, breaking through the tangle of roads and railroad tracks that has kept Philadelphians from their river. In recent years, some new interest has developed in the Delaware waterfront with the creation of Penn's Landing, which consists of a promenade, concert bandstand, ferry dock, and restaurants.

The future of Philadelphia's park and recreation programs is unclear. On the one hand, the city has a substantial amount of parkland and a large number of facilities—perhaps even too much land and too many facilities—and enjoys a high level of private interest and support, particularly from the foundation community, friends' groups, and Philadelphia Green. On the other hand, the bureaucracies are not working together, and there is no effective, unified park and recreation lobbying effort before the city council. Mayor Rendell, who left office at the end of 1999, was a tireless and effective booster of Philadelphia as a city, but he did not put parks at the top of his agenda and sometimes even tended to look at them as sources of revenue rather than as green infrastructure that needs constant tending. If the new mayor, John Street, provides the leadership to pull together divergent public agencies and private advocates, Philadelphia's system could flourish.

Notes

1. Jane Jacobs, *The Death and Life of Great American Cities* (New York: Modern Library Edition, 1993), p. 120.

2. For a detailed profile of Philadelphia Green, see Alexander Garvin et al., *Urban Parks and Open Space* (Washington D.C.: ULI–the Urban Land Institute, 1997), p. 158.

Miami

WHAT COULD BE more pleasurable—on a beautiful late fall Sunday in southern Florida—than kicking off your shoes; grabbing a blanket, a frisbee, and a picnic lunch; and heading off with family and friends to a delightful outing in a neighborhood park? Isn't this what life is all about? Not in Miami. Miami has less open space than any big city in the country. Miami's 109 city parks and one county park total only 1,329 acres, or only 3.5 acres for every 1,000 residents, the lowest ratio of any city profiled in this book. If Virginia Key Park is eliminated from the list, since much of that island's public space is closed to the public, the number of acres per 1,000 persons drops to less than two.

Certain defenses can be raised. Great weather, combined with wonderful views of

Bicentennial Park, a $29 million gift from the citizens of Miami to themselves, has been transformed from a lavish passive park to a Grand Prix racing course (shown here, circa 1985) to an abandoned property inhabited by derelicts and now being considered as the site for the Florida Marlins' baseball stadium.

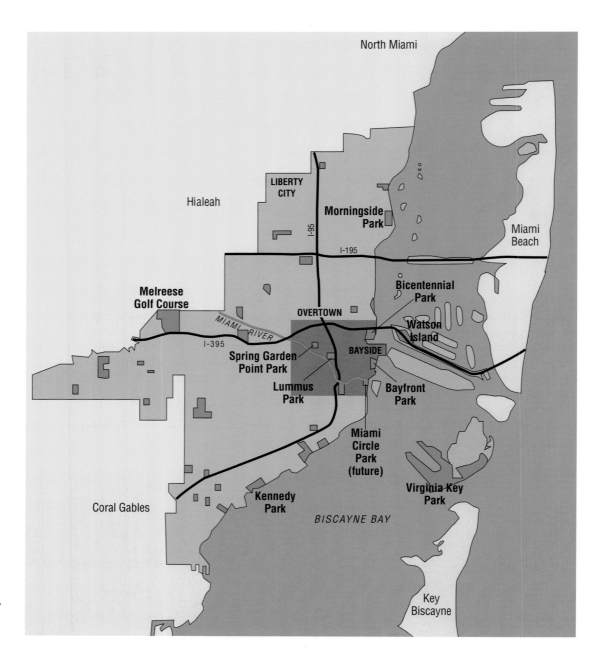

Miami's network of parks
and open space.

Biscayne Bay, diminish the need for parks to provide open-space relief. Miami–Dade County does provide regional oceanfront parks not far away in Miami Beach and Key Biscayne (both separate cities) and elsewhere. Some lovely small parks exist, including Morningside (across from Miami Beach) and Kennedy (in Coconut Grove). But the less-privileged inhabitants of Miami, those who do not live in waterfront neighborhoods and do not get to travel much, have precious little parkland to choose from.

Miami is such an unusual city that many Americans might assume that it holds no lessons for the rest of the nation. Almost 60 percent of Miami's population is foreign-born, and 48 percent of Miami's adults are not citizens. Its

principal language is Spanish not English. Its population density is by far the highest in the South and among the highest in the nation. With a 1996 poverty rate of 31.2 percent, the city had the lowest median household income of all U.S. cities. Adding in three authentic catastrophes—the Liberty City riot in 1980, the 100,000-refugee Mariel boatlift in 1981–1983, and Hurricane Andrew in 1992—makes the city's tribulations reach biblical proportions.

Nevertheless, Miami cannot be dismissed so easily as an aberration—the city may be a harbinger. The third youngest city in this book (see figure 9), Miami is a vibrant metropolis with an unending stream of entrepreneurial enthusiasm, a rough-and-tumble political arena, and a land development bubble that comes roaring back each time it bursts. Miami's multilingual culture, heavily influenced by Latin American immigrants, may give a glimpse of what the future holds for many American cities.

If so, it is a cautionary tale. Between the city's financial and political troubles—it was governed by six different mayors from 1980 to 1999 and has operated under a state financial control board since December 1996—Miami's park program and budget have dropped precipitously. Lummus Park along the Miami River was closed and locked for seven years because of crime and vandalism. Of two beaches at Virginia Key, one was closed for three years and the other remains shut to the present. In 1996, after a free-spending referendum campaign, the citizenry voted to turn over prime bayfront open space to a basketball team, the Miami Heat, for the construction of a sports arena. Adjacent to the arena, Bicentennial Park, expensively contoured and created in 1976, was allowed to be converted into the site of the Miami Grand Prix for several years and was never repaired or reopened. Other officially designated city parkland has been used for a highway depot dump site, a sewage treatment plant, and a medical center.

It is not easy to understand Miami. The city is not like St. Louis or Baltimore, which have a declining population and a waning economy. Instead, Miami is booming, with more people and jobs than ever and a Biscayne Bay skyline that is starting to look like a palm-tree version of Chicago's lakefront. However, Miami has not effectively captured enough of that private wealth, and the impoverished city government (which devotes 72 percent of the municipal budget to police and firefighting services) has not been able to hold its own with the prosperous and aggressive development industry. While many cities consciously attempt to stimulate economic activity adjacent to and near parkland, the pattern in Miami has been to treat the very parkland itself as an opportunity to generate revenue. Whether for housing, a health clinic, a sports venue, an office building, or a restaurant and entertainment complex, numerous parcels have been leased to developers and removed from the rolls of free, publicly available open space, particularly along Biscayne Bay. (Besides the loss of land to the basketball arena, the owner of the Marlins baseball team is eyeing Bicentennial Park, and part of Watson Island has been leased for Parrot Jungle.)

The principal downtown oasis is Bayfront Park, but the park has been contorted beyond recognition. Like Chicago's Grant Park on Lake Michigan, 62-acre Bayfront was created artificially in 1924, when sand was dredged from Biscayne Bay and placed behind bulwarks set in the harbor. From the 1920s through the 1940s, Bayfront Park appeared on virtually every Miami postcard—a lush, romantic park with a band shell, a lovely flower garden, concerts, dancing, strolling, and sparkling views of Biscayne Bay, as well as the premier site for political rallies and civic celebrations. After World War II, reduced maintenance, a changing population, and an increase in crime ultimately left the park almost abandoned. Bayfront still retained a powerful emotional grip, but with no indigenous citizens' organization to defend it (à la New York's Central Park Conservancy), it fell victim to corporate takeovers.

The first deal was with the Rouse Company, famous for pumping life into moribund centercities like it did with Faneuil Hall in Boston and Harborplace in Baltimore. Rouse leased about half of Bayfront Park (for $1 million a year) and built a restaurant and retail emporium called Bayside. In return for privatizing 31 of the most desirable waterfront acres in the state of Florida, city officials promised to use the profits to purchase an attractive and threatened hardwood hammock a few miles south. (Unfortunately, after protracted litigation against the owner, that property was lost, and the city has not acquired anything in its stead.) When even the Bayside emporium was unable to generate sufficient foot traffic and liveliness to restore a feeling of safety to the rest of the park, the

City Profile for Miami, Florida

City Population (1996)	365,000
City Area in Acres (1990)	22,784
City Population Density Level	16.0
County in Which City Is Located	Miami–Dade
County's Population (1996)	2,076,000
Metropolitan Area Population (1996)	2,076,000
City Relative Cost of Living (base = 100)	105.7
Number of Publicly Owned Vacant Lots	N.A.
Does the City Have a Developer Impact Fee for Parks?	Yes
Municipal Park Acres in City	1,291
National Park Acres in City	0
State Park Acres in City	0
County Park Acres in City	38
Total Park Acres in City	1,329

Miami Parks and Recreation Department

Address	444 Southwest 2nd Avenue, 8th Floor
Zip Code	33233
Telephone	(305) 416-1320
Fax	(305) 416-2154
Agency Acreage in City	1,291
Acreage as Percent of City	5.7%
Acres per 1,000 Residents	3.5
Number of Regional Parks	0
Number of Neighborhood Parks	24
Number of Recreation Centers	25
Number of Pools	10
Number of Golf Courses	1
Number of Tennis Courts	51
Number of Sports Fields	24
Number of Marina Slips	0
Number of Beaches	1
Miles of Bikeways/Greenways	4
Number of Skating Rinks	0
Number of Full-Time Employees	200
Number of Seasonal Employees	120
Number of Volunteers	10

Adjusted Budget for Fiscal Year 1998–1999

Revenue

General Funds	$9,607,000
Dedicated Taxes	0
Fees Retained by the Agency	1,746,000
Private Grants and Donations	0
State and Federal Support	472,000
Capital Income	1,735,000
Total	$13,560,000

Expenditure

Grounds and Facilities Maintenance and Repair	$5,563,000
Recreational Programming and Activities	5,690,000
Capital Construction and Acquisition	1,735,000
Total	$12,988,000

Expenditure per Resident $36

Note: Adjusted park budget includes the budget of the Bayfront Park Management Trust for the operation of Bayfront Park ($2.8 million).

city turned it over to a separate authority—the Claude and Mildred Pepper Bayfront Park Trust (Pepper, the city's beloved congressman, had landed a large federal grant for the park)—and hired famous environmental sculptor Isamu Noguchi to redesign the space completely.

Noguchi correctly convinced the city to tear down the view-blocking 1950s public library in the park, but he then proceeded to move so much dirt that the park now has hills—the city's highest—that still block the view of the bay. To make matters worse, because the Bayfront Trust was mandated to cover most of its costs through earnings from events, the entire character of the park was changed from free-flowing public space to a confusing layout of fenced outdoor theaters screened by thorny bougainvillea bushes. Large lockable gates were erected, making a walk in the park an aggravating exercise in avoiding dead-ends. The Pepper Trust has been successful in staging as many as 200 concerts and shows per year, but the only difference between Bayfront and a completely private outdoor theater is that Bayfront has a small slice of unlocked open space and that the Pepper Trust's excess revenues allow it to stage a few free events a year for all Miami residents.

Except for Bayfront, the city's parks are operated by the Miami Parks and Recreation Department, perhaps the most financially strapped of all the park agencies studied in this book. With an annual adjusted operating budget of under $13 million (or about $36 per resident, the third lowest of the 25 cities covered), Parks Director Alberto Ruder is hampered in every direction—park maintenance, recreation programs, planning, administration, and even public information. Financially, Miami's principal salvation is the $15 million to $20 million the city is slated to receive from the 1996 Miami–Dade County Safe Neighborhood Parks Bond Act, a measure carefully written to attract support from the normally tax-averse Hispanic community (and titled to reflect residents' concerns about crime and the need for young people's recreation). The city began spending the funds in 1998, constructing new tot lots with state-of-the-art equipment, repaving bicycling and walking paths, bringing in sand for an eroded beach, building a recreation center in underserved Liberty City, and renovating swimming pools (and keeping them open until December rather than only during the summer).

Miami's other potential source of revenue assistance is the Florida Communities Trust, perhaps the nation's most far-reaching state program designed to help city parks. Through

A small budget and a shortage of staff force Miami's Department of Parks and Recreation to close many of its parks on a revolving basis, often without notice to the public. The agency has erected miles of fencing in an effort to stem graffiti and vandalism.

the Communities Trust, which has quotas to ensure that a portion of the money will go to the urban core of big cities, $72 million worth of bonds is sold every year for land acquisition. Miami's first use of the money was in 1999 for Spring Garden Point Park, a one-acre parcel along the Miami River that had been designated for 64 townhouse residences. Created through private citizen initiative in the historic Spring Garden neighborhood, the property will be re-vegetated with mangroves and native plants and will serve as an ecological teaching site for the 22 schools in the surrounding area.

Best of all, Spring Garden Point Park may signal the breakthrough of the emerging new vision for the Miami River, a busy 5.5-mile waterway that could become the centerpiece of Miami's first greenway system. The driving force behind river revitalization is the need to dredge the waterway, but that economic cata-lyst is facilitating a community-wide dialogue about both pollution cleanup and park crea-tion; in 1997, the state created the Miami River Commission to consider all three goals. The successful reopening of Lummus Park, now the scene of a lively program for senior citizens, gives activists a glimmer of hope.

Another positive sign was the extraordinary campaign to save the Miami Circle. Located at the mouth of the Miami River, the Miami Circle is the site of an exceptional archaeological find, a 2,000-year-old carved limestone circle, seem-ingly aligned with the stars on the day of the equinox, and believed to be a Tequesta Indian ceremonial temple. The Circle was discovered

during a routine exploration just before two high-rise buildings were to have been erected, and only several lawsuits and an international outcry prevented Miami from allowing the con-struction project to proceed. Ultimately, when the city refused to take action, Miami–Dade County moved to acquire the land, buy out the developer, and preserve the site as an archael-ogical heritage park and museum.

Whether Miami has learned any lessons from Bayfront Park and from the Miami Circle will soon be tested at Virginia Key, the one large piece of green space left in the city. With a sew-age treatment plant, an abandoned marine sta-dium, a popular aquarium, and more, Virginia Key is by no means a pristine wilderness. Yet the 1,000-acre natural barrier island is still a treasure that features nesting grounds for sea turtles, tidal mud flats with mangrove forests, rare spoonbills normally seen only 60 miles away in the Everglades, and a breeding ground for manatees, plus the historic beach that was reserved as the only swimming spot for Miami's African Americans until the 1950s. Truly a slice of what southern Florida was like 150 years ago, Virginia Key is one of the few locales capable of sustaining a coalition of African American and environmental activists under the rubric of the newly formed Public Parks Coalition of the Urban Environment League. Nonethe-less, a wide variety of developers is intensely interested in Virginia Key as the site of more hotels, apartment buildings, or even a pricey "eco-campground." Theoretically, about half the island is protected by historical parkland

Hotels and banks tower over the Miami River and Biscayne Bay, leaving pre-cious little space for greenery in downtown Miami. However, Miami–Dade County's newest heritage park will be cre-ated among the high rises following the discovery of the Miami Circle, a 2,000-year-old Tequesta Indian ceremonial temple (the vacant parcel shown in the foreground), identified just days before construc-tion of two apartment buildings was to begin.

Figure 3. City Populations Compared with County Populations

City	City Population	County	County Population	City Population as Percentage of County Population
Baltimore	675,000	Baltimore City	675,000	100%
Denver	497,000	Denver	497,000	100
New York	7,381,000	5 counties	7,381,000	100
Philadelphia	1,478,000	Philadelphia	1,478,000	100
San Francisco	735,000	San Francisco	735,000	100
St. Louis	352,000	St. Louis City	352,000	100
Indianapolis	747,000	Marion/Unigov	815,000	92
Boston	558,000	Suffolk	643,000	87
Portland, Oregon	481,000	Multnomah	625,000	77
Kansas City, Missouri	441,000	Jackson	646,000	68
Atlanta	402,000	Fulton	718,000	56
Houston	1,744,000	Harris	3,127,000	56
Chicago	2,722,000	Cook	5,097,000	53
Dallas	1,053,000	Dallas	2,000,000	53
Detroit	1,000,000	Wayne	2,137,000	47
Phoenix	1,159,000	Maricopa	2,611,000	44
San Diego	1,171,000	San Diego	2,655,000	44
Cincinnati	346,000	Hamilton	858,000	40
Los Angeles	3,554,000	Los Angeles	9,128,000	39
Cleveland	498,000	Cuyahoga	1,402,000	36
Minneapolis	359,000	Hennepin	1,059,000	34
Seattle	525,000	King	1,619,000	32
Tampa	286,000	Hillsborough	898,000	32
Pittsburgh	350,000	Allegheny	1,296,000	27
Miami	365,000	Dade	2,076,000	18

Source: U.S. Census Bureau, 1996 estimates.

easements, but those easements have been ignored elsewhere in Miami and have force only if someone is prepared to take a case to court.

Miami represents only 18 percent of the population of Miami–Dade County (see figure 3). With the county and the state of Florida itself playing a more active role in the city, Miami's two-fisted politics may become somewhat moderated in the future. Of particular interest is the voluntary "Eastward Ho!" initiative of southern Florida's Regional Planning Council, designed to provide more ecologically for the 2 million new residents expected in the region. Through Eastward Ho! developers are being lured away from the delicate, western fringes of Dade County alongside the marshy Everglades and toward the "high ground" (by 12 feet) along the Interstate 95 north–south spine. This program could have a profound impact on places like Miami's impoverished Overtown neighborhood, where almost half the land is currently vacant.

Equally significant, under pressure from environmentalists, in late 1999, the city finally abided by its own charter and created a Parks Advisory Board. The long-overdue board, which has both appointed and elected members—including, uniquely, a required high school student representative and a historian—is expected to help the department prioritize its decisions and raise additional private funds for the system. If the board is successful in raising the public's consciousness about the value (and shortage) of parks, it may also spur the appropriation of more public money too. (At about the same time, the Urban Environment League became much more active and began a high-profile campaign to save Bicentennial Park from the Marlins' stadium.)

Miami is redeveloping as dramatically as any other city in the country. If construction follows the old model, Miami will stay at the bottom of U.S. park statistics lists for a long time. If development is carried out with proper planning and with real community input, and if the city's environmental consciousness continues to grow, a lively new network of pocket parks and greenways could emerge in Miami.

Baltimore

BALTIMORE HAS OFTEN been called the Cinderella of American cities because of its Inner Harbor, shimmeringly re-created from desolate, abandoned warehouses. This epithet may be true, but the city's park system has yet to attend Prince Charming's ball. Once the envy of mayors all over the country, Baltimore's park and recreation programs have been relentlessly underfunded, undermined, and underappreciated. And now, like Cinderella's slipper, they have been tried for a fit on other agencies like the Department of Public Works and the Police Department.

The outcome of the experiment could have an impact nationally. After all, Baltimore is a city more than willing to embark on new ideas, and in the past 30 years, at least four of them set the standard for the nation. It was Baltimore that went beyond the melting pot by pioneering jubilant ethnic festivals and the multicultural city fair; it electrified the country with its "abandoned-house-for-a-dollar" urban homesteading program; it jumpstarted a "gritty city" tourist economy with the highly successful renewal of the Inner Harbor; and it revolutionized sports marketing with the profoundly influential Orioles' stadium at Camden Yards, the first human-scale, walkable baseball park built anywhere in a generation.

None of those ideas included parks, however. In fact, transforming the ideas into reality seemed to leave fewer resources for park maintenance and recreational programs. (In 1998, only five of the 25 large cities spent less money per capita on parks and recreation than Baltimore.) Baltimore is not without greenery, however; of the densely populated metropolises the city is slightly above average with 7.5 acres of parkland for every 1,000 residents. Nevertheless, Baltimore does not *seem* all that green, and the

Rhodside & Harwell, Inc.

The Pagoda in Patterson Park is fenced off from the public as the park awaits a multimillion-dollar renovation. Years of deterioration are finally being reversed thanks to the emergence of an energetic citizens' organization, Friends of Patterson Park, but Baltimore's fractured park bureaucracy makes revitalization difficult and slow.

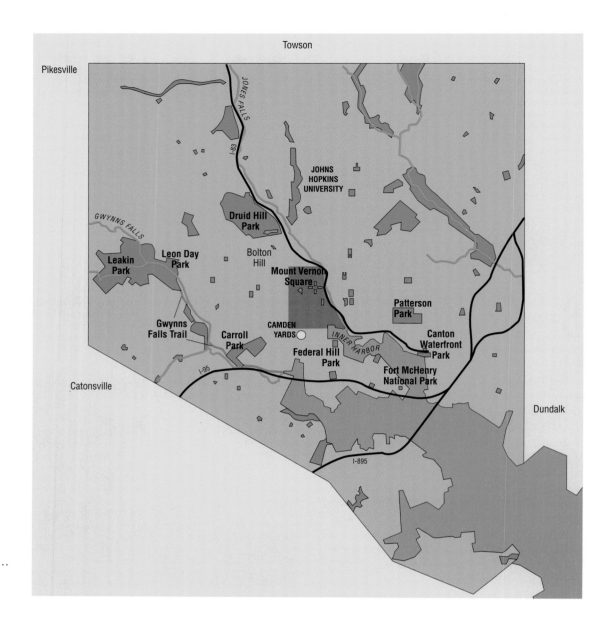

Baltimore's network of parks and open space.

city's fabled rowhouses—with their marble steps—are more famous than 650-acre Druid Hill Park, even with its zoo, conservatory, woodlands, lake, hiking trails, ballfields, pool, city farm, archery range, and picnic areas. In fact, one reason those marble steps may be so memorable is that too often they gleam brilliantly on sidewalks that are unshaded by a single tree.

More so than many cities, the history of Baltimore's parks is intertwined with the history of its transportation systems. It was Mayor Thomas Swann, former president of the B&O Railroad, who in 1860 imposed an unprecedented trolley tax that was dedicated to parkland acquisition. For 80 years, the levy generated millions of dollars, enabling the Park Commission to purchase and develop large tracts of land and also to hire top-notch landscape architects like Frederick Law Olmsted's firm. Swann also bucked controversy and led the effort to acquire Druid Hill Park.

But what transit gave the automobile took away. In the 1950s, the highway engineers commandeered the wooded Jones Falls Valley and constructed the Jones Falls Expressway (Interstate 83). In the process, they eliminated Mount Royal Park, severed Druid Hill Park from The Johns Hopkins University, relegated the venerable Jones Falls to the status of a hidden spillway, and eliminated the best opportunity for a park connection from the city to its harbor. Fortunately, a tenacious, multiracial citizens' alliance, called Movement Against Destruction, prevented the wildest of the freeway proposals, including one skyway literally over Fort McHenry National Park.

Fortunately, the Jones Falls Expressway was contorted through downtown so as to miss Baltimore's most attractive urban plaza, Mount Vernon Square, with its Washington Monument (predating the one in Washington, D.C.) and its elegant surrounding brownstone mansions and apartments. The interstate highways also bypassed the Inner Harbor and Federal Hill Park; the former has become the revitalized heart of the city, the latter a historic, beloved green space high on a steep hill overlooking the sports, culture, and shopping (not to mention the July 4th fireworks) found by the water.

Both Mount Vernon Square and Federal Hill Park clearly improve their surrounding neighborhoods, but not all green spaces in Baltimore are as successful. Carroll Park, in west Baltimore, needs extensive renovation and relandscaping as well as restoration or removal of a huge abandoned Montgomery Ward warehouse that looms over the trees and the unkempt fields. In east Baltimore, Patterson Park, an exceptionally striking and beloved 144-acre oasis, is showing the effects of undermaintenance, with its historic Chinese pagoda fenced off to the public, its pond infested with cattails and algal blooms, and its $9.6 million renovation plan largely unfunded. Tragically, it is almost impossible to sit in Patterson, the classic sitting park, with its winding pathways and unique vistas. After devoting a two-person full-time crew year-round to repair and paint vandalized benches, the Recreation and Parks Department gave up and removed them. Recently, however, through an intensive planning process, an energetic friends group has been formed, and the city has programmed $1.7 million to begin refurbishing the park's perimeter, its courts, and its three-acre waterway, the Boat Lake.

The Baltimore City Department of Recreation and Parks was created in 1948 through the merger of the Parks Department with the Department of Public Recreation. What should have been a strong, productive marriage turned out not to be; the intervening 50 years have witnessed not only a slowdown in the acquisition of land but also an erosion of facilities and infrastructure as well as a lack of momentum in the recreation program. Mayor William Donald Schaefer's administration (1971–1986) missed a critical opportunity when the department failed to land a role in the operation or event programming of the Inner Harbor. Later, under Mayor Kurt Schmoke (1987–1999), significant chunks of the recreation program were turned over to the Police Athletic Leagues, which were flush with funds from the U.S. Department of

Justice. (Under Schmoke, from 1988 to 1998, the Department of Recreation and Parks lost more staff—453 people—than any other agency in the city, even while the Police Department picked up 223 employees.)

In 1998, Mayor Schmoke, responding to a scathing report by a citizens' review team, removed the department's director and, in an attempt to save money, transferred more than 200 park maintenance staff to the city's Department of Public Works. The review team protested that the department needed more money, not fewer workers, but Schmoke justified the consolidation on efficiency grounds, because the move eliminated duplicate mowing, trimming, and trash removal functions. Of the big cities, only one other—Pittsburgh—has chosen this path; most managers believe that park values are lost when Public Works staff maintains green spaces. (Significantly, nearby Anne Arundel County, Maryland, made the same move in 1994 but switched back four years later, citing the large number of complaints about the reduced quality of park maintenance.)

Baltimore's problem is that it has not yet turned the corner in its economic transformation from grit to glitz. With a declining population, abandoned houses keep reverting to city ownership, and many of the 14,000 properties have become the responsibility of the Department of Recreation and Parks. As in Cleveland, Detroit, Philadelphia, and elsewhere, this scattered, unplanned inventory places a huge maintenance and cleanup burden on the department.

City Profile for Baltimore, Maryland

City Population (1996)	675,000
City Area in Acres (1990)	51,712
City Population Density Level	13.1
County in Which City Is Located	Baltimore City
County's Population (1996)	675,000
Metropolitan Area Population (1996)	2,474,000
City Relative Cost of Living (base = 100)	95.3
Number of Publicly Owned Vacant Lots	14,000
Does the City Have a Developer Impact Fee for Parks?	No
Municipal Park Acres in City	5,048
National Park Acres in City	43
State Park Acres in City	0
County Park Acres in City	0
Total Park Acres in City	5,091

Baltimore City Department of Recreation and Parks

Address	3001 East Drive
Zip Code	21217
Telephone	(410) 396-7931
Fax	(410) 889-3856
Agency Acreage in City[a]	5,048
Acreage as Percent of City	9.8%
Acres per 1,000 Residents	7.2
Number of Regional Parks	7
Number of Neighborhood Parks	384
Number of Recreation Centers	47
Number of Pools	24
Number of Golf Courses	5
Number of Tennis Courts	110
Number of Sports Fields	362
Number of Marina Slips	0
Number of Beaches	1
Miles of Bikeways/Greenways	4
Number of Skating Rinks	3
Number of Full-Time Employees	291
Number of Seasonal Employees	531
Number of Volunteers	672

Adjusted Budget for Fiscal Year 1999

Revenue

General Funds	$16,655,000
Dedicated Taxes	0
Fees Retained by the Agency	1,332,000
Private Grants and Donations[b]	0
State and Federal Support	2,896,000
Capital Income	4,586,000
Total	$25,469,000

Expenditure

Grounds and Facilities Maintenance and Repair	$4,708,000
Recreational Programming and Activities	16,176,000
Capital Construction and Acquisition	4,586,000
Total	$25,470,000

Expenditure per Resident	$38

[a]Park acreage excludes four parks totaling 659 acres located outside the city boundary in Anne Arundel and Baltimore counties.
[b]Not tracked separately; included with fees retained by agency.

Some of the lots have been turned over to the community for gardens or play lots, but most have simply become littered wastelands.

Not everything at Baltimore City Department of Recreation and Parks is bleak. On the bright side, the city has come to recognize that the Inner Harbor needs greening, and it now has a long-range plan to create pocket parks and a continuous five-mile greenway along the waterfront from Canton to Fort McHenry; the department finally has a role in Baltimore's spotlight. Second, during the tenure of Director Thomas Overton, the department improved its working relationship with other city agencies and even with private organizations. Private groups were minor actors in Baltimore for years, but park partnerships are now becoming pivotal. Leading the way in the late 1980s was the Urban Resources Initiative, a remarkable program connected with Yale University. The program generated some of the most dynamic new thinking about parks since Olmsted and Sons proposed a sweeping park and boulevard system for the city in 1903. The Urban Resources Initiative, in fact, revived several of the Olmsted firm's unfinished ideas, including a trail and greenway along the Gwynns Falls, one of the city's three principal streams. In 1991, the local Parks and People Foundation and the national Trust for Public Land adopted and sold the concept to the city. More than just a park effort, the greenway was considered an outstanding opportunity to revitalize neighborhoods and link communities to the Inner Harbor.

The two groups and the city's Planning Department went to work writing proposals and seeking to leverage funds for the Gwynns Falls Trail, and the results were spectacular—$8.4 million from Congress, the state of Maryland, the U.S. Department of Transportation, and a variety of private sources for the project. Slated to stretch 14 miles from the Baltimore County line to the Inner Harbor, the Gwynns Falls Trail is also expected to open up Leakin Park, Baltimore's beautiful but largely deserted 1,100-acre urban forest, to a populace that is only dimly aware of its existence. The first phase of the greenway opened in June 1999.

Other partnerships have followed suit. Capitalizing on the Gwynns Falls effort, a citizens' campaign coalesced around the mistreated Jones Falls. Operating out of the Greater Homewood Community Corporation, this plan seeks to provide the missing link in a rail trail greenway that will eventually run between the two capital cities of Annapolis, Maryland, and Harrisburg, Pennsylvania. A different group of well-

Richard Chamberlin

The Gwynns Falls, one of Baltimore's three principal streams, runs through the urban forest of Leakin Park on its way to Baltimore's Inner Harbor. The Gwynns Falls was first proposed as the site of a greenway by the Olmsted firm in 1903, but the idea did not bear fruit until 1999.

heeled park lovers set its sights on a major renovation of the Druid Hill Park Conservatory and raised $5 million in public and private money for the task. And in the middle-income neighborhood of Bolton Hill, the department is experimenting with a contract for the United Skates of America, a private organization, to renovate and operate a major skating facility.

Baltimore is at a crossroads. Most of the white-led private groups care more deeply about conservation values than about services for residents, such as midnight basketball; but the residents of this majority–African American city are more interested in high-quality recreation programs than in pristine parklands. Now that the department has been dismembered, it is overwhelmingly recreation oriented, but because of years of neglect, the recreation program has lost the confidence of Baltimore's citizens. Furthermore, the city has no effective outside recreation advocacy group to show up at city council meetings at budget time.

Parks and recreation *can* go hand in hand, something that the Gwynns Falls Trail advocates recognized when they renovated a large playing field alongside the stream and named it after local Negro League baseball star Leon Day. An endeavor like this requires a strong leader, however, and the agency has not had one for years. (Even visionary Director Chris Delaporte, who in the early 1980s built an indoor soccer arena, a boathouse, and an environmental center and who launched the city's

Bill McAllen

effort to land the Olympic Games, was criticized for ignoring the average Baltimorean.) Baltimore's corporate leadership, with occasional exceptions like the France-Merrick Foundation and the Abell Foundation, is noticeably disengaged from activities involving parks and recreation. And, unlike Philadelphia and Washington, D.C., Baltimore even lacks a vocal constituency agitating for bicycle trails.

This situation puts pressure on the Gwynns Falls and Jones Falls Trail efforts, not only to create outstanding new facilities but also, more important, to provide the physical, economic,

Baltimore City Department of Public Works

Address	600 Abel Wolman Municipal Building
Zip Code	21202
Telephone	(410) 396-5198
Fax	(410) 396-3314
Agency Acreage in City	0
Number of Full-Time Employees	120
Number of Seasonal Employees	80

Adjusted Budget for Fiscal Year 1997–1998

Revenue

General Funds	$6,000,000
Dedicated Taxes	0
Fees Retained by the Agency	0
Private Grants and Donations	0
State and Federal Support	0
Capital Income	500,000
Total	$6,500,000

Expenditure

Grounds and Facilities Maintenance and Repair	$6,000,000
Recreational Programming and Activities	0
Capital Construction and Acquisition	500,000
Total	$6,500,000

Expenditure per Resident	$9

Note: Baltimore City Department of Public Works maintains parkland for the Baltimore Department of Recreation and Parks. Budget and employee figures refer only to Public Works' parkland activities.

and psychological linkage between the Inner Harbor's vitality and the authenticity of the neighborhoods. Many Baltimoreans were disappointed with the results of the 12-year Schmoke administration, but their hopes were raised when a new mayor, Martin O'Malley, took office in late 1999 and immediately solicited recommendations from park and recreation advocates. At the top of the list were the tasks of reassembling the dismembered Recreation and Parks Department and giving it a higher level of funding.

Baltimore may be hurting, but it still has plenty of spunk. In 1998, when a few bicyclists asked that the Jones Falls Expressway be shut down on a Sunday morning, the Public Works Department was surprisingly supportive. As a result, 5,000 delighted bicyclists, runners, skaters, and baby stroller pushers got to enjoy the city from an unprecedented vantage point, many discovering Jones Falls—the creek, not the highway—for the first time. With cooperation like this and the pleasure of reexperiencing their city's natural values, Baltimoreans might be on the verge of a new period of innovation in the city's park system.

Los Angeles

I F THE AMERICAN DREAM is a single-family house on a quarter-acre lot with a two-car garage and a couple of television sets, does that dream include any room for parks? Nowhere does this question have more relevance than in Los Angeles. By almost any measure, Los Angeles is an extraordinarily successful city. In 1982, it surpassed "Second City" Chicago in population; many years earlier, it had passed both Chicago and New York in physical expanse. Los Angeles is a leader in the entertainment, music, fashion, and aircraft industries; the Port of Los Angeles/Long Beach is the nation's busiest; and in the 1990s, the city created more new jobs than any other city did.

The city's primacy does not extend to its parks, however. With only 10 percent of its total city land devoted to parks and open space, Los Angeles's park system trails all the other big cities of the West Coast (see figure 4 on page 61) and even scores below New York and Philadelphia. Moreover, the open space in this far-flung city is distributed very unevenly, with the bulk contained in the city's difficult-to-reach, mountainous midsection: Topanga State Park (9,470 acres), Santa Susana Mountains Park (1,026 acres), Franklin Canyon and its surrounding lands (2,753 acres), and Griffith Park (4,171 acres). (Of all this land, most is semiwilderness operated as state or federal parks or as watershed land; only Griffith Park is designed for heavy public use.)

Griffith Park is justifiably held out as one of America's great city parks. But a grand park

Los Angeles Department of Recreation and Parks

America's largest city park for 40 years, 4,171-acre Griffith Park is a recreational wonderland for the nation's second largest city, serving more than 12 million visitors a year. Besides bridle paths, the park has four golf courses, two nature camps, an observatory, a zoo, gardens, a bird sanctuary, and much more—all rising to a 1,625-foot, chaparral-covered peak.

Los Angeles's network of parks and open space.

alone does not constitute a system, and there are not many medium-sized and regional parks to provide backup for Griffith Park. The millions of residents of center-city and south central Los Angeles and of the San Fernando Valley must travel miles to reach even small park parcels. The 24-mile stretch from San Pedro on the south to Beverly Boulevard on the north has only a single city park larger than 100 acres. This lack of parks does not mean that Los Angeles's Department of Recreation and Parks does not provide the city with a great array of services, including 127 recreation centers, meals for 175,000 low-income seniors, a summer camp program for 1,400 boys and girls, a holiday light festival, more than 700 baseball and softball teams, jazz concerts, a senior citizens' rose garden, and much more. But the city needs more public open space that is easily accessible.

With hindsight, it is clear that Los Angeles's spectacular location and innovative lifestyle undermined the political will to create a quality park system, despite the efforts of George Hjelte, the internationally known playground and park advocate and innovator who first ran the city's Playground Department and later the Recreation and Parks Department on and off for 22 years between 1926 and 1962. For one thing, the city had the magnificent Pacific Ocean beach in addition to a seemingly endless stretch of mountain wilderness to the west, north, and east. In the 1940s and 1950s, it was hard to imagine that those natural resources would ever become overused or depleted and would need to be supplemented with artificial parks. In addition, there were all those backyards; Los Angeles seemed well on its way to becoming the first city with so much private lawn space that public parks would be unnecessary. Finally, there was Griffith Park, a glorious retreat so huge and varied that it seemed able to meet Angelenos' park needs forever.

In 1896, when self-made millionaire Colonel Griffith J. Griffith donated his 3,500-acre Rancho Los Feliz to the city, it was an isolated mountainous property several miles outside the city limits; Angelenos were so suspicious of his motives that they almost rejected the offer. For more than 40 years as the nation's largest municipal park (it has since slid to eighth), today Griffith Park lies in the center of the vast urban expanse and is visited annually by more than 12 million people, who delight in its bridle trails, car-free roads for walking and bicycling, four golf courses, two nature camps, a world famous observatory, a zoo, museums, gardens, a natural theater, a bird sanctuary, and "Shane's Inspiration"—a playground for all children with special swings that can accommodate wheelchairs. The park hosts the annual Jimmy Stewart Marathon, and from a different corner sells "Top-Gro," recycled greenwaste made ultra-potent by the addition of composted animal manure known locally as "zoodoo." The terrain is rugged, rising from relatively flat edges to a lofty 1,625-foot, chaparral-covered peak. Designed as an automobile-oriented facility with dramatic hairpin turns reminiscent of a national park, Griffith Park has experienced a growth in bicycling since the 1991 closing of several long stretches of internal roadway. (Earlier, in 1973, a successful car-free Sundays-in-the-Park program was terminated when money for the free transit shuttle dried up.) Even people who have never been to Los Angeles have most likely seen Griffith Park, because it is the location of the fa-

City Profile for Los Angeles, California

City Population (1996)	3,554,000
City Area in Acres (1990)	300,352
City Population Density Level	11.8
County in Which City Is Located	Los Angeles County
County's Population (1996)	9,128,000
Metropolitan Area Population (1996)	9,128,000
City Relative Cost of Living (base = 100)	126.2
Number of Publicly Owned Vacant Lots	N.A.
Does the City Have a Developer Impact Fee for Parks?	Yes
Municipal Park Acres in City[a]	17,309
National Park Acres in City	431
State Park Acres in City[b]	12,173
County Park Acres in City	208
Total Park Acres in City	30,121

[a]Includes lands of Los Angeles County Department of Water and Power.
[b]Includes lands of the Mountain Conservation and Recreation Authority and the Santa Monica Mountains Conservancy.

mous white Hollywood sign and is also a favorite filming spot; for example, in March 1995 (to pick a single month), the park hosted shoots for four movies, five television shows, two music videos, five advertisements, and four magazines. (The Los Angeles Recreation and Parks Department earns about $300,000 a year in fees from all these activities.)

Griffith Park is not perfect. For one thing, California state transportation planners used it as a convenient location for two freeways, paving over 260 acres (one-fifth of the park's level area) and permanently reducing the quality of hundreds more adjoining acres because

Figure 4. Total Parks and Open Space as Percentage of City Area for Five West Coast Cities

City	City Area (In Acres)	Total Park/ Open Space (In Acres)	Park/Open Space as Percentage of City Area
San Francisco	29,888	7,594	25.4%
San Diego	207,360	36,108	17.4
Portland, Oregon	79,808	12,591	15.8
Seattle	53,696	6,194	11.5
Los Angeles	300,352	30,121	10.0

Los Angeles Department of Recreation and Parks

Address	200 North Main Street, City Hall East, Room 1330
Zip Code	90012
Telephone	(213) 473-7070
Fax	(213) 473-7057
Web Site	www.ci.la.ca.us/dep/rap
Agency Acreage in City	14,987
Acreage as Percent of City	5.0%
Acres per 1,000 Residents	4.3
Number of Regional Parks	5
Number of Neighborhood Parks	352
Number of Recreation Centers	127
Number of Pools	58
Number of Golf Courses	13
Number of Tennis Courts	299
Number of Sports Fields	385
Number of Marina Slips	0
Number of Beaches	1
Miles of Bikeways/Greenways	14
Number of Skating Rinks	0
Number of Full-Time Employees	1,807
Number of Seasonal Employees	N.A.
Number of Volunteers	10,000

Adjusted Budget for Fiscal Year 1998–1999

Revenue

General Funds	$22,319,000
Dedicated Taxes	51,720,000
Fees Retained by the Agency	22,190,000
Private Grants and Donations	1,000,000
State and Federal Support	3,500,000
Capital Income	26,000,000
Total	$126,729,000

Expenditure

Grounds and Facilities Maintenance and Repair	$58,721,000
Recreational Programming and Activities	36,683,000
Capital Construction and Acquisition	30,625,000
Total	$126,029,000

Expenditure per Resident	$35

Note: Park acreage excludes Decker Canyon, High Sierra, Radford, Stoney Point, and Val Crest, all located outside the city boundary.

of noise and air and visual pollution. Moreover, the freeways irreparably separate the park from the Los Angeles River. Griffith Park also suffers from hundreds of millions of dollars of deferred maintenance, from pockmarked roads to invasive species, from a deteriorated irrigation system to sagging buildings, from eroded hillsides to washed-out trails. In addition, the park is the site of a 90-acre landfill crammed with 16 million tons of trash. (Sealed and seeded in 1985, the dump is gradually settling and should be available for public use in 2015.) The situation would have been even worse had it not been for the extraordinary defense of the park by Colonel Griffith's son, Van, and later descendants. Without the family's dedication, the park could have suffered the fate of nearby Elysian Park, which lost hundreds of acres to a police training academy, Dodger Stadium, and other encroachments.

A shortage of funds is not unique to Griffith Park. The entire recreation and park system in Los Angeles has, until recently, been starved of capital appropriations. Even with so-called Quimby Funds paid by developers to mitigate the loss of open space resulting from new housing construction, the Department of Recreation and Parks purchased less than 1,000 acres between 1972 and 1998, and repairs of recreation centers fell woefully behind. Recognizing that elected officials were not taking responsibility for the loss of open space, the conservation and environmental community sought to place matters directly in voters' hands. The first effort to pass a large, countywide park bond measure in 1990 failed. After the civil unrest following the Rodney King trial, however, the revamped campaign picked up many new proponents who felt that inadequate recreation outlets in south Los Angeles might have contributed to the riot. Supporters included Richard Riordan, a self-made millionaire, who was chair of the Recreation and Parks Commission at the time. Riordan threw himself into the effort enthusiastically. In 1992, Los Angeles County passed Proposition A, a $550 million assessment measure for parks (the largest ever county park authorization in the United States), of which $126 million was earmarked for the city.

In 1996, again with the support of Riordan, who by that time was mayor of Los Angeles, the coffers were opened even wider as recreation bond issues were passed in both Los Angeles County ($319 million) and Los Angeles city ($25 million a year for 30 years). This time the leader was the new president of the Recreation and Parks Commission, Steven

The channelized Los Angeles River has been so mistreated that one proposal called for using it as a freeway during the dry season. But given half a chance, the river's ecology can flourish—and educate—and there is a growing movement to develop parks and trails along its 51-mile length.

Soboroff, an enthusiastic and outspoken real estate professional, committed to pushing the department out of its old way of doing things. It took several years to get the money flowing, with no funds earmarked for the purchase of new land, but by early 1999, 100 construction and reconstruction projects were underway.

Capital expenditures are only half the picture, however. The city's yearly operating budget is equally important, and it is tight as well. Unlike most city agencies, the Los Angeles Department of Recreation and Parks has a guaranteed source of income under the city charter

(a direct payment of $0.13 for every $100 of city property valuation, for a total of $51.7 million in 1999) plus the authority to keep all fees that it receives. Nevertheless, even adding a $22 million appropriation by the city council, the department is still underfunded with per-capita spending of only $35 per resident, less than every other full-service park and recreation agency described in this book, except that in Indianapolis.

Not only is Los Angeles short of parkland, but also it seems to be short on a *vision* for parkland, at least in the area south of the Hollywood

Hills. The compelling dream and driving force for open space in the region is focused north and west of the city in the Santa Monica Mountains, and that effort, led by the state-chartered Santa Monica Mountains Conservancy, seems to have grabbed and channeled most of the conservationist energy and commitment of the residents of greater Los Angeles. The Santa Monica Mountains National Recreation Area is a laudable project, but it will do relatively little for the more than million lower-income people of color—and particularly their nondriving children—who live south of Hollywood.

One area that holds promise for new parkland lies along the Los Angeles River, which is mile for mile perhaps the nation's most maligned waterway. The area is now largely a concrete channel that was publicly suggested for highway use in the dry season, but the 51-mile river was once the centerpiece of a diverse riparian community. Breaking up some of the concrete, planting vegetation, reintroducing a community of animals, installing riverside trails, and creating a string of small and medium-sized parks along the waterway is a vision that, despite the average Angeleno's incredulity, is gaining momentum. More than half the river's length is within the city of Los Angeles (it also runs through 12 other jurisdictions), and the river has attractive, soft-bottom sections that support vegetation and over 200 species of birds. A potpourri of private organizations—including North East Trees and the Trust for Public Land—is taking the lead on saving the river and working under the umbrella leadership of the Friends of the Los Angeles River. So far, the only government agency that has successfully produced results is the city's Department of Transportation, which coordinated three miles of bikeway construction along the river and plans four more.

Thus far, virtually all projects along the Los Angeles River involve small parcels of land and incremental improvements (like sprucing up street stubs as they intersect the corridor), but one large tract holds promise: the Taylor Yard, an unused, 174-acre Union Pacific rail yard. The city is studying the site for a mixed-use development with housing, industry, retail, and 66 acres of parkland—the first significant new parkland to be created downtown in generations. If designed sensitively, the project could do for Los Angeles what the new Commons (also a former rail yard) promises to do for Denver, but the city must first find the political will to spend the $25 million to $30 million the land will cost.

With big parcels so expensive, some park advocates are setting their sights on microsites. In low-income communities, these frequently isolated abandoned properties could be used for basketball courts, baseball diamonds, or simply neighborhood picnicking and gathering places. Historically opposed to miniparks, the Recreation and Parks Department has recently bowed to pressure from citizens and the city council to do something—anything—for communities with almost no open space. (The department is also seeking to work with the school district to cooperate on the use, management, and maintenance of school properties, but the two bureaucracies have not yet succeeded in making the program work.) Another possible source of recreation fragments is the city's Department of Water and Power, which has several abandoned reservoir sites and also owns about 3,000 acres underneath its 100-plus miles of power lines in the city.

In downtown Los Angeles, a few developers are beginning to fashion public/private deals similar to those pioneered in New York City. Most dramatic was the 1993 renovation of the Los Angeles Public Library, which included a complete redesign of its adjoining park, plus the creation of the striking, five-story Bunker Hill Steps, a parklike pedestrian space inspired by the Spanish Steps in Rome. Maguire Thomas Partners privately financed the entire open-space scheme in return for the right to gain additional height for a new office tower and to construct a parking garage under the library's park.

As a result of that successful effort, Maguire Thomas is now turning its sights to Pershing Square, the city's second oldest park, which has fallen on protracted hard times. Once a lovely, forested square surrounded by exclusive hotels and shops, the square has been gradually denuded, de-benched, and paved over with concrete in a failing effort to control vagrants and panhandlers. Through a public/private partnership, the park was again redesigned in 1994, but thus far the effort has been unsuccessful. (However, the erection of a temporary ice skating rink during the 1998 Christmas season attracted thousands of delighted skaters, many of whom had not been downtown in years, and prompted much favorable coverage for the park and the department.)

Another lovely downtown space teetering between failure and rejuvenation is 32-acre MacArthur Park, once a center of family Sunday recreational promenading and boating but now surrounded by a low-income Central American community plagued by crime and drugs. The MacArthur Park neighborhood is the beneficiary of a station location on the city's new subway, offering the opportunity for park and economic development advocates to work together to create a vibrant, attractive urban village with jobs, opportunities, and hope. This will not happen without a strategic plan, however, and the department at present does not have one.

The consequences of operating without a plan have been twofold. First, the uncoordinated political requests of the 15 members of the city council have repeatedly buffeted the department. Instead of big, bold agency initiatives, park programs are reduced to small, "divided-by-15" miniprojects aimed at preserving parity among the council districts. Second, other public agencies have begun stepping into the void. The city's first rail-to-trail effort, the Exposition Boulevard Greenway, was undertaken not by the Recreation and Parks Department but by the Department of Environmental Affairs, which got the Metropolitan Transportation Authority, the Department of Transportation, and the University of Southern California to join in. Moreover, the lead agency on the Los Angeles River Bikeway, one of the mayor's pet projects, is the Department of Transportation.

After years of weak leadership, things may be changing in Los Angeles. For one thing, the Recreation and Parks Department spent much of the year 1999 undertaking an extensive Community Needs Assessment program, holding outreach meetings with each neighborhood to determine what people want, as a precursor to producing a plan of action. Recreation and Parks Commissioner Soboroff, who wants to move the agency forward expeditiously, asked that the much-delayed 1996 bond money be spent in

24 months instead of the 25 years the agency was planning on. Also, in June 1999, Mayor Riordan appointed a new general manager, Ellen Oppenheim, who has experience with both parks and event marketing.

The task of filling in a park system in such a large, underserved metropolis is too big a responsibility for any single department, and it would be preferable for the open-space needs assessment to be coordinated by a multiagency task force, or even directly out of the mayor's office. The effort requires a partnership of public and private agencies working on recreation, parks, water courses, roadways, trees, beaches, clean air, brownfields, community gardens, rail trails, school yards, utility corridors, and more—in short, every agency concerned with people and spaces in the city. Despite the challenge, if any American city has a "can-do" spirit, it is Los Angeles. Given the right leadership and tools, Los Angeles parks could thrive in the 21st century.

Though not a leader in landholdings, the Los Angeles Department of Recreation and Parks sponsors a wide array of programs for people of all ages, including a body-building course at Muscle Beach.

Part II
Medium-Density Cities

Detroit

IF CITIES WERE STARS, 20th-century Detroit would be a supernova, lighting the heavens with the flash of its brilliance and then collapsing in on itself in a mass of dark embers. Between 1920 and 1950, the Motor City's population ballooned from 993,000 to 1.8 million; but by 1999, it had tumbled back down to the 1 million mark. The industrial metropolis that has been credited with leading America to victory in World War II, today Detroit has a downtown that is stagnant, and large areas around the core are abandoned and vacant. Regionally, Detroit still has many strengths—a large, well-educated, and prosperous population in the surrounding suburbs, a felicitous location in the heart of the Great Lakes, and a border crossing with Canada—but the city's leaders are strug-

gling to define a new image and a new economy to replace the one the automobile industry left behind.

Part of the struggle is to define the role of Detroit's parks, particularly Belle Isle. An island in the Detroit River, Belle Isle is the nation's only major city park that is surrounded by water instead of by neighborhoods. Rather than the usual dozens of park entryways, Belle Isle has only one, MacArthur Bridge, and instead of being accessed by foot, bike, or skates, the park is overwhelmingly reached by car. As much a sylvan urban icon as Forest Park in St. Louis, Fairmount Park in Philadelphia, and others, Belle Isle resonates deeply in the hearts and collective memories of Detroiters. From family picnics to cultural outings to sports leagues to

Alexander Garvin

Belle Isle is the only major city park that is an island. Its location in the middle of the Detroit River makes the park a true resource for all the city's residents—but also makes it harder to reach and introduces severe problems with auto traffic and congestion. The city is considering charging a toll to help pay for improvements to the park.

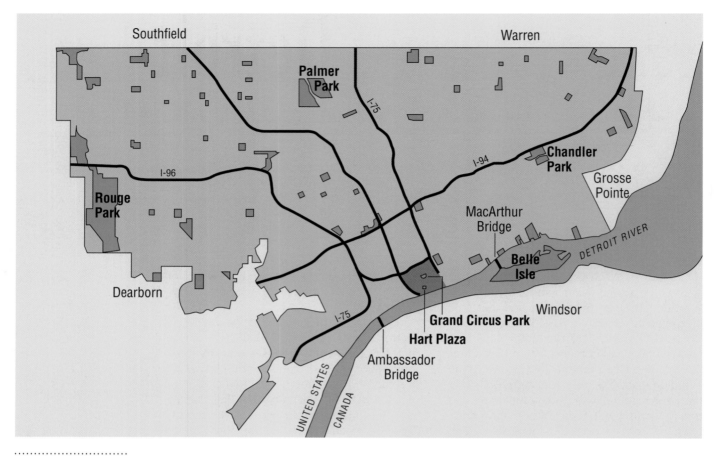

Southfield   Warren

Palmer Park

I-75

I-96

I-94

Chandler Park

Grosse Pointe

Rouge Park

MacArthur Bridge

DETROIT RIVER

Belle Isle

Dearborn

Windsor

I-75

Grand Circus Park

Hart Plaza

Ambassador Bridge

UNITED STATES

CANADA

Detroit's network of parks and open space.

cruising, Belle Isle is the destination of about 7 million users a year, including not only residents of greater Detroit but also virtually every out-of-town visitor who tours the city.

Master planned in 1883 by America's preeminent landscape architect, Frederick Law

City Profile for Detroit, Michigan

City Population (1996)	1,000,000
City Area in Acres (1990)	88,768
City Population Density Level	11.3
County in Which City Is Located	Wayne
County's Population (1996)	2,137,000
Metropolitan Area Population (1996)	4,318,000
City Relative Cost of Living (base = 100)	110.9
Number of Publicly Owned Vacant Lots	N.A.
Does the City Have a Developer Impact Fee for Parks?	N.A.
Municipal Park Acres in City	5,890
National Park Acres in City	0
State Park Acres in City	0
County Park Acres in City	0
Total Park Acres in City	5,890

Olmsted, the 982-acre oasis has forests, fields, picnic areas galore, the Whitcomb Conservatory, the mammoth Scott Fountain, a yacht club, the nation's oldest rowing club, the Livingstone Lighthouse, a zoo, an aquarium, two lakes, a lagoon, a golf course, a model yacht basin, and terrific views of both downtown Detroit and downtown Windsor, Ontario. Unfortunately, it also has the Detroit Grand Prix auto race. One three-day weekend each year, Belle Isle becomes "Bellow Isle," as more than 150,000 fans pay up to $150 each to watch 30 Indy-style cars battle it out at speeds of up to 200 miles per hour over a 2.4-mile course on the western quarter of the park, spewing exhaust, rubber dust, and deafening noise across what should be the city's premier retreat from the rat race. The racers use roads that were straightened and widened in 1991, when the Grand Prix was moved from downtown to Belle Isle, and the fans sit in stadium stands that take six weeks to erect and six more weeks to dismantle. In all, the race takes a big chunk of Belle Isle away from the public for three months of the year.

Even without the Grand Prix, over the decades Belle Isle has been pulled more and more out of the Olmstedian natural concept into the orbit of the automobile culture. Only 2.8 miles long, the island is encircled and crisscrossed by 15 miles of roadways, some of them as many as six lanes wide. Because of the roadways, much of Belle Isle's shoreline has no pathways for strolling, skating, or fishing. Even bicycling is difficult: during weekdays the straight, wide boulevards become virtual expressways; on warm weekend evenings, when the park is packed with recreationists and picnickers, car traffic is so intense that the island becomes gridlocked with double-, triple-, and quadruple-parked auto-socializers, forcing the police to close the entrance. Belle Isle, like all other big parks in the country, could accommodate far more than 35,000 users, but the Full sign goes up at the entrance because of the 13,000 cars needed to deliver the people. On the other hand, no other city park is as totally devoid of neighborhood-versus-outsider turf issues as Belle Isle, a public space that truly welcomes all in Detroit. In a city whose parks are often considered unsafe, Belle Isle is lauded for its perceived security.

Detroiters' love affair with their park blinds many of them to how much better Belle Isle could be. According to a detailed study carried out for the Detroit Recreation Department from 1996 to 1999, Belle Isle needs at least $180 million worth of infrastructure repair and replacement, building renovation or removal, forest and field improvement, roadway modification, shoreline stabilization, drainage corrections, pathway upgrades, graffiti removal, and much more.

Some of the work—such as unclogging and reestablishing the canals that Olmsted designed to drain the waterlogged island—has already been done. But much more money is needed, and everyone—from Mayor Dennis Archer to the Detroit City Council to Recreation Director Ernest Burkeen—is focusing on ways to fund such a massive program. Even though Detroit's economy seems to be climbing out of its 20-year slump, the upturn is too fragile to bear the full weight of fixing Belle Isle. (In other cities, a case can be made that park spending will boost surrounding property values and ultimately return higher tax proceeds to the city's coffers, but this argument does not work for Belle Isle because it does not have a surrounding neighborhood.) Many residents feel that Detroit's three newly established gambling casinos should devote a portion of their profits to city improvements, but the line of deserving applicant organizations and agencies is so long that Belle Isle would probably receive only a small part of the amount it needs. Heavy reliance on the private sector—following the example of conservancies in New York, Pittsburgh,

Atlanta, and elsewhere—does not offer a solution either, because Belle Isle does not have immediate neighbors willing to invest themselves totally in the park.

Faced with these realities, Recreation Director Burkeen supports an approach that is simultaneously obvious and shocking: putting up a tollbooth at the bridge. According to his consultants, a $3-per-car toll (with hefty reductions for senior citizens and purchasers of annual passes) would yield $14 million in annual revenue, enough steady income to pay the interest on $132 million in bonds for capital improvements. (The remainder would come from the state of Michigan, the federal government, and private grants and donations.) The concept of a fee mirrors the recent trend in national parks as well as in the respected Huron–Clinton Metropark System (which has facilities in Detroit's suburbs and from which Burkeen was hired),

Belle Isle provides many amenities, such as a youth baseball tournament, a day camp, and much more.

©Mick Kuskowski

The Detroit Grand Prix attracts more than 150,000 fans to watch Indy-style cars scream through Belle Isle at up to 200 miles per hour. Park lovers are horrified, but race enthusiasts (including Mayor Dennis Archer) counter that the event is good for Detroit's economy and that it also introduces millions of television viewers to the beauty of Belle Isle.

but Belle Isle would still become the first major city park to charge an admission. When asked if they would be willing to pay to use Belle Isle as it is today, residents overwhelmingly said no. When they were shown the long-range, 15-year vision—which includes beautifully upgraded facilities, fewer roads, more promenades, better flower gardens, an attractive welcome center, and much more—they said yes, as long as those improvements were made.

Failing city council approval or a massive philanthropic effort, the only other feasible alternative would be a substantial increase in the charges for corporate use of Belle Isle and its facilities, beginning with the Grand Prix. Although Grand Prix sponsors reimburse the city for its police and sanitation costs, pay reparations for physical damage, and provide an annual cash contribution of about $80,000 to the Recreation Department, park lovers, led by Friends of Belle Isle, maintain that those payments massively underrate the park values that are lost to the race. Park advocates point out that race promoters moved the Grand Prix from downtown Detroit to the park because of cost: the original location was too expensive and the park should be no cheaper. Race enthusiasts, including Mayor Archer, counter that the race is good for the city's economy and image, because it introduces thousands of suburban and out-of-

state spectators to a park they might otherwise never visit, and millions of television viewers get to see lovely Belle Isle as the backdrop for the thundering cars.

Of course, there is more to Detroit's park system than simply Belle Isle. Rouge Park, on the city's far west side, is actually the biggest park (1,200 acres) and the site of a major golf course, plus a largely undeveloped oasis of floodplain, wetlands, wooded valleys, and lovely upland areas. With significant improvement in the water quality of the once heavily polluted Rouge River, Rouge Park is attracting increasing attention and use. The Recreation Department is experimenting with alternatives to traditional park mowing by seeking to re-create the type of prairie ecology that existed in southeastern Michigan before modern cultivation. In addition, the city has three other major parks and dozens of smaller ones. The Detroit Recreation Department also has responsibility for a built-in web of roadway medians dating all the way back to the radiating series of boulevards laid out in 1805 by Judge Augustus Woodward (a friend of President Jefferson and admirer of Pierre L'Enfant), who wanted Detroit to reflect the design of Washington, D.C.

True to its name, the Recreation Department also operates a wealth of recreation programs for the city, including gymnastics, rowing, ice and roller hockey, a teen fashion show organized entirely by teenagers, an athletic team for persons with physical disabilities, weight training, swimming, and bowling, among others. Nevertheless, compared with other big cities, Detroit's park and recreation system could use a boost. Statistically it ranks low in parkland as percent of city land, dollars spent per resident, number of swimming pools, miles of bikeways, and particularly the amount of total city parkland per capita (5.9 acres per 1,000 residents, below all others except Chicago, Cleveland, and Miami). The city is about average only in the number of golf courses and recreation centers, although a recent foundation analysis revealed that the aged recreation centers need repairs that will cost hundreds of millions of dollars.

One area where Detroit is way *above* average is in the commitment and involvement of its professional basketball team. Through the corporate Piston Palace Foundation, the Detroit Pistons have donated $3.7 million and raised another $8 million from scores of companies and foundations. The funds were used to renovate 33 smaller parks and playgrounds and to establish a permanent endowment to provide light maintenance in the parks forever. The Pistons' staff participated in over 2,000 community meetings and events to help build neighborhood confidence and competence and to empower communities to resist vandalism, graffiti, and park misuse (but the road back to civic health remains long: at one tree-planting event the only persons to show up were students from suburban Ann Arbor). Pistons' owner William Davidson grew up in the city and lived near some of the playgrounds the team is refurbishing. No other big-league team is doing as much for its hometown as the Pistons.

The Detroit Recreation Department is also beginning to work more closely with its county counterpart, Wayne County Parks Department. In 1997, when the county took a proposed tax increase for park improvement to the voters, it announced that part of the proceeds would be used for two city projects: building an $8 million water park in Chandler Park and refurbishing Mariner's Park. Voters approved the rate increase, and Detroit got its first partnership with Wayne County.

For many years, Detroit's park advocates have had a long-term vision of greening the downtown Detroit riverfront from "bridge to bridge"—the four-mile stretch between MacArthur Bridge and Ambassador Bridge—and in the late 1970s the idea seemed on the verge of reality. Advocates hoped that the high-profile

Detroit Recreation Department

Address	65 Cadillac Square, Suite 3900
Zip Code	48226
Telephone	(313) 224-1100
Fax	(313) 224-1860
Web Site	www.ci.det.mi.us
Agency Acreage in City	5,890
Acreage as Percent of City	6.6%
Acres per 1,000 Residents	5.9
Number of Regional Parks	4
Number of Neighborhood Parks	274
Number of Recreation Centers	31
Number of Pools	14
Number of Golf Courses	6
Number of Tennis Courts	120
Number of Sports Fields	192
Number of Marina Slips	369
Number of Beaches	2
Miles of Bikeways/Greenways	11
Number of Skating Rinks	3
Number of Full-Time Employees	620
Number of Seasonal Employees	700
Number of Volunteers	64

Adjusted Budget for Fiscal Year 1998–1999

Revenue

General Funds	$38,130,000
Dedicated Taxes	0
Fees Retained by the Agency	6,024,000
Private Grants and Donations	645,000
State and Federal Support	3,283,000
Capital Income	15,100,000
Total	$63,182,000

Expenditure

Grounds and Facilities Maintenance and Repair	$26,328,000
Recreational Programming and Activities	21,654,000
Capital Construction and Acquisition	15,100,000
Total[a]	$63,082,000

Expenditure per Resident	$63

[a]Excludes the Detroit Zoo and Aquarium.

construction of the gleaming Renaissance Center in 1977 signified the "return of Detroit," and a park-filled riverfront seemed the perfect stimulus for additional downtown development. Unfortunately, the city's continuing economic distress, plus the lack of a clear civic vision, hampered most efforts. Under the leadership of a small group of dedicated Detroit boosters, including Peter Stroh (who kept his 150-year-old brewery downtown), three small riverfront parks were painstakingly established, but are not connected yet, and the predominant land use in the area continues to be the surface parking lot.

A new opportunity for the riverfront emerged in 1999. In the process of planning the celebration of Detroit's 300th birthday in 2001, a public/private consortium announced plans to raise $15 million for the Legacy Project, which consists of a new downtown waterfront promenade as well as a spruced up Heart of Downtown tree-lined concourse from Hart Plaza to Grand Circus Park. The commitment (which also included tree planting and beautification in ten neighborhood parks around town) involved raising enough extra money to create a permanent maintenance endowment so that the Legacy Project would never become a burden to the city.

Goals that Detroit has not been able to accomplish on its own may get a boost from the surrounding region, the state, and even the federal government. Thanks to Michigan's growing statewide trail movement, activists in greater Detroit have been promoting a seven-county Southeast Michigan Greenway Initiative that is designed to link the Detroit River to many other features and sites, including streams, abandoned rail lines, and parks. This effort overlaps a campaign to create a national heritage area, which would teach about and celebrate the automobile industry. These combined efforts have resulted in the federal government's designation of the Detroit River as a Heritage River (one of only 11 in a briskly contended national competition). The designation allows the government, including the National Park Service, to devote additional money and attention to the riverfront.

In early 1998, a momentous event took place. Bowing to pressure, Mayor Archer and the city council approved the establishment of casino gambling in the city. That one vote changed the entire development equation for the downtown area. On the positive side, the plan boosted an ambitious redevelopment scheme for Campus Martius, the old central business district that dates back to the very early days of Detroit. The plan depends on eliminating some roadways and reestablishing a central Campus Martius Park, which will be the focal and economic development engine for the whole project. On the other hand, the casino decision was not entirely helpful to parks, because it caused land prices to skyrocket. Soon after the vote, the increased cost of land acquisition caused Michigan Governor John Engler to pull the plug on the state's development of an important six-acre waterfront park.

High land values do not necessarily preclude park creation (as demonstrated in Boston, Chicago, and New York), but overcoming the challenge caused by the expense requires more than a free-market, laissez-faire approach. It remains to be seen if Detroit residents will rise up to demand a first-class park system and if Mayor Archer will exert the needed pressure on developers, casino owners, transportation planners, and others to build green space into their development schemes.

Minneapolis

BITTERLY COLD IN THE WINTER, hot and buggy in the summer, allergenic in the spring and fall, Minneapolis could be forgiven for simply writing off parks and recreation entirely. But, far from it, the city may come closer to urban park nirvana than any other metropolis in the United States. Compared with sunny Los Angeles, Minneapolis spends four times as much per capita on parks. Compared with the park agencies in balmy Tampa, the Minneapolis Park and Recreation Board owns almost four times the proportion of the city's land. Per capita, Minneapolis has twice as many public golf courses as retiree paradise San Diego, four times as many recreation centers as sports-crazed Portland, Oregon, and

Unlike most 19th-century cities, which filled in wetlands to squeeze in more housing, Minneapolis dredged swamps and ponds to form Lake Harriet (shown here) and the rest of the famous Chain of Lakes. Today, the waterway continues to generate property value and tax revenue across a swath of the city's west side.

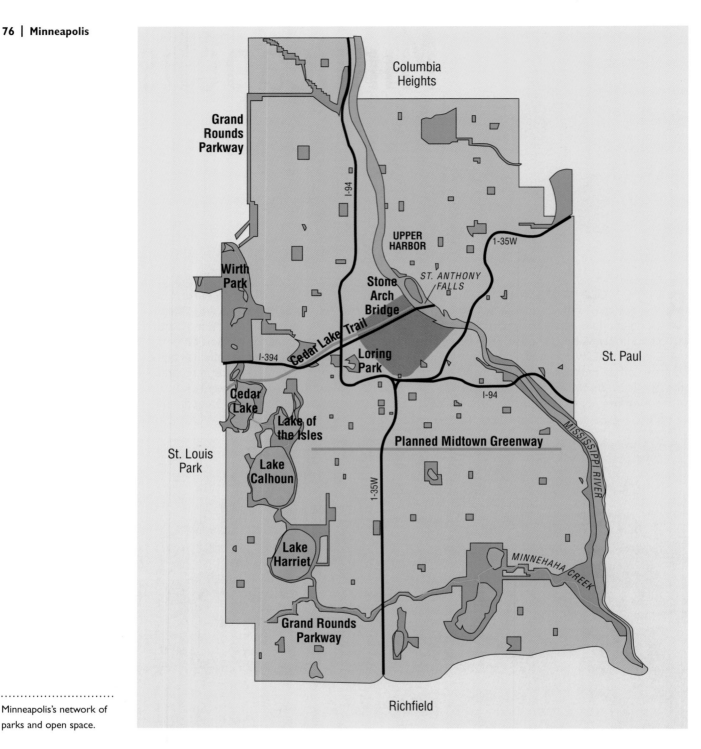

Minneapolis's network of parks and open space.

seven times the bikeway mileage of Olympic Games host Atlanta. And it is not worth trying to find a city that has more skiing or ice skating opportunities.

Why? The success of a park system has less to do with weather and topography than with community cohesion and leadership. Perhaps Minneapolis's harsh climate offers the unifying challenge (and the long winter evenings needed for endless planning meetings) that balmier

towns like Dallas and Tampa do not provide. Or perhaps Minneapolis's historically homogeneous population, culture, and economy have made it easier to reach political consensus on parks. Whatever the reason, from sparkling Lake Calhoun with its summertime windsurfers and wintertime iceboaters, to the auto-free Stone Arch Bridge across the Mississippi River, to the expansive sculpture garden near Loring Park, to the oldest wildflower garden in the country, to Minnehaha Falls (immortalized by Long-fellow), Minneapolis offers something for all its residents and visitors.

Minneapolis got started on its park system early. In 1883, when the city barely extended a few miles from St. Anthony Falls, an enlightened board of trade pressed not only for the creation of a park system but also for an independent, elected board to run it. That board structure, complete with its own taxing authority, survives today and gives Minneapolis park officials more autonomy and accountability than their peers in every other big city in the country. The board quickly made some good decisions, hiring landscape architect H. W. S. Cleveland (who had worked on New York's Prospect Park and Chicago's South Park Commission) to create a plan, and then bringing on Theodore Wirth as superintendent. (Wirth's extremely productive 29-year career set the tone for long tenures at the agency, which has had only eight superintendents since 1906.)

In modern times, the Park and Recreation Board has had to turn to the city to bolster its revenue stream but still retains an unusual level of independence. In the late 1960s, for example, reacting to the use of some of its property for freeway construction, the board adopted a policy of "no net loss of parkland"—an unimaginable concept in any other city. Minneapolis also set (and has virtually achieved) a goal unattained elsewhere: providing a park within six blocks of every resident of the city. (This was particularly important for a city that abolished community schools in the 1970s; for two decades community parks and recreation centers were the primary sites for neighborhood interaction.)

Minneapolitans started out on the right foot by thinking creatively about the land. Instead of filling all their natural wetlands, they dredged and shaped some of them into lakes. While other growing cities were obsessed with creating as much buildable land as possible and then building on it, Minneapolis set aside more than 1,000 acres of lakes and parkways to build *next to*, *across from*, and *down the street from*. In other cities, parkland was considered an expendable amenity that merely decreased the taxable property base. To the contrary, Minneapolitans felt that parkland added value to adjoining property and increased the tax base. The results are today's Chain of Lakes and the Grand Rounds Parkway system, areas that have virtually come to define the city.

Of the principal lakes in the chain, only Lake Harriet is completely natural. Lake of the Isles

and Lake Calhoun were shaped and deepened, and Cedar Lake was created from marshland. A complex set of pipes and channels was created to keep the water level steady; during droughts, water is piped in from the Mississippi River; during wet periods, lake water is piped out back to the Mississippi River through Minnehaha Creek. Over the years, increasing money and effort have been put into keeping the water quality high, and the city recently began creating artificial wetlands around the lakes to help filter and purify the water flowing in. The lakes are so popular that the Park Board has instituted one-way trails as well as separate treadways for bicyclists, roller skaters, and runners. The city has also passed height restrictions to protect the lakes from becoming entirely encircled by high-rise buildings.

The city's other circle is much larger. The 53-mile Grand Rounds Parkway system makes an almost complete loop, joining most of the larger parks plus the Mississippi River to most of the city's residential and business neighborhoods. Although the parkways are not as wide, well landscaped, or attractive as the boulevards of Kansas City—another parkway city—Minneapolis's system as a whole is better linked and more successful. In fact, noting that some of the most problematical neighborhoods are those not connected to the Grand Rounds, the Minneapolis Park and Recreation Board, in cooperation with Hennepin County, is engaged in a high-risk experiment to buy and tear down some housing in low-income northern Minneapolis.

City Profile for Minneapolis, Minnesota

City Population (1996)	359,000
City Area in Acres (1990)	35,156
City Population Density Level	10.2
County in Which City Is Located	Hennepin
County's Population (1996)	1,059,000
Metropolitan Area Population (1996)	2,765,000
City Relative Cost of Living (base =100)	103.4
Number of Publicly Owned Vacant Lots	N.A.
Does the City Have a Developer Impact Fee for Parks?	No
Municipal Park Acres in City	5,694
National Park Acres in City	0
State Park Acres in City	0
County Park Acres in City	0
Total Park Acres in City	5,694

Minneapolis Park and Recreation Board

Address	Suite 200, 400 South 4th Street
Zip Code	55415
Telephone	(612) 661-4800
Fax	(612) 661-4777
Agency Acreage in City	5,694
Acreage as Percent of City	16.2%
Acres per 1,000 Residents	16.0
Number of Regional Parks	26
Number of Neighborhood Parks	107
Number of Recreation Centers	50
Number of Pools	4
Number of Golf Courses	6
Number of Tennis Courts	167
Number of Sports Fields	396
Number of Marina Slips	0
Number of Beaches	11
Miles of Bikeways/Greenways	75
Number of Skating Rinks	31
Number of Full-Time Employees	500
Number of Seasonal Employees	1,000
Number of Volunteers	3,000

Adjusted Budget for Fiscal Year 1997–1998

Revenue

General Funds[a]	$1,162,000
Dedicated Taxes	18,775,000
Fees Retained by the Agency	11,881,000
Private Grants and Donations	370,000
State and Federal Support[b]	11,958,000
Capital Income	10,794,000
Total	$54,940,000

Expenditure

Grounds and Facilities Maintenance and Repair[c]	$24,091,000
Recreational Programming and Activities	20,034,000
Capital Construction and Acquisition	10,794,000
Total	$54,919,000

Expenditure per Resident	**$153**

[a]Includes transfers from other agencies and pension fund payments.
[b]Includes one-time $2 million payment from the Federal Emergency Management Agency for storm damage.
[c]Does not include additional $6.5 million spent on managing street and boulevard trees.

By building a new parkway, the city hopes to beautify and strengthen the neighborhood, and thereby stimulate private reinvestment.

Even though the auto-based Grand Rounds is still preeminent, auto-free trails and greenways—including the Stone Arch Bridge, recreational trails around the lakes, and the high-speed Cedar Lake Trail commuting bicycle path—are gaining ascendancy in Minneapolis. In winter, scores of miles of cross-country ski trails are fashioned out of the Park Board's golf courses.

The history of Cedar Lake Trail is particularly instructive. When the Burlington Northern Railroad put up for sale 28 acres of an old switching yard in 1986, the Park Board was not interested, because the attractive but unremarkable land was located on the west side of town, which had, if anything, more than its share of parks. However, the neighbors, who had come to love the area for its peaceful solitude, opposed plans to build houses there and sought to raise money privately. Then, to the residents' dismay, the railroad added a lengthy panhandle-shaped parcel —an abandoned railroad track—significantly raising the land's cost and dimming chances for a purchase. Up to that point, the park effort had been purely a neighborhood endeavor; the addition of the panhandle, however, got the attention of commuter bicyclists, who brought with them the political clout to deliver federal transportation money. Observing the gradual coalescing of these disparate forces, the Park Board began to see the value of the new park and agreed to seek funds to match any raised by the community. Ultimately, after scores of meetings and consultations with outside landscape designers from as far away as Seattle and Connecticut, the board created a unique new park combining top-of-the-line bicycling, skating, and running lanes with, among other things, contemplative forests, restored prairie and wildlife habitat, and memorial groves. Cedar Lake Trail will eventually link directly to the Stone Arch Bridge—railroad baron James J. Hill's historic gateway to the Pacific Northwest—and it has also spawned the creation of other trails to suburban jurisdictions.[1]

In fact, trails and greenways have become so important to Minneapolitans that the city is trying to use them as tools for the economic revitalization of the city's poorer near south and near north neighborhoods, in some cases with no reliance on the Park Board. For instance, when the Park and Recreation Board was reluctant to take the lead on the 5.5-mile Midtown Greenway, another trail based on an abandoned

Named after Minneapolis's great park superintendent, Theodore Wirth, Wirth Park is the city's largest. Its expansive golf fairways double as cross-country ski trails during the city's long winter.

railroad, the Public Works Department took on design and funding responsibilities, in cooperation with the private Midtown Greenway Coalition and Hennepin County (which owns the right-of-way).

An even more important current trend in Minneapolis is the gradual shift of emphasis from the lakes to the Mississippi River. Since 1976, the Park Board has been busily acquiring riverfront land, and from downtown to the city's southern border, virtually everything on both sides of the Mississippi is owned by either the board or the University of Minnesota. The city is now turning its attention to the two miles of river that lie north of downtown, the so-called Upper Harbor. In the early days, when Minneapolis's elite sought views of the water, they would not consider locating near the polluted river, with its banks blanketed by industry. Today, however, most of the grain mills have closed, the shipping terminals are fading, and the river is cleaner; in contrast, the prestigious lake-fronts are congested and expensive.

Once again practical economic calculations are tilting the equation toward parkland on the Mississippi. It turns out that riverside parks in Minneapolis actually provide what economists call a "higher and better use" than commerce does. Whereas port facilities currently employ about one person per acre along the Upper Harbor, new light industry set back from the river and served by parks and parkways could

provide 17 jobs per acre. The addition of up-scale housing, offices, and entertainment and retail establishments might generate as much as $10 million annually in tax revenue for the city, about four times the amount generated now. In fact, the Park Board's research indicates that, over the past 30 years, for every $1 the public has invested in green space along the river, private developers have invested $10. As of 1998, nearly $1 billion of private funds had been spent or programmed along the new Mississippi River Park frontage acquired since 1970. Interestingly, relatively little of that money has gone toward hotels, convention centers, stadiums, museums, monuments, or other glamorous tourist-oriented facilities that commonly take advantage of—and often overwhelm—riverfront locations. The Mississippi River Park is designed for the use of the people of Minneapolis.

Compared with other big-city park agencies, the Minneapolis Park and Recreation Board consistently comes out at or near the top. This does not mean that the system is trouble-free, however. Auto traffic, particularly around the lakes, is a contentious issue because of conflicts with other users as well as street runoff, which is the primary source of the lakes' pollution. In addition, a lively debate is ensuing over the conversion of dozens of park sites from turf, which is neat but expensive in both staffing and chemicals, to native grasses and plants, which are more ecologically sound but appear unkempt to

Built in 1883 to carry the Northern Pacific Railroad across the Mississippi River, the Stone Arch Bridge was closed to trains in 1981. The bridge now serves bicyclists, roller skaters, and pedestrians traveling between downtown Minneapolis and the University of Minnesota. Its conversion mirrors the gradual evolution of the city's entire waterfront from industrial uses to recreational ones.

some eyes. Perhaps most significant, because of the Park Board's many successes, Minneapolitans have much higher expectations of their agency than residents elsewhere. In most other cities, taxpayers are pleased if park roads are simply plowed in the winter; in Minneapolis, residents have come to expect perfectly groomed ski trails as well.

For 19 years, David Fisher was the superintendent who kept the system humming but also worked to deflect the highest of the expectations and demands of the populace. A skilled and diplomatic administrator, Fisher steered the Park and Recreation Board past numerous political pitfalls, which had damaged other park agencies during the years when most cities were going through painful transition and decline. (Minneapolis is not immune to urban decline, but it is somewhat shielded by Minnesota's Fiscal Disparities Act, which partially balances the economies of the older cities and the newer suburbs of the Twin Cities region. In fact, as an official regional facility, Minneapolis's Grand Rounds Parkway system gets some funds from the region.) Fisher retired in 1999 and was replaced by Mary Merrill Anderson, a 26-year veteran of the agency, who came up primarily through its recreation ranks rather than the park side. Anderson is the first female, African American superintendent in Minneapolis (mirroring Sharon Sayles Belton, the city's first female, African American mayor), which is appropriate for a community that is belatedly moving toward greater racial and ethnic diversity.

Nevertheless, as other cities have found, a diversity of users can produce enormous strains on a park system. It will be interesting to see if the Minneapolis Park and Recreation Board's strong team and historical successes can transcend these growing strains, or if the board will fall victim to them.

Note

1. For a detailed narrative on the creation of the Cedar Lake Trail, see Alexander Garvin et al., *Urban Parks and Open Space* (Washington, D.C.: ULI–the Urban Land Institute, 1997), p. 58.

Cleveland

AFTER A FOUR-DECADE population slide that claimed half its residential population and almost darkened its downtown, Cleveland is starting to blossom again. Housing starts are higher today than any time since the 1930s, the striking Great Lakes Science Museum and the Rock and Roll Hall of Fame twinkle on the lakefront, and the historic five-theater Playhouse Square complex has been beautifully renovated. But for a city that was first laid out around ten-acre Public Square in 1796, the role parks and open space will play in the city's revitalization is still open to question.

Parkland within the city is overseen not only by the Cleveland Department of Parks, Recreation, and Property (with 1,394 acres) but also by two other agencies: Cleveland Metroparks,

operator of a large multicounty system (1,017 acres of which are in the city), and the Ohio Department of Natural Resources with 476 acres along Lake Erie. Even taken together, however, Cleveland's park statistics are near the bottom of the big cities in two critical categories— acres of parkland per person (23rd out of 25) and parkland as a percent of city area (20th). Given its recent success at attracting new residents, one can only imagine the ability of a revitalized local park system to contribute to the city's rejuvenation.

Cleveland has rebounded from a deficiency in open spaces once before. In 1890, the city's park commission reported that Cleveland stood "at the foot of the list" of the then biggest cities when it came to parks. By 1916, thanks to an

Cleveland Metroparks

The 88-mile-long Ohio and Erie Canal (center foreground) weaves its way past oil tank farms and other present or past industrial enterprises on its way to downtown Cleveland and Lake Erie. The corridor is not yet fully open for public recreation, but planners are working on it

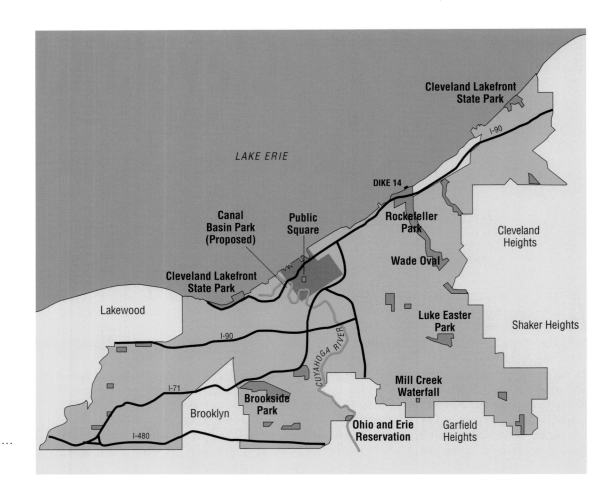

LAKE ERIE

Cleveland Lakefront
State Park

DIKE 14

Canal
Basin Park
(Proposed)

Public
Square

Rockefeller
Park

Cleveland
Heights

Wade Oval

Cleveland Lakefront
State Park

Lakewood

Luke Easter
Park

Shaker Heights

I-90

CUYAHOGA RIVER

I-71

Mill Creek
Waterfall

Brookside
Park

Brooklyn

I-480

Ohio and Erie
Reservation

Garfield
Heights

Cleveland's network of
parks and open space.

invigorated commission, substantial state and local appropriations, wealthy citizens' generous donations of land, and the leadership of legendary Mayor Tom Johnson (who built pools, playgrounds, dance halls, and skating rinks and ordered the removal of all Keep off the Grass signs), the system had mushroomed to 2,160 acres, 12th largest in the United States.

Unfortunately, the renaissance did not last. To score a second rebound Cleveland will have to resolve issues about the development of open spaces in three specific areas: the Erie lakefront, the Cuyahoga riverfront, and the neighborhoods.

It is instructive to compare Cleveland with Chicago. Both cities have similar lakefront topography; both were industrial powerhouses and are in the midst of an economic transition; and, from the standpoint of parks and recreation, both have similarly challenging weather caused by their proximity to the Great Lakes: long, snowy winters that take their toll on facilities. However, sightseeing trips on Lake Michigan and Lake Erie on sparkling weekends reveal dramatic differences. Chicago's lakefront, draped in almost continuous greenery, is teeming with park users, bicyclists, museum visitors, and tour-

ists. In contrast, Cleveland's few shorefront park parcels are broken up and partly blocked by highways, railroad tracks, an airport, port facilities, sewage treatment plants, and private boat clubs. The parks have a handful of users, most of whom drive to a particular location to catch the view. Cleveland is trying to catch up by gradually establishing a shoreline bikeway and planning to create a new park, but a visionary lakefront plan that was put forth in the 1970s has never been implemented. In addition, the impact of the lakefront parks goes far beyond their capacity to provide fun and games. Standing over much of Chicago's waterfront is a phalanx of apartment buildings that house tens of thousands of middle- and upper-class residents, who help provide an economic base and support a retail core in the central city. The sparse housing behind Cleveland's lakefront is run-down and attracts almost no middle-class residents.

The combination of physical impediments, fiscal constraints, and political crosscurrents makes greening Cleveland's 14-mile lakefront difficult. About two miles currently consist of a collection of six parks known as Cleveland Lakefront State Park, which has been operated by the Ohio Department of Natural Resources for the past two decades. Statistically, Lakefront Park is the most heavily used park in the state's system, yet, in recent years, these lands have not received the investment or staffing that their high usership demands. Happily, Dike 14, an 80-acre parcel of newly filled land, is likely to be added when the U.S. Army Corps of Engineers completes a dredging project. With luck, converting this wild landscape into an attractive park will serve as a catalyst for increased development of lakefront parks, including completion of the partially finished Cleveland Lakefront Bikeway.

The second opportunity to expand green space in Cleveland lies along the Cuyahoga River. The Cuyahoga made national headlines in 1969, when a floating oil slick caught fire and burned a bridge, but since then, the river has been significantly cleansed. Upstream from the city, the river now even serves as the center spine of a 30,000-acre bucolic national recreation area. Within Cleveland, the Cuyahoga valley could not be more centrally located. The combination of natural, historical, and cultural resources along the river—most prominently the well-preserved Ohio and Erie Canal, built between 1825 and 1832—along with the gradual diminution of industrial uses in the river valley, has led to increased interest in new parks and trails.

The parks effort is proceeding from two directions. On the south, Cleveland Metroparks has established a new 325-acre Ohio and Erie

City Profile for Cleveland, Ohio

City Population (1996)	498,000
City Area in Acres (1990)	49,280
City Population Density Level	10.1
County in Which City Is Located	Cuyahoga
County's Population (1996)	1,402,000
Metropolitan Area Population (1996)	2,233,000
City Relative Cost of Living (base = 100)	112.6
Number of Publicly Owned Vacant Lots	20,000
Does the City Have a Developer Impact Fee for Parks?	No
Municipal Park Land in City	1,394
National Park Land in City	0
State Park Land in City	476
County Park Land in City[a]	1,017
Total Park Land in City	2,887

[a]Land held by Cleveland Metroparks.

Reservation, which provides a link to the city from the Cuyahoga Valley National Recreation Area. Park advocates are working to extend the reservation northward and to connect it to a city park (and the striking 45-foot Mill Creek waterfall) through trails, on-street bicycle lanes, and the reclamation of an old slag heap and an abandoned hospital site. On the north, near the mouth of the river at Lake Erie, local nonprofit organizations, in cooperation with the National Park Service, have proposed the creation of a ten-acre Canal Basin Park near the

Cleveland Metroparks

In 1999, 25,000 people turned out to celebrate the ribbon cutting for the first trail segment along the Ohio and Erie Canal within the city of Cleveland.

Cleveland Department of Parks, Recreation, and Property

Address	500 Lakeside Avenue
Zip Code	44114
Telephone	(216) 664-2487
Fax	(216) 664-4086
Agency Acreage in City[a]	1,394
Acreage as Percent of City	2.8%
Acres per 1,000 Residents	2.8
Number of Regional Parks	4
Number of Neighborhood Parks	114
Number of Recreation Centers	18
Number of Pools	41
Number of Golf Courses	2
Number of Tennis Courts	133
Number of Sports Fields	142
Number of Marina Slips	0
Number of Beaches	0
Miles of Bikeways/Greenways	14
Number of Skating Rinks	2
Number of Full-Time Employees	330
Number of Seasonal Employees	110
Number of Volunteers	N.A.

Adjusted Budget for Fiscal Year 1998

Revenue

General Funds	$25,943,000
Dedicated Taxes	0
Fees Retained by the Agency	2,248,000
Private Grants and Donations	0
State and Federal Support	0
Capital Income	3,000,000
Total	$31,191,000

Expenditure

Grounds and Facilities Maintenance and Repair	$15,315,000
Recreational Programming and Activities	12,603,000
Capital Construction and Acquisition	3,000,000
Total[b]	$30,918,000

Expenditure per Resident	**$62**

[a]Does not include Highland Park Golf Course, Seneca Golf Course, Camp George Forbes, Raus Playfield, and Washington Park, all located outside the city boundary.
[b]Excludes the Convention Center, East Side Market, West Side Market, public parking, and funds used to clean up vacant lots. The figure includes only the park-oriented activities of the Division of Property Management (45 percent of the division's budget).

old boat turnaround. Located amid a vast assemblage of bridges, railroads, and industrial equipment and artifacts, Canal Basin Park could become the kind of recreational and historical meeting place that Seattle created with Gas Works Park and Minneapolis is developing with its abandoned flour mills along the Mississippi River.

The largest (at 130 acres) and best-known park in the system is Rockefeller Park. Acquired as part of a seven-mile chain of green space from Lake Erie to Shaker Heights, the park was paid for by John D. Rockefeller with a stipulation that, if it were not properly maintained, it would revert to him or his heirs. For the first half of the 20th century, the park was nationally famous for its handsome carriage roads and a unique set of cultural gardens that celebrates through horticulture the heritages of Cleveland's many different ethnic groups. By the late 1970s, however, the park had deteriorated to the point that one portion was turned over to the state and another was managed in partnership with University Circle, Inc., a private, nonprofit consortium of cultural institutions in and around Wade Oval. Community-wide discussions about the rest of the park revealed that money from the estate of a former landowner, William Holden, was being erroneously spent elsewhere; the city of Cleveland sued and, in the resulting settlement, a new Holden Trust was established to benefit Rockefeller Park specifically. The trust generates about $300,000 a year to assist the city with facility rehabilitation, stream erosion control, repair of the cultural gardens, and more. The most significant improvements have been an attractive bicycle path constructed along the length of the park, the narrowing of the park roadway, and the reduction of its speed limit. By 1995, the Holden Trust and the city had put $4 million into Rockefeller Park (with estimates that another $10 million was needed).

In the recreation arena, Cleveland's performance is at or above big-city standards for provision of recreation centers, tennis courts, and swimming pools. Although the infrastructure is old (several recreation centers are actually converted bathhouses from the 1940s), one major new recreation center was opened in the 1990s, and another is scheduled to be dedicated in 2001. The park department also has a program to renovate and modernize the city's 114 playgrounds, installing state-of-the-art safety surfaces around all play equipment. There is no formal bond program for renovation of facilities, but the department has about $3 million a year to spend on emergency repairs when they

are needed. Because of the small land base, there is also a severe shortage of ballfields.

One reason for the predicament with Cleveland's parks is that the city lacks a single-purpose agency to carry out the task. The huge Department of Parks, Recreation, and Property not only manages parks and playgrounds but also runs the municipal parking garages and parking lots. The department is also responsible for keeping the city's 20,000 tax-defaulted vacant lots clean, for operating the football stadium and the convention center, and for overseeing the construction of a new convention center.[1] Identifying the department's core mission is

Rockefeller Park's cultural gardens offer a unique smorgasbord of horticulture, history, and statuary from the many ethnic communities that make up Cleveland's population. With each garden tended by its own committee, the gardens have strong emotional ties; in 1991, for example, when the former Yugoslavia dissolved as a nation, so did the Yugoslavian cultural garden.

Cleveland Lakefront State Park

Address	8701 Lakeshore Boulevard, N.E.
Zip Code	44108
Telephone	(216) 881-8141
Fax	(216) 881-9256
Agency Acreage in City	476
Acreage as Percent of City	1.0%
Acres per 1,000 Residents	1.0
Number of Marina Slips	335
Number of Beaches	3
Miles of Bikeways/Greenways	N.A.
Number of Full-Time Employees	34
Number of Seasonal Employees	N.A.
Number of Volunteers	N.A.

Adjusted Budget for Fiscal Year 2000

Revenue

General Funds	$2,700,000
Dedicated Taxes	0
Fees	0
Grants and Donations	0
State and Federal Support	0
Capital Income	2,300,000
Total	$5,000,000

Expenditure

Grounds and Facilities Maintenance and Repair	$2,700,000
Recreational Programming and Activities	0
Capital Construction and Acquisition	3,300,000
Total	$5,000,000

Expenditure per Resident	$10

Cleveland Metroparks
(Within Cleveland)

Address	4101 Fulton Parkway
Zip Code	44144
Telephone	(216) 351-6300
Fax	(216) 351-2584
Agency Acreage in City	1,017
Acreage as Percent of City	2.1%
Acres per 1,000 Residents	2.0

Adjusted Budget for Fiscal Year 1998

Revenue	N.A.
Expenditure	N.A.

Note: Facility and financial breakouts for the city of Cleveland are not available.

difficult, and staff morale is not as high as it should be.

The issues confronting the Department of Parks, Recreation, and Property are not lost on Mayor Michael R. White, himself an avid gardener and bicyclist. In 1996, White advocated the creation of an independent parks advocacy group similar to those in New York, San Francisco, and elsewhere. Two years later, ParkWorks Cleveland was unveiled, the metamorphosis of an existing nonprofit organization, which had successfully beautified a railroad corridor, planted trees, and built playgrounds. With the goal of increasing the resources devoted to the city's open space, ParkWorks' first major initiative was "School Yards as Community Parks," modeled after Chicago's School Park Program. The initiative will result in about 200 acres of additional neighborhood park and recreation facilities by greening and redesigning some 80 elementary school grounds.

Many Clevelanders believe that the city should have three priorities for its park system: making the lakefront network cohesive and continuous, extending the Towpath Trail to Lake Erie and creating feeder connections, and improving the pocket parks and playgrounds. Unfortunately, there is no overall agreement on this program and no plan for achieving its goals. It will be up to the mayor to fashion an agreed-upon vision for open space in Cleveland and then to build the coalition that can make it happen.

Note

1. To keep comparisons accurate, all the agency's expenditures and staffing that do not involve parks and recreation activities have been eliminated from the statistics used in this book.

Pittsburgh

IN THE VAST AREA that is Appalachia, 200,000 square miles of craggy uplands from central New York to northern Alabama, there is only one big city—Pittsburgh. Like the rest of the region, Pittsburgh struggles daily to maintain its critical mass. From Appalachia, it is downhill in all directions, and normally everything —including water, wood, coal, wealth, and people—flows out of the highlands. (In fact, the city has suffered a greater percentage of population loss since 1950 than any other city covered in this book, except St. Louis. See figure 5.) But Pittsburgh has one great survival advantage: its location. Positioned on a rugged triangle where the Monongahela and Allegheny Rivers converge to form the Ohio River, Pittsburgh's site has been called one of the nation's three most natural locations for a city (along with New York and San Francisco).

Back in the early days—when Pittsburgh's around-the-clock blast furnaces belched so much soot and noise that the street lights stayed on 24 hours a day and the city was known as "hell with the lid off"—parks were a minor sidelight to the mercantile struggles of industrial titans and unionized workers. Today, with heavy industry so diminished that the city's air quality is better than that of Washington, D.C., and with the city frequently topping lists of the best places to live, Pittsburgh's dramatic parks and miles of increasingly green riverfronts might emerge as the city's salvation.

The operative word is "might," because, when it comes to park and recreation numbers, Pittsburgh is not yet there. Compared with Cincinnati (whose topography is similar and whose population is almost identical), Pittsburgh has fewer recreation centers, fewer tennis courts, and fewer swimming pools. Cincinnati has seven

Pittsburgh's shoreline, once entirely given over to industry, is being steadily transformed into parkland. Here, skaters use the Three Rivers Heritage Trail, which, when completed, will extend for 35 miles along the Allegheny, Monongahela, and Ohio Rivers.

Melissa Farlow

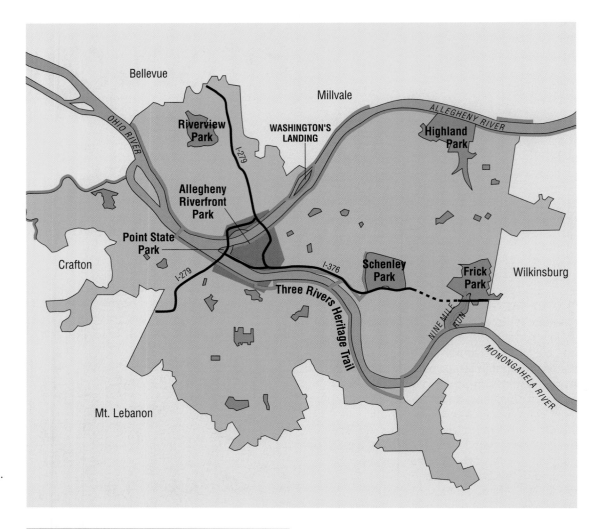

Pittsburgh's network of parks and open space.

City Profile for Pittsburgh, Pennsylvania

City Population (1996)	350,000
City Area in Acres (1990)	35,584
City Population Density Level	9.8
County in Which City Is Located	Allegheny
County's Population (1996)	1,296,000
Metropolitan Area Population (1996)	2,379,000
City Relative Cost of Living (base = 100)	N.A.
Number of Publicly Owned Vacant Lots	N.A.
Does the City Have a Developer Impact Fee for Parks?	No
Municipal Park Acres in City[a]	2,699
National Park Acres in City	0
State Park Acres in City	36
County Park Acres in City	0
Total Park Acres in City	2,735

[a]Includes land operated by the Urban Redevelopment Authority.

public golf courses, whereas Pittsburgh has only one. More significant, per capita, Pittsburghers have about one-third the park acreage that Cincinnatians have. Even taking into account Pittsburgh's smaller physical size, Cincinnati is almost twice as "green," with 15 percent of its area covered by parks, compared with only 7.7 percent for Pittsburgh. Worse, Pittsburgh spends less than half as much on parks and recreation, per capita, as Cincinnati does (and, in fact, spends less per capita than every other medium-density big city).

The numbers, though challenging, do not give the full picture, however. Under the leadership of Mayor Tom Murphy, Pittsburgh is scrambling to make up for lost time and for some unfortunate past decisions regarding resource allocation. A runner and bicyclist whose lifestyle matches his political rhetoric, Murphy sits on the board of the national Rails-to-Trails Conservancy. In 1999, he took five days off from his busy schedule to join the bike team inaugurating a 320-mile off-road trail linking Pittsburgh with Washington, D.C. Murphy is so committed

Figure 5. Comparison of 1996 Population with Peak Population

City	1996 Population	Peak Population	Year of Peak Population	1996 Population as Percentage of Peak Population
St. Louis	352,000	857,000	1950	41%
Pittsburgh	350,000	676,000	1950	52
Detroit	1,000,000	1,849,000	1950	54
Cleveland	498,000	914,000	1950	54
Cincinnati	346,000	503,000	1950	69
Minneapolis	358,000	521,000	1950	69
Boston	558,000	801,000	1950	70
Baltimore	675,000	949,000	1950	71
Philadelphia	1,478,000	2,071,000	1950	71
Chicago	2,721,000	3,620,000	1950	75
Atlanta	401,000	496,000	1970	81
Kansas City, Missouri	441,000	507,000	1970	87
New York	7,380,000	7,894,000	1970	93
Seattle	524,000	557,000	1960	94
San Francisco	735,000	775,000	1950	95
Denver	497,000	514,000	1970	97
Indianapolis	746,000	746,000	1996	100
Dallas	1,053,000	1,053,000	1996	100
Houston	1,744,000	1,744,000	1996	100
Los Angeles	3,553,638	3,553,000	1996	100
Miami	365,000	365,000	1996	100
Phoenix	1,159,000	1,159,000	1996	100
Portland, Oregon	481,000	481,000	1996	100
San Diego	1,171,000	1,171,000	1996	100
Tampa	285,000	285,000	1996	100

to an uninterrupted system that he has been known to call corporate chiefs to ask them to redesign planned buildings to make room for trails. When the Three Rivers Heritage Trail is completed, it will form a 15-mile network using all the riverfronts to link parks, stores, schools, housing, two new planned sports stadiums, and downtown offices.

Trails are not the way Pittsburgh used to think. This city had a magnificent potential promenade frontage on three rivers, yet methodically walled off virtually all the opportunities with railroad yards, massive industrial tracts, highways, and parking lots. Stream valleys that could have linked neighborhoods were filled with tons of industrial slag instead, and islands in the rivers housed dumps and slaughterhouses rather than parks. However, Pittsburgh is the city that invented reinvention, and no amount of change seems impossible. Beginning in 1943, the city's corporate leadership, led by Richard King Mellon, began to recognize that Pittsburgh's famous extraction-based, "environment-be-damned" economy

was not sustainable and that the city would need a new vision of itself.

Italy needed only one Renaissance to emerge from its Dark Ages, but Pittsburgh needed three. Its first renaissance, an unprecedented partnership between Republican corporate leaders and Democratic Mayor David Lawrence, took place from the 1950s through the 1970s and was primarily a slum-clearance program that resulted in a glittering downtown with a great new urban focus, Point State Park. The second renaissance, under Mayor Richard Caliguiri, resulted in more and bigger corporate high rises, even as a fledgling preservation movement began raising awareness about the wealth of historic resources that needed protection not demolition. Only in the 1990s, under Mayor Murphy's leadership, did a third renaissance shift the focus to the city's 88 neighborhoods and to repair of the city's parks.

Pittsburgh's park system, while small in total acreage, has a mythology almost larger than life. Schenley Park came into being in 1889, when an agent of the public works director raced

Pittsburgh Department of Parks and Recreation

Address	400 City–County Building, 414 Grant Street
Zip Code	15219
Telephone	(412) 255-2539
Fax	(412) 255-2307
Web Site	www.city.pittsburgh.pa.us/parks
Agency Acreage in City	2,691
Acreage as Percent of City	7.6%
Acres per 1,000 Residents	7.7
Number of Regional Parks	4
Number of Neighborhood Parks	152
Number of Recreation Centers	19
Number of Pools	32
Number of Golf Courses	1
Number of Tennis Courts	138
Number of Sports Fields	126
Number of Marina Slips	1
Number of Beaches	0
Miles of Bikeways/Greenways	35
Number of Skating Rinks	1
Number of Full-Time Employees	150
Number of Seasonal Employees	459
Number of Volunteers	2,800

Adjusted Budget for Fiscal Year 1998

Revenue

General Funds	$5,195,000
Dedicated Taxes	0
Fees Retained by the Agency	1,213,000
Private Grants and Donations	580,000
State and Federal Support	1,737,000
Capital Income	1,139,000
Total	$9,864,000

Expenditure

Grounds and Facilities Maintenance and Repair	$0
Recreational Programming and Activities	9,864,000
Capital Construction and Acquisition	0
Total	$9,864,000

Expenditure per Resident	**$28**

by steamship to London to personally ask Mary Schenley to donate the land, arriving just before a rival land developer who was offering to buy it for housing. (Even though the citizenry had just voted down a park bond issue to pay for the land, Schenley was generous to give it to the city.) Frick Park came into being through the entreaty of the young daughter of steel tycoon Henry Frick. Before her debut into society, when her father offered her anything she desired as a gift, Helen Frick asked him to donate his spectacular wooded hilltop holdings to the people of Pittsburgh for a park. (However, when deciding where to leave his great art collection, he chose his mansion in Manhattan in order to protect the paintings from Pittsburgh's smoke, much of which came from his factories.) Finally, Point State Park, at the tip of the Golden Triangle, is a living testament to perseverance. Originally proposed in the inaugural speech of Pittsburgh's first elected mayor on March 31, 1836, the park was finally dedicated 138 years later, on August 30, 1974.

The extraordinarily difficult creation of Point State Park required not only the acquisition and demolition of hundreds of run-down structures but also the replacement of two long bridges and the complete redesign of the downtown traffic system. The project resulted in 36 acres of open space, but more than that, it revolutionized the city's relationship with its rivers. For the first time, Pittsburghers could physically get to the water. With its fountain, fireworks display, myriad festivals, and pedestrian proximity to Three Rivers Stadium, the Point quickly and appropriately became the city's civic gathering place. Moreover, its success later prompted the Allegheny Conference to commission a study of Schenley Park, formerly the city's flagship green space but in relentless decline since World War II, a shadow of its former greatness. The 1991 study revealed significant deferred maintenance as well as some management problems and estimated a repair bill of $20 million. Although modest when compared with similar park studies done in Detroit, St. Louis, and elsewhere, the figure frightened Mayor Sophie Masloff, and the report was never officially released.

During the Masloff administration, the city's tight finances led to another decision that continues to affect Pittsburgh's parks today: the entire 202-person park maintenance staff was merged into the Public Works Department. The theory behind the move seemed elegant—the combined maintenance staff could mow grass and trim trees in the summer, then sweep

snow and fix potholes in the winter, when it was assumed that nothing was happening in the parks—but the reality has turned out to be quite different. In today's big cities there is no off-season for parks; they may be more or less busy at various times, but they always need attention. Unfortunately, Pittsburgh's parks are now regularly found second in line behind streets and other responsibilities of the Public Works Department. In addition, it turns out that a large number of park maintenance and repair projects can only be taken care of when facilities are not heavily booked. With maintenance in a separate agency, it became more difficult to coordinate the work of the parks staff and the recreation staff—that is, the people who prepare the fields and the people who program their use. The departmental transfer (which has since been emulated by the city of Baltimore and may be considered elsewhere) has not been entirely negative—the staff now has the use of better equipment than was available from the Parks and Recreation Department—but observers believe that park maintenance has deteriorated, and the city has agreed to study whether the arrangement should be continued or reversed.

Tom Murphy's inauguration as mayor in 1994 was like a breath of fresh air for city parks, but his tenure began with a tragedy. Soon after the election, a dilapidated playground slide fell over and killed a young girl. Emergency meetings in the neighborhoods revealed that run-down playgrounds—what Murphy calls "the most tangible thing to touch the families of Pittsburgh"—were at the top of residents' grievance list. In response, he launched a $20 million program to replace all of the city's 169 playgrounds; the project is scheduled to be completed in 2001.

Between playgrounds and rail trails, residents suddenly discovered a new parkland optimism that transcended city government. Influenced by private park advocacy groups in New York, Atlanta, and elsewhere, a group of east-side activists formed the Schenley Park Conservancy, which Mayor Murphy then proposed to expand to cover all four of the city's regional parks—Schenley, Frick, Highland, and Riverview. Thus was born the Pittsburgh Parks Conservancy, which in its first year raised $300,000 in cash and $400,000 in in-kind contributions. Under a guiding principle of taking on achievable projects and completing them to the

One of the great accomplishments of Pittsburgh's first renaissance, Point State Park allowed residents to connect with their three rivers for the first time. Originally proposed in 1836, it took 138 years for the city to find the money and the political will to tear down slums, demolish bridges, and move roadways to create the park.

Pittsburgh Department of Public Works

Address	611 Second Avenue
Zip Code	15219
Telephone	(412) 255-2726
Fax	(412) 255-8981
Web Site	www.city.pittsburgh.pa.us/pw
Number of Full-Time Employees	202
Number of Seasonal Employees	21
Number of Volunteers	0

Adjusted Budget for Fiscal Year 1998

Revenue

General Funds	$5,365,000
Dedicated Taxes	620,000
Fees Retained by the Agency	0
Private Grants and Donations	0
State and Federal Support	350,000
Capital Income[a]	2,830,000
Total	$9,165,000

Expenditure

Grounds and Facilities Maintenance and Repair[b]	$6,335,000
Recreational Programming and Activities	0
Capital Construction and Acquisition[a]	2,830,000
Total	$9,165,000

Expenditure per Resident	**$26**

[a]Includes $2.2 million for playground construction from the Department of Engineering and Construction.
[b]Includes $140,000 for tree removal.

Herr's Island in the Allegheny River, a former brownfield site of rail yards and a slaughterhouse, has been renamed Washington's Landing and completely redeveloped. Thanks to its location, amenities, and park system (including a car-free trail bridge to the mainland), housing on the Landing is selling briskly.

highest quality, the Conservancy selected four high-visibility undertakings, one in each park, including an entry garden, an entry fountain, and a welcome center.

With the Conservancy focusing on the four large regional parks, the Department of Parks and Recreation itself created a Partners for Parks program to mobilize volunteers for the 152 neighborhood parks and playgrounds that are, if anything, suffering even more from lack of maintenance. Through the Partners program, which began in 1992, more than 2,800 volunteers have undertaken 600 projects, including restoring historic bridle trails, picking up litter, planting trees, and pruning bushes. The successful program has helped keep up the parks, although union officials and some others question whether the use of so many volunteers

merely takes the pressure off the city to provide a sufficient number of paid workers. (Because of these concerns, certain tasks, such as painting, are not assigned to volunteers.)

Even though existing parks need attention, Pittsburgh has been seeking to increase its total resource base by building parks and trails into most of its urban redevelopment projects. An island in the Allegheny River that formerly held rail yards and a slaughterhouse was acquired by the city's Urban Redevelopment Authority, renamed Washington's Landing, and redeveloped with housing, low-rise office buildings, restaurants, a marina, and even a special bicycle and pedestrian bridge to the mainland. Because of its great location and a lovely new park and trail system (funded in perpetuity through a permanent endowment), the Landing's houses are selling as fast as they become available at top-of-the-market prices. Downtown, a new strip of green is being created by way of the Allegheny Riverfront Park between Point State Park and the planned new Convention Center. The park is being squeezed out of frontage that had formerly been a parking wharf as well as through the relocation of Fort Duquesne Drive (after the state's Department of Transportation refused the city's request to close the drive entirely). The new park is being built as part of a new walkable downtown arts district spearheaded by the Pittsburgh Cultural Trust.

Near the Monongahela River, a much larger effort is underway to combine new housing, a park, and the restoration of a badly mistreated stream. For more than a century, the steep Nine Mile Run valley had been considered nothing more than a good place to dump millions of tons of slag left over from steelmaking. When the steel mills closed, the city purchased the 238-acre dump and initiated an ambitious project to create forests and wetlands and restore the ecology while constructing a new community and providing a trail linking the river to landlocked Frick Park. Ultimately, Frick will be enlarged by about 100 acres. Although it is unclear if the city will ever recoup all the public funds invested in the project, the gain from property and other taxes will at least significantly cover the ecological cleanup costs that would have been required in any case.

By their very nature, citizens of Pittsburgh fight rather than switch: one study has shown that, of all the cities in the country, Pittsburgh residents have the lowest relocation rate. In the past, the fight was to build a city; later, it was to re-create downtown and to clean the air and water; today, the task is to build a top-notch park and trail system.

Seattle

NORMALLY, SEATTLE GIVES the impression of a community that is calmly progressing toward urban perfection. With a steady influx of environmentally conscious newcomers to their stunning region, Seattleites have long believed that they can fashion a different kind of city, one that looks beautiful, functions smoothly, and operates in a political climate that is civil and respectful. Ironically, Seattle was the scene of the nation's most bitter city park debate—and most wrenching setback—of the 1990s.

It all began with a newspaper column in 1991. Picking up on an idea first suggested in

Seattle Parks and Recreation Department

The sun does not always shine, but Seattle's parks do, thanks to the highest per-capita park and recreation expenditure of the nation's biggest cities —$164 per resident, per year.

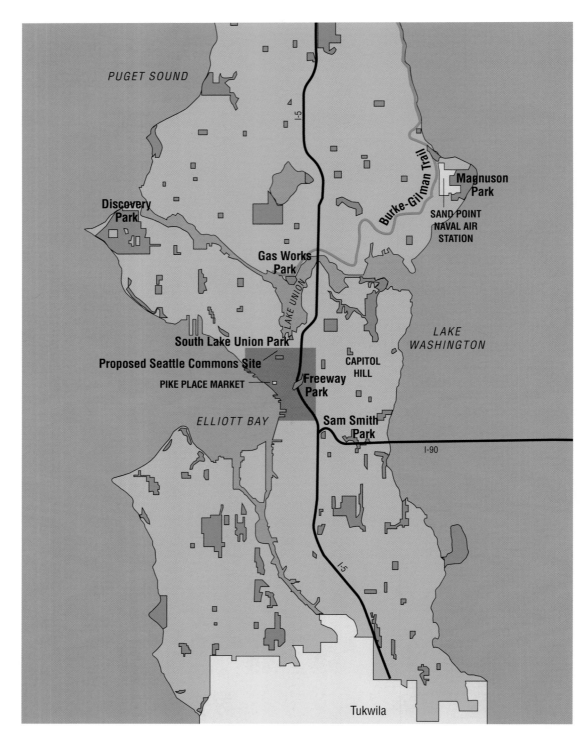

PUGET SOUND

Discovery Park

Burke-Gilman Trail

Magnuson Park

SAND POINT NAVAL AIR STATION

Gas Works Park

LAKE UNION

I-5

LAKE WASHINGTON

South Lake Union Park

Proposed Seattle Commons Site

CAPITOL HILL

PIKE PLACE MARKET

Freeway Park

ELLIOTT BAY

Sam Smith Park

I-90

I-5

Tukwila

Seattle's network of parks and open space.

1911, *Seattle Times* columnist John Hinterberger proposed converting a ragtag neighborhood of parking lots and small warehouses between Lake Union and the center of the city into an attractive focal park that would become the city's central meeting space. The park could also stimulate a housing and commercial revitalization just a few blocks from downtown. Hinterberger dubbed the plan the Seattle Commons.

Many residents felt that the Commons was just what Seattle needed. Though not deficient in parks, the city is certainly not rich in them. (With 11.5 percent of its area covered by parkland, Seattle is slightly above the average of the medium-density cities, but by population—11.8 acres per 1,000 residents—it is slightly below average, and way below archrival Portland, Oregon.) More important, Seattle lacks any kind of significant park downtown. Proponents envisioned that the Commons would do at least as much for Seattle as Point State Park has done for Pittsburgh.

In short order, the pieces of a political campaign fell into place. An organization was created, a blue-ribbon board of directors assembled, a staff hired, and significant financial backing secured, much of it from Paul Allen, the billionaire cofounder of Microsoft Corporation. More than 1,000 volunteers gave time and money to the vision of an 85-acre park with meadows, trees, gardens, a stream, playgrounds, ball courts, an amphitheater, a beach, and a public pier—all of it surrounded by a 470-acre, pedestrian-scale business and residential neighborhood with a population of about 15,000. With Allen's pledge to purchase and donate much of the needed land, Mayor Norm Rice and the city council both signed on to the project. The Planning Department approved the concept, and all that remained was a citywide referendum on a $100 million levy to pay for it. Then a strange series of mishaps conspired to bring down the entire effort.

Most significantly, many small-business owners in the affected area were opposed to the plan. Although only a tiny group, it was so vocal that Mayor Rice lost some of his initial enthusiasm (though he continued to pay lip service to the idea). In addition, because the city's priority was education, the administration decided to delay the park bond vote until after the passage of a school bond referendum, thus frittering away some of the political momentum that had built up. Finally, a year after the school bond vote, the Commons suddenly became entangled in that demon of modern urban statecraft—stadium politics. When the new owners of the Seattle Mariners baseball team threatened to leave town if they were not given a new stadium, that $300 million item was also placed on the 1995 ballot. Even though the Commons would cost only one-third as much, there was a sense that the city could afford only one such extravagance. With so many crosscurrents, and thinking of their wallets, the voters rejected both proposals (the Commons losing by a razor-thin 1,700 votes).

The scale of this taxpayer revolt was unacceptable in Olympia, the state capital. The legislature quickly devised a new package for stadium funding and sent it back for approval not to Seattle but to the King County Council, which passed it. Thus, the vote of Seattle's citizens had been overridden in two fell swoops. The result was a sudden, deep cynicism over the political process. Organizers of the Commons

City Profile for Seattle, Washington

City Population (1996)	525,000
City Area in Acres (1990)	53,696
City Population Density Level	9.8
County in Which City Is Located	King
County's Population (1996)	1,619,000
Metropolitan Area Population (1996)	2,235,000
City Relative Cost of Living (base = 100)	N.A.
Number of Publicly Owned Vacant Lots	N.A.
Does the City Have a Developer Impact Fee for Parks?	No
Municipal Park Acres in City	6,189
National Park Acres in City	0
State Park Acres in City	0
County Park Acres in City	5
Total Park Acres in City	6,194

bravely redesigned their proposal, shrank its size to 41 acres, and reduced its cost to $49 million; however, by that time public paranoia had begun to creep in. Would the state simply override the voters no matter what they did? What was Paul Allen's real motivation in buying so much land? Why did the city want to displace tax-paying small businesses with a park anyway? What good would a new downtown Commons do for people in outlying neighborhoods? Why did a park proposal include housing, new streets, and other changes?

The moment had been lost, and the proposal was defeated again the following year, this time fatally. A hundred small, unrelated concerns had conspired to defeat one big idea. There will be a residue of incremental benefits to the city—an addition of a few acres to existing South Lake Union Park, the opening of a new recreation center in the neighborhood, and possibly some open space built in connection with the new biotechnology complex being built by Paul Allen (who kept the land he had purchased). Hinterberger's city-changing vision will not be realized, however.

Perhaps one reason for the rejection of the Seattle Commons tax is the generous amount that Seattleites already allocate to their Parks and Recreation Department, almost $165 per resident, more than every other city described in this book. (In fact, if nonbudgeted expenses are included, the amount is even higher; Seattle also has a network of Recreation Advisory Councils, which collect $7 million in activity fees and employ 1,500 part-time instructors and event leaders, who work in city community centers.) In general, Seattle's parks are well kept and suffer from far less deferred maintenance than parks in most Eastern cities, but some critics feel

Seattle Department of Parks and Recreation

Address	100 Dexter Avenue North
Zip Code	98109
Telephone	(206) 684-4075
Fax	(206) 233-7023
Web Site	www.pan.ci.seattle.wa.us
Agency Acreage in City	6,189
Acreage as Percent of City	11.5%
Acres per 1,000 Residents	11.9
Number of Regional Parks	17
Number of Neighborhood Parks	168
Number of Recreation Centers	24
Number of Pools	10
Number of Golf Courses	4
Number of Tennis Courts	165
Number of Sports Fields	185
Number of Marina Slips	3
Number of Beaches	9
Miles of Bikeways/Greenways	8
Number of Skating Rinks	0
Number of Full-Time Employees	910
Number of Seasonal Employees	600
Number of Volunteers	2,600

Adjusted Budget for Fiscal Year 1998

Revenue

General Funds	$26,692,000
Dedicated Taxes	22,582,000
Fees Retained by the Agency	10,748,000
Private Grants and Donations	152,000
State and Federal Support	262,000
Capital Income	26,759,000
Total	$87,195,000

Expenditure

Grounds and Facilities Maintenance and Repair	$37,196,000
Recreational Programming and Activities	19,478,000
Capital Construction and Acquisition	29,164,000
Total	$85,838,000
Expenditure per Resident	**$164**

that the city should take better care of what it has before taking on more.

Regardless of that opinion, Seattle's Parks and Recreation Department *has* been taking on more, thanks to King County voters' passage of a large Open Space and Trails bond in 1989. Shrewd management of the $41 million earmarked for the city allowed Seattle to more than double its allotment with county, state, and federal matches and to use the money to acquire nearly 600 acres of parkland. In fact, since 1970, the size of Seattle's park system has increased by nearly 50 percent. The system will grow again soon, when the decommissioned Sand Point Naval Air Station on Lake Washington becomes a 153-acre addition to Magnuson Park. The city bears none of the cost for the transfer, thanks to the federal Lands-to-Parks Act, although developing ballfields and a beach and sailing facility, restoring wetlands, and retrofitting many of the old base's buildings into cultural facilities and housing will cost upwards of $100 million. (Washington's late Senator Henry Jackson specifically wrote the Lands-to-Parks Act in 1970 to enable Seattle to create its largest green space, Discovery Park, out of old Fort Lawton.)

Seattle is one of a handful of cities in the United States whose population density is increasing. (Most of the Sunbelt cities that are gaining population are also gaining in land area, and this keeps their density low.) Despite the contentiousness of the debate about the Seattle Commons—or perhaps because of it—the city is now going through an impressive neighborhood planning process. City officials are seeking greater development density along the central spine of the city (and maintaining lower density, lower building heights, and more views along the shores of Puget Sound and Lake Washington), and planners are meeting with community leaders from the 37 affected neighborhoods and asking them, in effect, "What amenities do you want in compensation for greater density?" Of thousands of responses, the second most common is more parkland. (Number one is protection from too much traffic.) As in all fully built-out cities, Seattle can create more parkland only by recycling old properties into new uses or by making more efficient use of existing land, and the city is doing both.

Seattle's most famous recycled park is the Burke–Gilman Trail, a car-free recreation and transportation corridor fashioned from an abandoned railroad corridor along Lake Washington. The Burke–Gilman Trail, which attracts over a million users a year, is one of several rail trails

design and its thoughtful placement, which reduced the impact of the busy, noisy interstate highway on downtown Seattle (and helped to add development value to the core). Freeway Park's success was duplicated 15 years later, when Interstate 90 was completed across Lake Washington. After the highway comes ashore, it first tunnels through a large hill, then continues under a 28-acre deck, upon which sits Sam Smith Park, an "urban peace park" consisting of tennis courts, bike trails, and a memorial sculpture of Martin Luther King, Jr., made from the melted-down barrels of guns. The newest idea for park decks is over the city's five municipal reservoirs, starting with one in the park-sparse Capitol Hill neighborhood. Even though the reservoirs are attractive, health advocates and the Environmental Protection Agency would prefer to have them covered to reduce the chances of contamination; the neighbors would welcome more space for sports, games, children, and dogs.

The dog issue—or, more precisely, the issue of off-leash dog areas in parks—is contentious in Seattle and, as in San Francisco, is getting more so. As of mid-1999, the city's parks had seven off-leash areas, with three more planned. Promoted by proponents as a way to reduce the number of illegally unleashed dogs throughout the rest of the system, the experiment's success or failure seems to lie primarily in the eye of the beholder. Dog owners wax poetic about these areas, talking of their community-building joys and calling them the singles bars of the 1990s. Park professionals wince at what dog parks do to the land; off-leash areas—generally about a half acre in size and often fenced—quickly become denuded of grass (thanks both to the dogs and to the large numbers of owners standing and talking in one small corner). As the earth turns to dust in July and to mud the rest of the year, the Parks and Recreation Department responds by laying on wood chips or sand. On the other hand, neither dog fights nor dog litter seems to be a problem. At the same time, illegal off-leash dog use has not decreased elsewhere in the city. Like most agency heads in other cities, Parks and Recreation Superintendent Ken Bounds is not enthusiastic about the off-leash areas ("There's virtually no place in our entire system where dogs are banned," he says, "we just prefer them on a leash."), but for the time being, a city council resolution has overruled him. The next big flashpoint is likely to be in Magnuson Park—the converted military site—where advocates for a restored wetland-and-salmon-breeding system are squaring off

More than most other cities, Seattle involves its residents in community planning, particularly in neighborhoods where the population density is increasing. When asked what amenities would compensate for greater numbers of people, the second most frequent response from Seattleites was "more parks."

in the city and one reason for Seattle's constant rating near the top of the list of best bicycling cities. (In 1993, when the Burlington Northern Railroad sold off a piece of track that had been slated as an extension of the Burke–Gilman Trail, cyclists chained their bikes across the entrance to the company's headquarters and raised so much opposition that the railroad was forced to cancel the sales contract. Since then, the city used a federal grant to equip every bus with a bicycle rack, and the bus system now transports 40,000 cyclists a month.)

The trail runs past another Seattle landmark, Gas Works Park, a hilly patch of green space on Lake Union that incorporates the hulking remains of an old, soot-belching natural gas cracking plant. Another land recycling project is currently underway on Elliott Bay, just blocks from the famous Pike Place Market: the conversion of a six-acre former oil transfer station into a sculpture garden to be operated by the Seattle Art Museum.

As for making better use of existing public land, Seattle is a leader in building parks on decks. The most celebrated of these is Freeway Park—a five-acre, almost sculptural amalgam of textured concrete, trailing ivy, cascading water, trees, shrubs, flowers, and bushes, built directly over Interstate 5 in the center of downtown. Opened in 1976, making it one of the earliest such interstate overlays, Freeway Park was extremely influential because of both its dramatic

Seattle has seven off-leash dog areas and plans three more. As in other cities, the off-leash issue is contentious, with emotions on both sides running high. Trying to put the dispute into context, Parks and Recreation Superintendent Ken Bounds has stated, "There's virtually no place in our entire system where dogs are banned —we just prefer them on a leash."

against dog proponents, who want access to Lake Washington.

Dog owners aside, one of the strongest new sentiments among park advocates seems to be coming from the environmental side of the spectrum, not the recreation side. The shortage of soccer fields and other play spaces (and Seattleites, like city dwellers everywhere, are being forced to play league games at increasingly bizarre early-morning and late-night time slots) is widely acknowledged, but residents are clamoring just as loudly for the restoration of natural processes in the city, including forestland, wetlands, healthy streams, and ecologically productive tidelands. The trend is partly demographic, as the percentage of children in the city continues to drop, but it also reflects the desire to have both urbanity and nature within walking and bicycling distance right in town.

The bottom line is the need for more money for all types of parkland in Seattle. This issue harks back to the early days of Seattle's park system, when landscape architect John C. Olmsted fretted that the city was undertaking only about half of his ideas and plans. Today, the fundrais-

ing goal is being pursued both publicly and privately. On the private side, park advocates are reviving from the Seattle Commons setback and establishing, for the first time, a Seattle Park Foundation, which will be positioned to tap into the region's growing corporate and individual wealth. On the public side, Mayor Paul Schell is proposing the creation of a Metropolitan Park District, which would have authority from the state to institute a permanent levy and to issue bonds for capital improvements and land acquisition. The city's and county's bond measures in 1989 and 1991 pumped significant funds into construction and renovation of community centers, but Schell believes the scale of the improvements can only be ratcheted up through an ongoing levy, similar to those that currently exist in Minneapolis and Chicago.

To many Americans, the views of snow-capped mountains and sparkling waters in all directions would make Seattle the most beautiful city in the United States, even if it had no parks at all. To Seattleites, that backdrop serves as an inspiration to keep weaving parkland into their daily lives.

St. Louis

NO BIG CITY in the country has been as devastated by population loss as St. Louis. From a high of 857,000 in 1950, the city dropped to only 352,000 inhabitants in 1996, a mind-numbing decrease of 59 percent (see figure 5). As far back as 1978, it was reported that the weathered bricks from demolished rowhouses were a notable St. Louis export. As a result, today hundreds of city blocks retain only the occasional building amid a sea of vacant properties. A few neighborhoods are experiencing reinvestment, and some new buildings have been erected downtown, but even the highest-profile new ventures—the Union Station and Laclede's Landing retail developments—are barely holding on.

In contrast, the entire metropolitan area of St. Louis is still growing modestly in population, gaining jobs, and retaining wealth. In fact, more so than in other cities, suburban sprawl seems to be exacerbating urban decay; just when the city's economy picked up slightly in the late 1970s, General Motors relocated its 10,000-employee assembly plant to rural Wentzville, Missouri, 40 miles on the fringe. Part of St. Louis's problem stems from its small physical size—40,000 acres, sixth smallest of the cities covered in this book—and the fact that it is legally blocked from absorbing its wealthier suburbs. If it were as expansive as, say, Kansas City (Missouri), St. Louis would have a population of nearly 1 million and much greater fiscal strength. Ironically, the city fathers set the boundaries in 1876 because they did not want to pay for services in St. Louis County, which was nearly empty at the time.

As the city tries to fight its way back, however, one of the weapons in its arsenal is a park. Forest Park, 1,293 acres of greenery and culture, strikes a deep chord with residents of St. Louis.

And it has an incredible bounty: two outstanding museums, a science center, a planetarium, a world famous zoo, an outdoor theater, a stunning art-deco conservatory, several lakes, two golf courses, a tennis center, miles of bike paths, scores of ballfields, a renovated pavilion from the 1904 Louisiana Purchase Exposition, a waterfall, and a brand new playground with

Forest Park Forever

The 1,293-acre Forest Park, including a stream cascading through the Seven Pools, has captured the hearts of St. Louis citizens since 1868. The park's resonance with residents past and present led to the formation of Forest Park Forever in 1986.

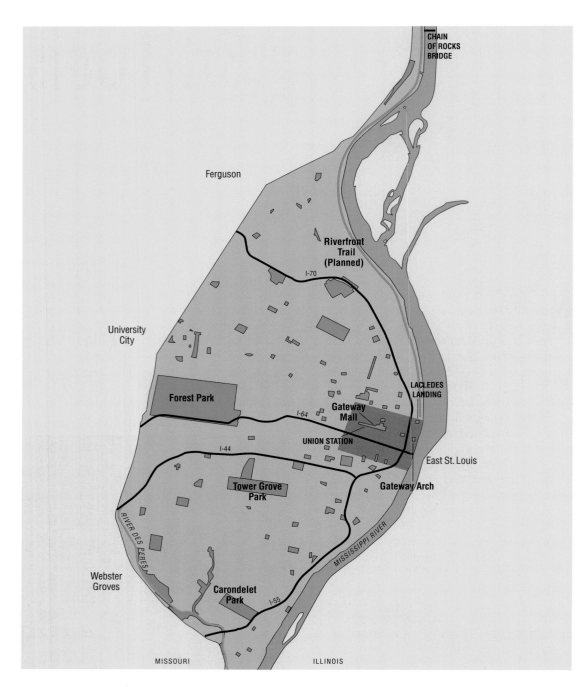

St. Louis's network of
parks and open space.

huge climbable turtles.[1] Forest Park attracts
10 million users a year and has played a part in
the life of almost every resident of the region.

Yet it is not surprising that not all is well with
Forest Park. The walls of Grand Basin are crumbling, and its waterway link to Post-Dispatch
Lake is blocked by silt. The ponds are stagnant
and their water quality is poor. Drains have
cracked and failed, resulting in flooding and
erosion. The boathouse, docks, and boats are
in disrepair. Roadways are potholed and fields
sometimes unplayable. The famous Jewel Box
Conservatory has leaky windows and a dripping
roof. Worse, the park is still suffering from the

impact of the 1904 Exposition, which brought
19 million people to "meet me in St. Louis" and
burdened the western half of Forest Park with
hundreds of buildings, severely modified roadways, and the undergrounding of the flood-
prone Des Peres River. Most buildings were
promptly removed, but the excessive blacktop
remained and the river was never brought back
to the surface; it still flows through giant concrete culverts directly below the stagnant pools
that replaced it.

Thus, in 1986, when prominent local residents and the city's private-sector leaders established a nonprofit friends' organization, Forest

Park Forever, there was a tremendous ground-swell of support from the entire region. Matters did not fall into place simply and quickly, however. It turned out that, even though everyone loved Forest Park, not all of them loved the same features of the sanctuary. Some worshipped it for its bucolic natural features, others for its active recreation, and others for its cultural institutions. Each of the three groups had very different ideas about what it meant to "fix" the park—ranging from removal of facilities to addition of more structures. Everyone agreed that cars in the park were a problem, but some wanted to solve the predicament with more parking spaces and some with less. Although individuals were happy to donate to the park's improvement, most felt that the city itself should carry at least a portion of the burden—and city taxpayers had stubbornly turned down every capital bond initiative proposed since 1958.

The first effort to devise a master plan for Forest Park had ended in failure; a document was produced in 1981 but nothing came of it. For over a decade, the decline continued with only stopgap emergency repairs by Forest Park Forever or the city's Department of Parks, Recreation, and Forestry. Finally, in 1993, under the prodding of Mayor Freeman Bosley, Jr., St. Louis voters passed a half-cent increase in the city sales tax to finance desperately needed capital improvements (of which parks were allotted $17 million). The signal was weak but it was enough for the business establishment, including NationsBank, McDonnell Douglas, and the Danforth Foundation, which agreed to invest

City Profile for St. Louis, Missouri

City Population (1996)	352,000
City Area in Acres (1990)	39,616
City Population Density Level	8.9
County in Which City Is Located	St. Louis City
County's Population (1996)	352,000
Metropolitan Area Population (1996)	2,548,000
City Relative Cost of Living (base = 100)	96.9
Number of Publicly Owned Vacant Lots	17,000
Does the City Have a Developer Impact Fee for Parks?	N.A.
Municipal Park Acres in City	3,290
National Park Acres in City	91
State Park Acres in City	0
County Park Acres in City	4
Total Park Acres in City	3,385

in a broad partnership through Forest Park Forever. Mayor Bosley also called for the creation of a revised Forest Park master plan, which was adopted in 1995 after painstaking negotiations. According to the plan, the city and the private sector each agreed to raise half the needed $86 million, and all participants agreed to the principle of "no net loss of parkland" to automobiles or to building expansion. (Although several museums plan to expand, the open space that is lost will be recovered by eliminating some roadways and parking lots.)

With the divisions and political impediments finally removed, Forest Park Forever was able to jump into the fundraising effort enthusiastically and creatively. The organization landed tax incentives from the state legislature, solicited penny collections from schoolchildren and other groups, arranged challenge grants from foundations and corporations, spurred a television documentary, and more. (Forest Park Forever was so creative that a corporation that uses tax credits and the Danforth match can leverage $150,000 for the park at a net cost of only

Forest Park includes broad expanses of playing fields and the Jewel Box Conservatory. Hammering out a revitalization master plan that balanced open space and development took more than 14 years.

St. Louis Department of Parks, Recreation, and Forestry

Address	5600 Clayton Avenue
Zip Code	63110
Telephone	(314) 289-5310
Fax	(314) 535-3901
Web Site	http://stlouis.missouri.org/citygov/parks/
Agency Acreage in City[a]	3,290
Acreage as Percent of City	8.3%
Acres per 1,000 Residents	9.3
Number of Regional Parks	2
Number of Neighborhood Parks	103
Number of Recreation Centers	10
Number of Pools	8
Number of Golf Courses	3
Number of Tennis Courts	99
Number of Sports Fields	57
Number of Marina Slips	3
Number of Beaches	0
Miles of Bikeways/Greenways	15
Number of Skating Rinks	4
Number of Full-Time Employees	192
Number of Seasonal Employees	100
Number of Volunteers	100

Adjusted Budget for Fiscal Year 1998–1999

Revenue

General Funds	$9,263,000
Dedicated Taxes[b]	0
Fees Retained by the Agency	120,000
Private Grants and Donations	940,000
State and Federal Support	926,000
Capital Income	14,387,000
Total	$25,636,000

Expenditure

Grounds and Facilities Maintenance and Repair	$7,245,000
Recreational Programming and Activities	3,273,000
Capital Construction and Acquisition	15,274,000
Total[c]	$25,792,000

Expenditure per Resident	**$73**

[a]Includes Tower Grove Park (289 acres, $2.04 million), a public park operated by the Tower Grove Park Commission (4255 Arsenal Street, St. Louis, Missouri 63116; telephone: 314-771-2679).
[b]The department and the Tower Grove Park Commission received an aggregate of $774,000 in dedicated taxes, which can be used only for capital construction. The funds have been listed under capital income.
[c]Excludes the Forestry Division's "Operation Greenlot" program ($3.1 million) to clean vacant lots.

$29,000.) Major contributions are flowing in from residents of not only the city of St. Louis but also St. Louis County and the rest of the region, as well as from former St. Louisans living throughout the United States and the world. As of April 2000, the campaign, dubbed "Restoring the Glory," had raised $37 million.

If Forest Park were the only park in St. Louis, there might be hope that the entire system could be refurbished by 2004—the 200th anniversary of the Lewis and Clark expedition and the 100th anniversary of the Louisiana Purchase Exposition—a year that is shaping up as St. Louis's next moment in the sun. Unfortunately, the St. Louis Department of Parks, Recreation, and Forestry has five other midsized parks and 97 smaller ones, all of which need as much attention as Forest Park but do not have the benefit of a private fundraising and stewardship organization.

As St. Louis has gained vacant, abandoned land, the city has been forced to devote more and more resources to its unplanned open space. As in Cleveland, those responsibilities have fallen on the shoulders of the Parks, Recreation, and Forestry Department. Besides tending 35,000 park trees and 154,000 street trees, the department's Forestry Division mows 17,000 vacant lots every month and 9,000 properties with vacant but still standing buildings every eight weeks. The division also carts away more than 16,000 tons of illegally dumped debris each year. Dubbed "Operation Greenlot," the program now consumes fully 60 percent of the Forestry Division's budget (although those numbers have been taken out of this book's financial analysis in order to make the St. Louis parks and recreation program equal to that of other cities). Interestingly, even though few staffers initially joined the Forestry Division because of their desire to remove trash, the program is remarkably successful: flying over the city's slums in the summer reveals a vast pattern of green that is as attractive as it is jarring, and the department is proud of its contribution to urban livability. If and when jobs return to the inner city, St. Louis has an impressive supply of open space available for neighborhood parks and urban greenways, as well as for redevelopment.

Another group working to put that open space to good use is Gateway Greening, St. Louis's 15-year-old gardening advocacy organization, which has helped community groups establish 100 gardens on school yards and vacant, city-owned parcels. Ranging in size from a single property to a full square block with 80 plots and a variety of hands-on programs for children and others, the gardens have helped to strengthen neighborhoods, to stave off dumping and drug dealing, and even to stimulate reinvestment in adjacent homes and apartment buildings.

St. Louis has one major public park that the city does not manage. Tower Grove Park, although eclipsed by Forest Park, actually predates it by eight years and is every bit as special, featuring a greater diversity of tree species than any other park in the country. Donated by Henry Shaw, a prominent business owner and horticulturalist, who placed the property into a special trust to shield it from city politics, Tower Grove Park is one of the few remaining large gardenesque parks in the United States. Unlike the predominant Olmstedian style (as represented by Forest Park), which emphasizes serene countrylike vistas amid forest patches, gardenesque parks feature highly stylized gates, huge urns, artificial well houses, extravagant pavilions, and even replicas of Roman ruins. The effect is not unlike having a huge, fancy garden as the backyard for an entire neighborhood, and Tower Grove has helped maintain its near-south community's cohesion and value even as the neighborhood has experienced ethnic and racial transition.

Because of St. Louis's financial woes, neither the parks and recreation agency nor the Tower Grove Park Commission is in any kind of expansionist mood—both have their hands full maintaining the acreage and programs they already have. Nevertheless, under the leadership of a private nonprofit organization—Trailnet—an active effort is underway to increase parkland in the city and to make better use of the neglected and run-down Mississippi riverfront. At the top of the list is the Confluence Greenway, a multi-pronged trail system that runs on both sides of the Mississippi River and also crosses the Missouri River a few miles north. (It may one day link with the 200-mile-long Katy Trail heading toward Kansas City.) The city's 12-mile segment of the greenway, called the Riverfront Trail, runs from the Gateway Arch to the Chain of Rocks Bridge. In an amazing feat of vision and per-

severance, Trailnet converted the abandoned bridge (which used to carry famous Route 66) into a pedestrian/bicycle span, one of only two car-free crossings of the Mississippi River (the other being in Minneapolis), and has a 20-year lease on the facility. Of the $4 million needed

Forest Park Forever

An $86 million "Restore the Glory" campaign is showing results throughout Forest Park. Here the once dilapidated World's Fair Pavilion from 1904 shines resplendent once again.

Forest Park Forever

for renovation, by mid-1999 Trailnet had raised all but $300,000 and had already made $1.5 million worth of repairs. In a symbolic nod toward the new prominence of the Mississippi, the city's 1999 Earth Day festival took place on the Chain of Rocks Bridge instead of the usual location in Forest Park.

Figure 6. City and Metropolitan Populations (1996)

City	City Population	Metro Population	City Population as a Percentage of Metro Population
New York	7,381,000	8,643,000[a]	85%
Indianapolis	747,000	1,492,000	50
Houston	1,744,000	3,792,000[a]	46
San Francisco	735,000	1,655,000[a]	44
San Diego	1,171,000	2,655,000	44
Phoenix	1,159,000	2,747,000	42
Los Angeles	3,554,000	9,127,000[a]	39
Chicago	2,722,000	7,734,000[a]	35
Dallas	1,053,000	3,048,000[a]	35
Philadelphia	1,478,000	4,953,000[a]	30
Portland, Oregon	481,000	1,759,000[a]	28
Baltimore	675,000	2,474,000[a]	28
Denver	497,000	1,867,000[a]	27
Kansas City, Missouri	441,000	1,690,000	26
Seattle	525,000	2,235,000[a]	24
Detroit	1,000,000	4,318,000[a]	23
Cleveland	498,000	2,233,000[a]	22
Cincinnati	346,000	1,597,000[a]	22
Miami	365,000	2,076,000[a]	18
Boston	558,000	3,263,000[a]	17
Pittsburgh	350,000	2,379,000	15
St. Louis	352,000	2,548,000	14
Tampa	286,000	2,199,000	13
Minneapolis	359,000	2,765,000	13
Atlanta	402,000	3,541,000	11

[a]Indicates a Primary Metropolitan Statistical Area (PMSA), a subset of the larger Consolidated Metropolitan Statistical Area. All others are Metropolitan Statistical Areas. All population figures are 1996 U.S. Census Bureau estimates.

Taking Trailnet a step further is Gateway Parks and Trails 2004, an effort to create new regional agencies in both Missouri and Illinois in order to develop a broad, interconnected trail system in greater St. Louis, which would link the city and the suburbs with the region's major rivers. If voters approve the measure in November 2000, a small sales tax surcharge would fund new land acquisition and development. The effort could serve to begin breaking down some of the physical and psychological barriers between the scores of governmental agencies that make up the St. Louis region.

Thus far, despite the trail and greenway effort, St. Louisans have not yet made a meaningful connection between their downtown and the Mississippi riverfront. The soaring Gateway Arch would be the natural link, but, except for fireworks on July 4, the National Park Service has been reluctant to turn the 91-acre memorial grounds into the kind of civic gathering place that Chicago has with Grant Park on the lakefront or Cincinnati is creating with Central Riverfront Park. The dilemma could be solved by linking the riverfront with the city's Gateway Mall, a long, rectangular green space that has been evolving over the years with the gradual demolition of obsolete buildings between the arch and Union Station. Because the cost for that project is $70 million, including $25 million to put a deck over Interstate 70, it may entail waiting until the Forest Park campaign is completed. At that time, perhaps, the slogan "Forest Park Forever" will be broadened to "St. Louis Forever."

Note

1. For a detailed description of the creation of Turtle Park, see Alexander Garvin et al., *Urban Parks and Open Spaces* (Washington, D.C.: ULI–the Urban Land Institute, 1997), p. 196.

Cincinnati

Named after an ancient Roman, Cincinnati is a bit reminiscent of an Italian hill town. Where old European hilltops held fortresses, however, virtually all of Cincinnati's most dramatic heights are crowned by parks. For example, Ault Park has beautiful gardens, an Italian-style pavilion, a water cascade, and a 360-degree vista. Mount Echo Park provides spectacular views of the Ohio River's sweeping S-curve. The 1,470-acre Mount Airy Forest was the site of the first municipal reforestation project in the United States and is now a mecca for hikers. Finally, Eden Park stands atop another summit with its picturesque gazebo, striking water tower, conservatory, museums, gardens, and playhouse.

Cincinnati's challenge today is to find a way to link these isolated peaks by adding connecting greenways through its hillsides and valleys and along the mighty Ohio River. The city's heyday was back in the 1850s, when a constant flow of paddle wheelers on the Ohio River made Cincinnati the biggest city west of the Appalachians. It seemed destined to become the Queen City of the heartland, but Cincinnati was awkwardly located between the North and South during

Cincinnati Park Board

Endowed with more open space per capita than most of the nation's other big cities, Cincinnati is also blessed with dramatic hilltops that are frequently crowned by parks, such as Mount Echo Park with its great views of the Ohio River.

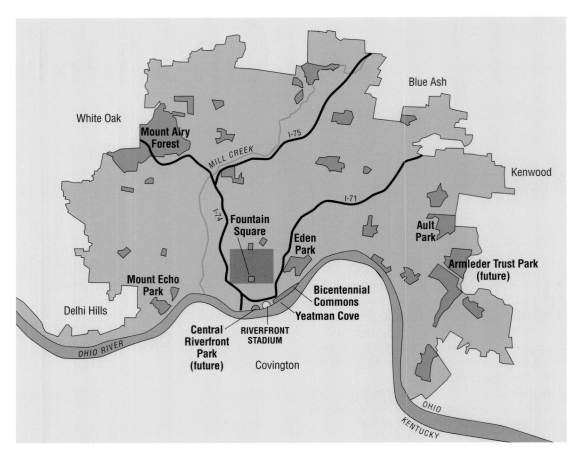

Cincinnati's network of parks and open space.

the Civil War and, after failing to transform from riverboat to railroad technology, it found itself surpassed by St. Louis and Chicago.

It may be just as well. Had Cincinnati's growth spurt continued into the frenetic 20th century, hillsides might have been leveled, ra-

City Profile for Cincinnati, Ohio

City Population (1996)	346,000
City Area in Acres (1990)	49,408
City Population Density Level	7.0
County in Which City Is Located	Hamilton
County's Population (1996)	858,000
Metropolitan Area Population (1996)	1,597,000
City Relative Cost of Living (base = 100)	98.7
Number of Publicly Owned Vacant Lots	N.A.
Does the City Have a Developer Impact Fee for Parks?	No
Municipal Park Acres in City	7,246
National Park Acres in City	3
State Park Acres in City	0
County Park Acres in City	142
Total Park Acres in City	7,391

vines filled, ridgeline apartment blocks constructed, and much of the city's special quality lost. As it is, only three major gashes—the 19th-century rail yards along Mill Creek, the 20th-century freeway system, and the blank concrete cylinder of Riverfront Stadium—marred Cincinnati's form, and all of these are now being mitigated through greenways, parks, landscaping, or complete reconstruction.

Cincinnati today is considered a conservative city, propelled into the nation's memory by its ban of *Hustler* magazine and indictment of a museum director for exhibiting Robert Mapplethorpe photographs that were termed pornographic. The city is also thought to be provincial: Mill Creek divides east from west, and steep hillsides delineate 51 sharply defined communities that tend toward an inward-looking insularity.

Cincinnati's willingness to spend money, however, shows that the city is not traditionally conservative. For example, on a per-capita basis, Cincinnati has more swimming pools than any other city. The pools are small and may be inefficient and expensive to operate, but each community likes having its own, and residents are willing to pay for the privilege. At $130 per person, Cincinnatians spend more on parks and recreation than big-city taxpayers everywhere else, except Minneapolis, Seattle, and Portland, Oregon, and they also get more. For every 1,000 residents, Cincinnati has 21 acres of parkland, a better ratio than any other medium-density city, and fifth best of all the cities studied in this book. Cincinnatians have more golf courses and pools, per capita, and are tied for third highest in tennis courts. In addition, the city is embarking on a variety of new programs, including beautifying its freeway gateways and supporting community garden efforts. Cincinnati is even gradually creating a new White Blossom Festival to challenge Washington's Cherry Blossom Festival by promoting the citywide planting of thousands of white-blossomed trees, such as Japanese tree lilacs, fringe trees, Kousa dogwoods, and yellowwoods.

The relatively steady level of funding over the years has enabled Cincinnati's park and recreation programs to avoid the kind of system-wide collapse suffered at one time or another by Chicago, Boston, New York, and virtually all older cities. Like the others, Cincinnati has a long list of unmet capital needs (including the complete renovation of the beloved but decrepit Tyler Davidson Fountain in Fountain Square, and millions of dollars of upgrades to recreation centers), but the challenge seems manageable, especially in light of citizens' extraordinary generosity over the years. Private individuals have donated about 40 percent of Cincinnati's park system over the years, and the Park Board has more than $40 million in trust funds earmarked in perpetuity for upkeep and maintenance of specific parcels of land.

It is not easy to get a handle on Cincinnati's park and recreation system, because it consists of two programs, not one. In theory, the Cincinnati Park Board, with a staff of 125 responsible for 4,686 acres, operates all the passive and ornamental parks; the Cincinnati Recreation Commission, with a staff of 255 and responsibility for 2,560 acres, operates all the active spaces plus the pools, recreation centers, community programs, and more. In reality, many of their tasks overlap, some logically, some not. Of the big cities, the vast majority houses both programs under the same roof, and most Americans assume that park and recreation offices are joined at the hip.[1] But the Cincinnati experience is strong enough to at least question the notion. Using analogies like "Parks is wine-and-cheese; Recreation is beer-and-pretzels," Cincinnati officials point out that each agency can focus more clearly on its core mission and deliver better results

Cincinnati Recreation Commission

At $130 per person, per year, Cincinnatians spend more on parks and recreation than taxpayers in all but three of the big cities; and they get a lot in return, including more golf courses and pools per capita than any of their urban counterparts. Here youngsters cool off in the new Dyer Sprayground.

by eliminating the need to make internal trade-offs as in other cities. They also note that modern park management is moving more toward preserving open spaces and ecological purity, while modern recreation management is increasingly merging with such community services as vocational education, gang control, programs for persons with disabilities, and language instruction. (Interestingly, as in Philadelphia, the recreation system generates far more political support and funding than the parks system does; as one staff member put it, "Trees are nice, but children sell.") Furthermore, debates over priorities that usually take place behind closed doors in other cities occur publicly in Cincinnati. For example, in 1988, when the city council proposed merging the parks and recreation agencies, park supporters went into a frenzy, worrying that all the trees in Mount Airy Park would be chopped down to create ballfields, and the idea was shelved.

Cincinnati's recent focus is on the Ohio riverfront, once the city's welcome mat but increasingly, after World War II, the site of an impenetrable tangle of highways, off-ramps, and parking areas. As in Pittsburgh, New York, Portland (Oregon), and other locales where the citizens were cut off from their water tradition, it

Cincinnati Park Board

Address	950 Eden Park Drive
Zip Code	45202
Telephone	(513) 352-4079
Fax	(513) 352-4096
Web Site	www.cinci-parks.org
Agency Acreage in City[a]	4,686
Acreage as Percent of City	9.5%
Acres per 1,000 Residents	13.5
Number of Regional Parks	12
Number of Neighborhood Parks	106
Number of Beaches	0
Miles of Bikeways/Greenways	50
Number of Full-Time Employees	125
Number of Seasonal Employees	92
Number of Volunteers	500

Adjusted Budget for Fiscal Year 1998–1999

Revenue

General Funds	$6,500,000
Dedicated Taxes	0
Fees Retained by the Agency	1,000,000
Private Grants and Donations	1,400,000
State and Federal Support	0
Capital Income	5,300,000
Total	$14,200,000

Expenditure

Grounds and Facilities Maintenance and Repair	$6,700,000
Recreational Programming and Activities	2,200,000
Capital Construction and Acquisition	5,300,000
Total	$14,200,000

Expenditure per Resident	**$41**

[a]Excludes 368 acres owned by the Cincinnati Park Board but managed by the Cincinnati Recreation Commission.

took many years to reach consensus on whether and how to make the reconnection in Cincinnati. The effort has been proceeding fitfully, first with Yeatman Cove and the Serpentine Wall (1971), then with Bicentennial Commons, the Olympic Rowing Center, tennis courts, and a skating rink (1989). International Fellowship Park is next on the agenda (slated for 2001), followed by the 3.5-mile Eastend Walkway (date undetermined). The centerpiece of the effort is Central Riverfront Park, which will

emerge from the construction of two new stadiums along the river.

The stadium replacement ritual is being played out in no less than a dozen of the 25 cities covered in this book, but in Cincinnati the undertaking is at least resulting in some additional parkland. Built in 1970, Riverfront Stadium was placed on the downtown Ohio River shore specifically to prop up the sagging fortunes of the center city. Unfortunately, its suburban design—a circular, blank-walled, concrete fortress surrounded by acres of windswept parking—only managed to block the view and intimidate pedestrians. Planners had assumed that downtown would change to accommodate the stadium but they misjudged. A few years later, Baltimore and Cleveland demonstrated how to design city-friendly ballparks that could pump liveliness and money—not just cars—into local economies. When the Reds (baseball) and the Bengals (football) began to complain about sharing Riverfront Stadium and threatened to leave town, the city launched an emergency campaign. The result was a $600 million plan to tear down the stadium, build two modern ones, place much of the parking underground, narrow the highway that separates the downtown area from the river, fill in the area with a new park (and possibly a new museum), and pay for it all with a half-cent increase in Hamilton County's sales tax.

Naturally, developing the park must await completion of the stadiums in 2001 and 2004. The park is budgeted at $65 million, but other details are much more vague, including which agency will build and operate it—the Park Board, the Recreation Commission, the Ohio Department of Natural Resources (which would provide a state park neatly mirroring the one established across Ohio on the Cleveland waterfront), or the Hamilton County Parks Department. Because Cincinnati is within Hamilton County, city residents provide about a third of the county agency's tax receipts, but they have long been resentful that the agency buys land almost entirely outside the city limits. There is a growing feeling among Cincinnatians that Central Riverfront Park might be the way for Hamilton County to compensate. (The city has increasing leverage in the tug-of-war, because the county park levy expires in 2003, and Cincinnati voters make up 40 percent of the county's electorate.)

Beyond the ownership question, the Central Riverfront Park project raises other tough issues. For one thing, the Ohio River is a difficult, fluctuating partner, usually rising at least 20 feet every spring. In 1937, for example, the river rose 50 feet above flood stage and inundated a large part of the downtown area; another season saw the river reach flood stage on seven different occasions. Therefore, every riverfront park on the Ohio must be designed to minimize damage, resist erosion, counter rust, and remain easy to clean up after the debris-filled waters subside. The city also has a plan to build a Freedom Center to memorialize its role in the Civil War–period Underground Railroad, and the park must conform to the design of that center. Finally, if skeptics can be overcome, Cincinnati hopes to begin constructing the region's first light-rail line, which would run directly through this central location.

Even though residents' attention is on a few key acres downtown, the near-term project that most excites the Recreation Commission and the Park Board is a 350-acre property along the Little Miami River, which will become the city's second largest park. A former landfill that long has been jointly owned by the Park Board and the Recreation Commission, the property is now being developed as a result of a $4 million gift from the Armleder Trust. The Little Miami River

Cincinnati Park Board

Mount Airy Forest, the largest park in Cincinnati, was created in 1911 as the first urban reforestation project in the United States. Today, Mount Airy not only serves as a mecca for hikers seeking a quick getaway from the city but also stems soil erosion that formerly polluted Mill Creek and the Ohio River.

Cincinnati Recreation Commission

Address	Two Centennial Plaza, 805 Central Avenue, 8th Floor
Zip Code	45202
Telephone	(513) 352-4000
Fax	(513) 352-1634
Web Site	www.cincyrec.org
Agency Acreage in City[a]	2,560
Acreage as Percent of City	5.2%
Acres per 1,000 Residents	7.2
Number of Regional Parks	15
Number of Neighborhood Parks	235
Number of Recreation Centers	30
Number of Pools	47
Number of Golf Courses	7
Number of Tennis Courts	125
Number of Sports Fields	188
Number of Marina Slips	30
Number of Beaches	0
Miles of Bikeways/Greenways	20
Number of Skating Rinks	3
Number of Full-Time Employees	255
Number of Seasonal Employees	900
Number of Volunteers	5,000

Adjusted Budget for Fiscal Year 1998

Revenue

General Funds	$13,245,000
Dedicated Taxes	0
Fees Retained by the Agency	10,470,000
Private Grants and Donations	141,000
State and Federal Support	100,000
Capital Income	8,675,000
Total	$32,631,000

Expenditure

Grounds and Facilities Maintenance and Repair	$1,804,000
Recreational Programming and Activities	21,154,000
Capital Construction and Acquisition	7,931,000
Total	$30,889,000

Expenditure per Resident	**$89**

[a]Includes 368 acres owned by the Cincinnati Park Board but managed by the Cincinnati Recreation Commission.

is also subject to annual flooding, and the agencies are planning state-of-the-art removable facilities—concession stands and even toilet buildings that can be unhooked from utilities and rolled up to high ground in the spring. The new park will combine natural lands with desperately needed sports fields.

The other new partnership in Cincinnati involves industrial, neglected Mill Creek, historically the city's sharpest dividing line and, in 1997, named the most threatened urban stream in North America. Spearheaded by the privately funded Mill Creek Conservancy, the campaign for a regional greenway is the first such effort in greater Cincinnati and, significantly, one in which neither the Park Board nor the Recreation Commission has become involved. The long-term vision includes not only creekside trails but also gardens, water-retaining forests and wetlands, removal of some of the $100 million worth of concrete channels dug by the Army Corps of Engineers, plus environmental education for children and work training programs

for local residents in the low-income communities that adjoin the creek. Even before it is completed, the Mill Creek Restoration Project hopes to accomplish something that no other entity in the city has done: link people and neighborhoods through parkland.

Cincinnati is a middle-aged city, entering its third century. From lovely hilltop parks Cincinnatians can clearly see their city's successes as well as its failures. As they now turn their attention to connecting greenways along streams and the Ohio River, residents have the opportunity to break down neighborhood barriers and build a good system into a great one.

Note

1. The only other big cities that have two distinct park and recreation agencies are Philadelphia and Tampa; Boston has a regular Department of Parks and Recreation as well as a Department of Community Centers.

Portland, Oregon

AS THE UNITED STATES gropes to develop a post-sprawl new urbanism, Portland is the city that is trying to blaze a trail. The two hallmarks of Portland's approach are elected regional governance and a clearly articulated growth boundary, and, since 1972, this strategy has been having an increasingly profound impact on the shape, feel, and economy of the city and its parks.

Portland defies stereotypes. Even though it is a rapidly growing West Coast metropolis, Portland's downtown was built before the introduction of automobiles and has a distinct East Coast feel. In fact, before 1972, Portland was experiencing virtually all the symptoms of older, established cities of the Northeast and Midwest, including decline of industry, deterioration of downtown, loss of population to the suburbs, and rise in the poverty rate. Since the institution of the growth boundary, the construction of a light-rail system, and the establishment of Metro (the regional government), the city has begun moving in a direction different from most others today: its population is growing *and* its density is increasing, generally around transit-oriented neighborhood nodes. (At the same time, there is markedly less suburban sprawl outside the growth line than around other big cities.) Although most Portlanders consider these changes positive, many also fear the population influx and feel a strong emotional need to preserve the greenery around them—not only the immutable, picture-perfect silhouette of Mount Hood standing on the eastern horizon, but also smaller parks, squares, and greenways within the city. (This is, after all, the region dubbed "Ecotopia" in the novel of the same name by Nicholas Katzenbach.)

Portland's transformation is affecting the city's park system, 77 percent of which is operated

Resembling Hansel and Gretel, these youngsters are taking part in the Recreation Department's Totwalk program in Forest Park. With nearly 5,000 acres, Portland's Forest Park is the fifth largest municipal park in the United States and one reason that the city provides a generous 26 acres of parkland for every 1,000 residents.

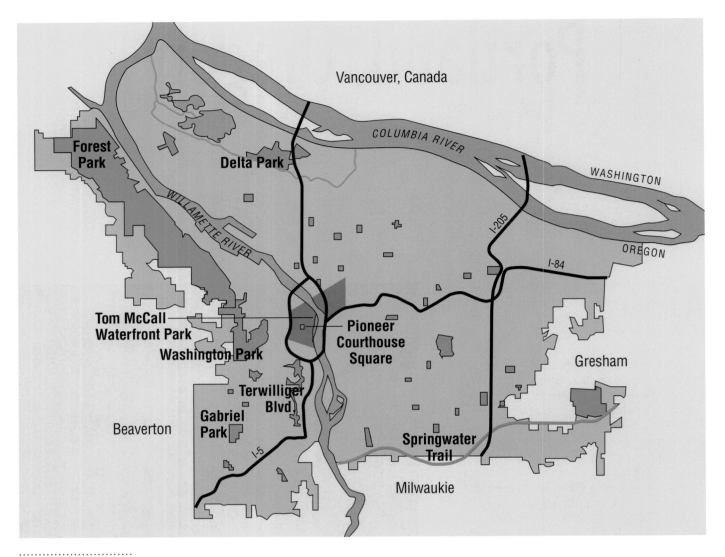

Vancouver, Canada

COLUMBIA RIVER

WASHINGTON

Forest Park

Delta Park

WILLAMETTE RIVER

I-205

OREGON

I-84

Tom McCall Waterfront Park

Pioneer Courthouse Square

Washington Park

Gresham

Terwilliger Blvd

Gabriel Park

Beaverton

I-5

Springwater Trail

Milwaukie

Portland's network of
parks and open space.

by the Portland Parks and Recreation Department and 18 percent by Metro. (The remaining 5 percent is a state park within the city limits.) Portland Parks and Recreation has a longer history and a broader mandate, but Metro now has much more money for land acquisition, both inside and outside the city limits.

Among the medium-density cities, Portland devotes a larger percentage of its land area to parkland than all but Minneapolis; per capita, Portland tops that group with 26 acres for every 1,000 residents, twice the average. Two parks are preeminent in Portland's system, and between these two extremes lie the 246 other parcels that provide the natural and recreational outlets for the city. One is Forest Park, 4,836 acres of verdant woods on a mountain overlooking the Willamette River valley; the other is Pioneer Courthouse Square, 1.5 acres of red brick hardscape in the center of town, surrounded by high rises and featuring a coffee bar and a flower wagon.

The story of Forest Park is the story of the tenacious power of a great idea. As early as 1903, only four years after the formation of the Municipal Park Commission, landscape architect John Olmsted (stepson of Frederick Law Olmsted) visited the city and drew up a master plan for the park, which called for a circuit of connecting parks (the so-called "40-Mile Loop") and the acquisition of the high hills west of the Willamette for a wildland park. In response, voters approved $1 million in park bonds in 1907, but most of the money went into developing existing parks not buying new ones. Small portions of the Olmsted plan were accomplished, but within a few years the enthusiasm had diminished. By 1913, when the next bond issue was proposed, the electorate voted it down. Even worse, the city set up a wood-cutting camp for the unemployed on Tualatin Mountain, and developers proposed large subdivisions throughout the area and sold hundreds of lots. The idea of developing a park seemed doomed.

The proposed subdivisions depended on the construction of a private road through the rugged forest, but building the road cost the developer twice what he had budgeted. To make matters worse, the road was devastated by a landslide. Reeling financially, the developer raised the assessment on all the vacant lots; in response, hundreds of them were forfeited to the city. Meanwhile, other land on the mountain, stripped of its timber and burned by wildfires, was abandoned and ended up as property of Multnomah County by default.

The next Easterner to dispense out-of-town advice was Robert Moses, New York City's ironfisted park commissioner, who, in 1943, revived the vision of converting Portland's striking hills into a large wooded park. The timing was propitious. A few elite business leaders favored the plan, and the Federation of Western Outdoor Clubs began lobbying for the effort. In 1948, all the defaulted city and county properties, as well as other donated lands, were combined into Forest Park.

Upon its dedication, Forest Park catapulted past Los Angeles's Griffith Park and Philadelphia's Fairmount Park to become the largest municipal park in the country. It has since fallen to fifth place (behind even larger parks in Phoenix, Houston, and San Diego), but Forest Park continues to offer Portlanders a wealth of benefits. Essentially undeveloped and closed to cars, it is not as heavily used as Washington Park and other gathering places in Portland, but its roads and trails offer runners, mountain bikers, hikers, and equestrians a 60-mile network for escape right in the city. Equally important, it provides the kind of large unbroken habitat so important to maintaining the viability of animal and plant species. Forest Park continues to grow thanks to gifts and land acquisition; when ultimately completed, it will encompass 6,000 acres.

At the other end of the spectrum is Pioneer Courthouse Square, an almost treeless block that hosts more (and more diverse) visitors in a day than Forest Park gets in a month. Created only in 1984, the square quickly became the city's outdoor living room, partly because of its central location and partly because it was born of a true grass-roots groundswell. The entire Portland community first lamented the demolition of the grand but decrepit Portland Hotel on the site, then rose up to protest the planned construction of an 11-story parking garage. The strong reaction induced the city to purchase the block, and the citizenry then bought—individual by individual and company by company—

65,000 bricks to pave the square and to pay for its other amenities.

With a whimsical, postmodern design that includes a waterfall, a bowl-shaped sitting area, and pillars reminiscent of the ruins of a Greek temple, Pioneer Courthouse Square gives users the immediate sense that anything can happen. And it does; events range from celebrations, concerts, and memorials to product rollouts, political rallies, presidential speeches, and a sand castle festival. Even when no programmed activities are scheduled, the square is busy because of its location at the confluence of the transit mall, the light-rail system, and the city's two biggest department stores.

Owned by Portland Parks and Recreation, the square is operated under contract by Friends of Pioneer Courthouse Square, a nonprofit corporation that handles programming, maintenance, and security. The organization derives the bulk of its $900,000 annual budget from event fees and leases (to two shops and several vendor carts). A simple rule governs the square's balance between commercial activities and free speech: using an amplifier requires payment, not using one does not. There are no impediments for jugglers, mimes, guitar strummers, and soapbox preachers; but for others, the daily fee ranges from about $100 (for a nonprofit group not selling anything) to $2,000 (for a large corporate extravaganza). The group's executive director, Karen Whitman, a former advertising

City Profile for Portland, Oregon

City Population (1996)	481,000
City Area in Acres (1990)	79,808
City Population Density Level	6.0
County in Which City Is Located	Multnomah
County's Population (1996)	625,000
Metropolitan Area Population (1996)	1,759,000
City Relative Cost of Living (base = 100)	111.7
Number of Publicly Owned Vacant Lots	N.A.
Does the City Have a Developer Impact Fee for Parks?	Yes
Municipal Park Acres in City	9,659
National Park Acres in City	0
State Park Acres in City	645
County Park Acres in City[a]	2,287
Total Park Acres in City	12,591

[a]Operated by Metro Regional Parks; total excludes 254 acres managed jointly by the Portland Parks and Recreation Department and counted as municipal park acres.

Portland Parks and Recreation Department

Address	1120 SW Fifth Avenue, Suite 1302
Zip Code	97204
Telephone	(503) 823-5379
Fax	(503) 823-6007
Web Site	www.portlandparks.org
Agency Acreage in City	9,659
Acreage as Percent of City	12.1%
Acres per 1,000 Residents	21.4
Number of Regional Parks	20
Number of Neighborhood Parks	196
Number of Recreation Centers	15
Number of Pools	16
Number of Golf Courses	4
Number of Tennis Courts	122
Number of Sports Fields	223
Number of Marina Slips	3
Number of Beaches	1
Miles of Bikeways/Greenways	105
Number of Skating Rinks	1
Number of Full-Time Employees	371
Number of Seasonal Employees	1,308
Number of Volunteers	3,500

Adjusted Budget for Fiscal Year 1997–1998

Revenue

General Funds	$25,436,000
Dedicated Taxes	0
Fees Retained by the Agency[a]	18,893,000
Private Grants and Donations	0
State and Federal Support	2,103,000
Capital Income	18,828,000
Total	$65,260,000

Expenditure

Grounds and Facilities Maintenance and Repair	$25,613,000
Recreational Programming and Activities	13,877,000
Capital Construction and Acquisition	25,770,000
Total	$65,260,000

Expenditure per Resident	$136

[a]Includes payments by other agencies for interagency services.

executive, is clear about the group's mission. "Our aspiration," she says, "is to become the Rockefeller Center of the West."

The success of Pioneer Courthouse Square followed from an even more remarkable achievement ten years earlier—the conversion of a downtown highway to a park. A center-city freeway loop, completed in the early 1970s, diverted enough traffic from the old Harbor Drive to allow highway engineers—under the prodding of environmentalists, city officials, and Governor Tom McCall—to agree to close down the six-lane roadway. Converted to Waterfront Park (named for Governor McCall after his death), the 22-block, 37-acre facility has transformed Portland's appearance, reconnected the city with the Willamette River, and spurred the construction of additional downtown housing and shops, a marina, and an esplanade. The park today hosts the city's Rose Festival, Blues Festival, and numerous other events attracting tens of thousands of visitors. By the late 1990s, Boston, Chicago, and a few other places were gingerly converting roadways to parks, but in 1974 the concept was revolutionary. The success of the experiment is leading planners to look into somehow providing similar green space on the east side of the Willamette River, which is still blocked by a tangle of roadways and ramps.

The soul of Portland's parks is Charles Jordan, director of the Parks and Recreation Department since 1989 and previously one of the city's five elected commissioners. A six-foot-seven-inch African American with the oratorical skills of a preacher, Jordan packs a wallop speaking for youth and community partnerships. Memorable phrases, such as "I may not have the resources and skills to turn around the gang member, but I can save his little brother from following in those footsteps" and "We're the second largest landowner in Portland—how can we not teach our children about land stewardship?" have landed Jordan on numerous boards and commissions from Oregon to Washington, D.C., and have made him one of the country's most influential city park advocates. He convenes an annual "leisure industry summit" every year, where scores of youth service providers—from Scouts to Police Athletic Leagues to Boys and Girls Clubs—come together to compare notes and ensure the best possible cooperation and service. To sweeten the pot, Jordan created a $250,000 Youth Trust Fund (generated by a surcharge of 50 cents per nine holes on every round of golf in the city) that pays for special programs.

Alexander Garvin

Although it contains only 1.5 acres of brick hardscape, Pioneer Courthouse Square has a central location, a whimsical design, and a diversity of programs, all of which have turned it into Portland's public living room. The park was created after Portlanders raised an outcry over a proposed 11-story parking garage on the site.

Portland also has many other notable facilities, including the new 16-mile Springwater Trail created from an abandoned rail line; spacious Delta Park, one of whose eight soccer fields was recently converted to Astroturf as an experiment in field preservation; lovely Terwilliger Boulevard, designed by the Olmsteds; the handsome Park Blocks, whose "cathedral of elms" has graced downtown since 1848; and tranquil rose and Japanese gardens in Washington Park. Although the Olmsteds' 40-Mile Loop plan sat largely unrealized for almost a century, city and regional planners are now seeking to complete the greenway and even extend it far into the surrounding counties by another 100 miles.

Portland's Parks and Recreation Department is one of the few city park agencies empowered to keep all the revenue it raises rather than send most of it to the city's general treasury. For this reason the department is the third best funded of those studied in this book (after the agencies in Seattle and Minneapolis). Nevertheless, because of the city's tightening budget, the department is considering raising additional income from the private sector, through corporations like Nike, Adidas, and the Portland Trailblazers as well as through higher individual fees for certain uses. Park advocates are also exploring the creation of a nonprofit foundation, which could solicit and accept donations for the creation and maintenance of parkland.

Despite its many strengths, Portland's park program is at a political crossroads. With the rise of Metro and its metropolitan-area-wide park and open-space program, the appropriate role for the Portland Parks and Recreation Department is unclear. On paper it looks easy: Metro provides undeveloped open space, Portland Parks provides developed facilities for recreation and culture. However, Portland's Parks Department owns the greatest single natural area in the region—Forest Park—and the city is not likely to turn it over to Metro. Conversely, when Portland Parks attempted to build a recreation center in a corner of Gabriel Park in 1998, some neighborhood activists protested the loss of three acres of habitat.

Voters in the three-county Metro area fully understand and support Metro's $110 million land acquisition program, under which 6,000

Portland Department of Parks and Recreation

A double row of cherry trees and a 22-block promenade have replaced old six-lane Harbor Drive, reconnecting downtown Portland with the Willamette River. Named for the visionary governor who made it happen, Tom McCall Waterfront Park spurred the construction of additional downtown housing and shops and has become the city's front porch.

more acres will be bought by 2015. A broad-based Greenspaces Advisory Committee had agreed upon the program in 1995 after scores of public hearings. A year earlier, in 1994, city voters had similarly passed a $65 million bond issue to rebuild and refurbish ailing and run-down park facilities in Portland.

In 1998, however, the next city bond measure was narrowly defeated, and this put the brakes on finishing the repairs. Parks were only one casualty of an apparent across-the-board taxpayer revolt, but the psychological impact on the department was undeniable. In response, the Parks and Recreation Department is under-taking a major public outreach process to come up with a 2020 plan and a new vision for operating in the 21st century. Director Jordan is also exploring the creation of a parks commission that could help him look at big-picture issues beyond the day-to-day concerns of the department. (Portland is one of the few cities without such a commission.)

As Portland's Parks and Recreation Department struggles to redefine its role within the new metropolitan government of greater Portland, many park advocates in other cities are watching to see what the future may hold for their areas as well.

Tables

Table 1. City Park Agencies and Their Holdings
(In Acres)

Agency	Acreage[a]
Atlanta Department of Parks, Recreation, and Cultural Affairs	3,122
Baltimore City Department of Recreation and Parks	5,048
Boston Department of Parks and Recreation	2,693
Chicago Park District	7,329
Cincinnati Park Board[b]	4,686
Cincinnati Recreation Commission[b]	2,560
Cleveland Department of Parks, Recreation, and Property	1,394
Dallas Parks and Recreation Department	21,828
Denver Parks and Recreation Department	5,643
Detroit Recreation Department	5,890
Houston Parks and Recreation Department	20,363
Indianapolis Parks and Recreation Department	11,547
Kansas City, Missouri, Department of Parks, Recreation, and Boulevards	11,047
Los Angeles Department of Recreation and Parks	14,987
Miami Parks and Recreation Department	1,291
Minneapolis Park and Recreation Board	5,694
New York City Department of Parks and Recreation	28,126
(Philadelphia) Fairmount Park Commission[b]	8,900
Philadelphia Department of Recreation[b]	1,464
Phoenix Parks, Recreation, and Library Department	34,901
Pittsburgh Department of Parks and Recreation	2,691
Portland Parks and Recreation Department	9,659
San Diego Park and Recreation Department	32,650
San Francisco Recreation and Park Department	3,317
Seattle Department of Parks and Recreation	6,189
St. Louis Department of Parks, Recreation, and Forestry	3,290
Tampa Parks Department[b]	1,760
Tampa Sports Authority[b]	423

[a]Acreage does not include landholdings outside city boundaries.

[b]Denotes cities that have more than one municipal park or recreation agency that manages land.

Table 2. Total Parks and Open Space
(In Acres, by City)

City	Acreage Held by City Park Agency	Acreage Held by All Other Park Agencies[a]	Total Acreage of Park/Open Space Land
Atlanta	3,122	25	3,147
Baltimore	5,048	43	5,091
Boston	2,693	2,172	4,865
Chicago	7,329	4,300	11,629
Cincinnati	7,246	145	7,391
Cleveland	1,394	1,493	2,887
Dallas	21,828	0	21,828
Denver	5,643	0	5,643
Detroit	5,890	0	5,890
Houston	20,363	1,427	21,790
Indianapolis	11,547	1,692	13,239
Kansas City, Missouri	11,047	2,282	13,329
Los Angeles	14,987	15,134	30,121
Miami	1,291	38	1,329
Minneapolis	5,694	0	5,694
New York	28,126	24,812	52,938
Philadelphia	10,364	321	10,685
Phoenix	34,901	1,600	36,501
Pittsburgh	2,691	44	2,735
Portland, Oregon	9,659	2,932	12,591
San Diego	32,650	3,458	36,108
San Francisco	3,317	4,277	7,594
Seattle	6,189	5	6,194
St. Louis	3,290	95	3,385
Tampa	2,183	907	3,090

[a]Includes land held by county, regional, state, and federal park agencies within city boundaries.

Table 3. City Population Density
(Persons per Acre)

City	Area[a] (In Acres)	Population[b]	Persons per Acre
High-Density Population			
New York	197,696	7,381,000	37.3
San Francisco	29,888	735,000	24.6
Chicago	145,408	2,722,000	18.7
Boston	30,976	558,000	18.0
Philadelphia	86,464	1,478,000	17.1
Miami	22,784	365,000	16.0
Baltimore	51,712	675,000	13.1
Los Angeles	300,352	3,554,000	11.8
Medium-Density Population			
Detroit	88,768	1,000,000	11.3
Minneapolis	35,156	359,000	10.2
Cleveland	49,280	498,000	10.1
Pittsburgh	35,584	350,000	9.8
Seattle	53,696	525,000	9.8
St. Louis	39,616	352,000	8.9
Cincinnati	49,408	346,000	7.0
Portland, Oregon	79,808	481,000	6.0
Low-Density Population			
San Diego	207,360	1,171,000	5.6
Denver	98,112	497,000	5.1
Houston	345,536	1,744,000	5.0
Dallas	218,880	1,053,000	4.8
Atlanta	84,352	402,000	4.8
Phoenix	268,736	1,159,000	4.3
Tampa	69,568	286,000	4.1
Indianapolis	231,488	747,000	3.2
Kansas City, Missouri	199,360	441,000	2.2

[a]From 1990 U.S. Census.

[b]From 1996 U.S. Census estimates.

Table 4. Largest Parks in the Largest Cities in the United States

Name	City	Acres
South Mountain Preserve Park	Phoenix	16,283
Cullen Park	Houston	10,534
North Mountain Preserve Park	Phoenix	7,500
Mission Trails Park	San Diego	5,700
Forest Park	Portland, Oregon	4,836
Eagle Creek Park	Indianapolis	4,813
Mission Bay Park	San Diego	4,600
Griffith Park	Los Angeles	4,171
Fairmount Park–Wissahickon Valley	Philadelphia	4,167
Trinity River Park	Dallas	3,653
White Rock Lake Park/Greenbelt	Dallas	2,956
Pelham Bay Park	New York	2,766
Los Peñasquitos Canyon Preserve	San Diego	2,572
San Pasqual Open Space	San Diego	2,341
Sepulveda Dam Recreation Area	Los Angeles	2,031
Greenbelt Park	New York	1,778
Swope Park	Kansas City, Missouri	1,769
Upper Fall Creek	Indianapolis	1,660
Pennypack Park	Philadelphia	1,618
Mount Airy Forest	Cincinnati	1,472
Hansen Dam Recreation Area	Los Angeles	1,463
Memorial Park	Houston	1,431
Forest Park	St. Louis	1,293
Flushing Meadows–Corona Park	New York	1,255
Lincoln Park	Chicago	1,212
Rouge Park	Detroit	1,200
Van Cortland Park	New York	1,146
Golden Gate Park	San Francisco	1,107
Gwynns Falls/Leakin Park	Baltimore	1,100
Balboa Park	San Diego	1,048
Richmond Parkway	New York	984
Rochester Park	Dallas	983
Belle Isle Park	Detroit	981
Riverfront Park	Kansas City, Missouri	955
Eisenhower Park	Houston	883
Central Park	New York	840

Note: Data cover only the cities profiled in this book, the 25 largest cities in the United States, excluding Milwaukee and Washington, D.C. There are other city parks that are as large as some of the parks on this list.

Table 5. Parks and Open Space per 1,000 Residents
(In Acres, by City)

City	Population	Total Acreage within City[a]	Acres per 1,000 Residents
High-Density Population			
San Francisco	735,000	7,594	10.3
Boston	558,000	4,865	8.7
Los Angeles	3,554,000	30,121	8.5
Baltimore	675,000	5,091	7.5
Philadelphia	1,478,000	10,685	7.2
New York	7,381,000	52,938	7.2
Chicago	2,722,000	11,629	4.3
Miami	365,000	1,329	3.6
Average, High-Density Cities			7.2
Medium-Density Population			
Portland, Oregon	481,000	12,591	26.2
Cincinnati	346,000	7,391	21.4
Minneapolis	359,000	5,694	16.0
Seattle	525,000	6,194	11.8
St. Louis	352,000	3,385	9.6
Pittsburgh	350,000	2,735	7.8
Detroit	1,000,000	5,890	5.9
Cleveland	498,000	2,887	5.8
Average, Medium-Density Cities			13.0
Low-Density Population			
Phoenix	1,159,000	36,501	31.5
San Diego	1,171,000	36,108	30.8
Kansas City, Missouri	441,000	13,329	30.2
Dallas	1,053,000	21,828	21.3
Indianapolis	747,000	13,239	17.7
Houston	1,744,000	21,790	12.5
Denver	497,000	5,643	11.4
Tampa	286,000	3,090	10.8
Atlanta	402,000	3,147	7.8
Average, Low-Density Cities			19.3
Average, All Cities			13.4

[a]Includes lands owned by city, county, regional, state, and federal park agencies within the city boundaries.

Table 6. Parks and Open Space per 1,000 Residents
(In Acres, by Agency)

Agency	Population	Acreage within City	Acres per 1,000 Residents
High-Density Population			
Baltimore City Department of Recreation and Parks	675,000	5,048	7.2
Fairmount Park Commission (Philadelphia)[a]	1,478,000	8,900	5.8
Boston Department of Parks and Recreation	558,000	2,693	4.9
San Francisco Recreation and Park Department	735,000	3,317	4.5
Los Angeles Department of Recreation and Parks	3,554,000	14,987	4.2
New York City Department of Parks and Recreation	7,381,000	28,126	3.8
Miami Parks and Recreation Department	365,000	1,291	3.5
Chicago Park District	2,722,000	7,329	2.7
Philadelphia Department of Recreation[a]	1,478,000	1,464	1.0
Average, High-Density Cities			4.2
Medium-Density Population			
Portland Parks and Recreation Department	481,000	9,659	20.1
Minneapolis Park and Recreation Board	359,000	5,694	16.0
Cincinnati Park Board[a]	346,000	4,686	13.5
Seattle Department of Parks and Recreation	525,000	6,189	11.8
St. Louis Department of Parks, Recreation, and Forestry	352,000	3,290	9.3
Pittsburgh Department of Parks and Recreation	350,000	2,691	7.7
Cincinnati Recreation Commission[a]	346,000	2,560	7.4
Detroit Recreation Department	1,000,000	5,890	5.9
Cleveland Department of Parks, Recreation, and Property	498,000	1,394	2.8
Average, Medium-Density Cities			10.5
Low-Density Population			
Phoenix Parks, Recreation, and Library Department	1,159,000	34,901	30.1
San Diego Park and Recreation Department	1,171,000	32,650	27.9
Kansas City, Missouri, Department of Parks, Recreation, and Boulevards	441,000	11,047	25.0
Dallas Parks and Recreation Department	1,053,000	21,828	21.7
Indianapolis Parks and Recreation Department	747,000	11,547	15.4
Houston Parks and Recreation Department	1,744,000	20,363	12.0
Denver Parks and Recreation Department	497,000	5,643	11.4
Atlanta Department of Parks, Recreation, and Cultural Affairs	402,000	3,122	7.8
Tampa Parks Department[a]	286,000	1,760	6.2
Tampa Sports Authority[a]	286,000	423	1.5
Average, Low-Density Cities			15.8
Average, All Agencies			10.5

[a]Denotes cities that have more than one municipal park or recreation agency that manages land.

Table 7. Parks and Open Space as Percentage of City Area (By City)

City	Area of City (In Acres)	Total Park/Open Space Acreage within City[a]	Park Acreage as Percentage of City Acreage
High-Density Population			
New York	197,696	52,938	26.8%
San Francisco	29,888	7,594	25.4
Boston	30,976	4,865	15.7
Philadelphia	86,464	10,685	12.4
Los Angeles	300,352	30,121	10.0
Baltimore	51,712	5,091	9.8
Chicago	145,408	11,629	8.0
Miami	22,784	1,329	5.8
Average, High-Density Cities			14.2%
Medium-Density Population			
Minneapolis	35,156	5,694	16.2%
Portland, Oregon	79,808	12,591	15.8
Cincinnati	49,408	7,391	15.0
Seattle	53,696	6,194	11.5
St. Louis	39,616	3,385	8.5
Pittsburgh	35,584	2,735	7.7
Detroit	88,768	5,890	6.6
Cleveland	49,280	2,887	5.9
Average, Medium-Density Cities			10.9%
Low-Density Population			
San Diego	207,360	36,108	17.4%
Phoenix	268,736	36,501	13.6
Dallas	218,880	21,828	10.0
Kansas City, Missouri	199,360	13,329	6.7
Houston	345,536	21,790	6.3
Denver	98,112	5,643	5.8
Indianapolis	231,488	13,239	5.7
Tampa	69,568	3,090	4.4
Atlanta	84,352	3,147	3.7
Average, Low-Density Cities			8.2%
Average, All Cities			11.0%

[a]Includes land owned by city, county, regional, state, and federal park agencies within city boundaries.

Table 8. Parks and Open Space as Percentage of City Area (By Agency)

City Agency	Area of City (In Acres)	Agency Land (In Acres)	Park Acreage as Percentage of City Acreage
High-Density Population			
New York City Department of Parks and Recreation	197,696	28,126	14.2%
San Francisco Recreation and Park Department	29,888	3,317	11.1
Fairmount Park Commission (Philadelphia)[a]	86,464	8,900	10.3
Baltimore City Department of Recreation and Parks	51,712	5,048	9.8
Boston Department of Parks and Recreation	30,976	2,693	8.7
Miami Parks and Recreation Department	22,784	1,291	5.7
Chicago Park District	145,408	7,329	5.0
Los Angeles Department of Recreation and Parks	300,352	14,987	5.0
Philadelphia Department of Recreation[a]	86,464	1,464	1.7
Average, High-Density Cities			7.9%
Medium-Density Population			
Minneapolis Park and Recreation Board	35,156	5,694	16.2%
Portland Parks and Recreation Department	79,808	9,659	12.1
Seattle Department of Parks and Recreation	53,696	6,189	11.5
Cincinnati Park Board[a]	49,408	4,686	9.5
St. Louis Department of Parks, Recreation, and Forestry	39,616	3,290	8.3
Pittsburgh Department of Parks and Recreation	35,584	2,691	7.6
Detroit Recreation Department	88,768	5,890	6.6
Cincinnati Recreation Commission[a]	49,408	2,560	5.2
Cleveland Department of Parks, Recreation, and Property	49,280	1,394	2.8
Average, Medium-Density Cities			8.9%
Low-Density Population			
San Diego Park and Recreation Department	207,360	32,650	15.7%
Phoenix Parks, Recreation, and Library Department	268,736	34,901	13.0
Dallas Parks and Recreation Department	218,880	21,828	10.0
Houston Parks and Recreation Department	345,536	20,363	5.9
Denver Parks and Recreation Department	98,112	5,643	5.8
Kansas City, Missouri, Department of Parks, Recreation, and Boulevards	199,360	11,047	5.5
Indianapolis Parks and Recreation Department	231,488	11,547	5.0
Atlanta Department of Parks, Recreation, and Cultural Affairs	84,352	3,122	3.7
Tampa Parks Department[a]	69,568	1,760	2.5
Tampa Sports Authority[a]	69,568	423	0.6
Average, Low-Density Cities			6.8%
Average, All Agencies			7.8%

[a]Denotes cities that have more than one municipal park or recreation agency that manages land.

Table 9. Adjusted Agency Budgets[a]
(Selected Agencies)

Agency	Adjusted Budget[a]	Budget Year
Atlanta Department of Parks, Recreation, and Cultural Affairs	$25,250,000	1998
Baltimore City Department of Public Works[b]	6,500,000	1997–1998
Baltimore City Department of Recreation and Parks[b]	25,470,000	1999
Boston Department of Community Centers[b]	13,712,000	1998–1999
Boston Department of Parks and Recreation[b]	26,638,000	1998–1999
Chicago Park District[b]	293,632,000	1998–1999
Cincinnati Park Board[b]	14,200,000	1998–1999
Cincinnati Recreation Commission[b]	30,889,000	1998
Cleveland Department of Parks, Recreation, and Property[b]	30,918,000	1998
Cleveland Lakefront State Park[b]	5,000,000	2000
Cook County Forest Preserve District (Chicago portion only)[b]	17,996,000	1999
Dallas Parks and Recreation Department	49,470,000	1998
Denver Parks and Recreation Department	51,358,000	1998
Detroit Recreation Department	63,082,000	1998–1999
Gateway National Recreation Area (New York portion only)[b]	16,878,000	1999
Golden Gate National Recreation Area (San Francisco portion only)[b]	N.A.	N.A.
Houston Parks and Recreation Department	73,183,000	1998
Indianapolis Parks and Recreation Department	24,147,000	1999
Kansas City, Missouri, Department of Parks, Recreation, and Boulevards	40,734,000	1998–1999
Los Angeles Department of Recreation and Parks	126,029,000	1998–1999
Metropolitan District Commission (Boston portion only)[b]	13,267,000	1998
Miami Parks and Recreation Department	12,988,000	1998–1999
Minneapolis Park and Recreation Board	54,919,000	1997–1998
New York City Department of Parks and Recreation[b]	305,812,000	1999–2000
Philadelphia Department of Recreation[b]	50,255,000	1998
(Philadelphia) Fairmount Park Commission[b]	18,752,000	1997–1998
Phoenix Parks, Recreation, and Library Department	80,304,000	1998–1999
Pittsburgh Department of Public Works[b]	9,165,000	1998
Pittsburgh Department of Parks and Recreation[b]	9,864,000	1998
Portland Parks and Recreation Department	65,260,000	1997–1998
San Diego Park and Recreation Department	96,639,000	1998
San Francisco Recreation and Park Department[b]	70,180,000	1998–1999
Seattle Department of Parks and Recreation	85,838,000	1998
St. Louis Department of Parks, Recreation, and Forestry	25,792,000	1998–1999
Tampa Parks Department[b]	15,440,000	1999
Tampa Recreation Department[b]	8,835,000	1997–1998
Tampa Sports Authority[b]	3,900,000	2000

[a]Includes both operating and capital expenditures but excludes stadiums, zoos, museums, and aquariums.
[b]Cities with more than one agency on the list.

Table 10. Park-Related Expenditure per Resident
(By City)

City	Population	Total of Adjusted Budgets of Park Agencies within City[a]	Expenditure per Resident
High-Density Population			
Chicago	2,722,000	$311,628,000	$114
Boston	558,000	53,617,000	96
San Francisco	735,000	70,180,000	95
Baltimore	675,000	31,970,000	47
Philadelphia	1,478,000	69,007,000	47
New York	7,381,000	322,690,000	44
Miami	365,000	12,988,000	36
Los Angeles	3,554,000	126,029,000	35
Average, High-Density Cities			$64
Medium-Density Population			
Seattle	525,000	$85,838,000	$164
Minneapolis	359,000	54,919,000	153
Portland, Oregon	481,000	65,260,000	136
Cincinnati	346,000	45,089,000	130
St. Louis	352,000	25,792,000	73
Cleveland	498,000	35,918,000	72
Detroit	1,000,000	63,082,000	63
Pittsburgh	350,000	19,029,000	54
Average, Medium-Density Cities			$106
Low-Density Population			
Denver	497,000	$51,358,000	$103
Tampa	286,000	29,773,000	99
Kansas City, Missouri	441,000	40,734,000	92
San Diego	1,171,000	96,639,000	83
Phoenix	1,159,000	80,304,000	69
Atlanta	402,000	25,250,000	63
Dallas	1,053,000	49,470,000	47
Houston	1,744,000	73,183,000	42
Indianapolis	747,000	24,147,000	32
Average, Low-Density Cities			$70
Average, All Cities			$80

[a]Agency operating budgets plus capital budgets, excluding zoos, stadiums, museums, and aquariums.

Table 11. Park-Related Expenditure per Resident
(By Agency)

Park Agency	Budget Year	Adjusted Budget	Dollars per Resident
Seattle Department of Parks and Recreation	1998	$85,838,000	$164
Minneapolis Park and Recreation Board	1997–1998	54,919,000	153
Portland Parks and Recreation Department	1997–1998	65,260,000	136
Chicago Park District[a]	1998–1999	293,632,000	108
Denver Parks and Recreation Department	1998	51,358,000	103
San Francisco Recreation and Park Department	1998–1999	70,180,000	95
Kansas City, Missouri, Department of Parks, Recreation, and Boulevards	1998–1999	40,734,000	92
Cincinnati Recreation Commission[a]	1998	30,889,000	89
San Diego Park and Recreation Department	1998	96,639,000	83
St. Louis Department of Parks, Recreation, and Forestry[b]	1998–1999	25,792,000	73
Phoenix Parks, Recreation, and Library Department	1998–1999	80,304,000	69
Atlanta Department of Parks, Recreation, and Cultural Affairs	1998	25,250,000	63
Detroit Recreation Department	1998–1999	63,082,000	63
Cleveland Department of Parks, Recreation, and Property[a]	1998	30,918,000	62
Tampa Parks Department[a]	1999	15,440,000	54
Boston Department of Parks and Recreation[a]	1998–1999	26,638,000	48
Dallas Parks and Recreation Department	1998	49,470,000	47
Houston Parks and Recreation Department	1998	73,183,000	42
Cincinnati Park Board[a]	1998–1999	14,200,000	41
New York City Department of Parks and Recreation[a]	1999–2000	305,812,000	41
Baltimore City Department of Recreation and Parks[a]	1999	25,470,000	38
Miami Parks and Recreation Department	1998–1999	12,988,000	36
Los Angeles Department of Recreation and Parks	1998–1999	126,029,000	35
Philadelphia Department of Recreation[a]	1998	50,255,000	34
Indianapolis Parks and Recreation Department	1999	24,147,000	32
Tampa Recreation Department[a]	1997–1998	8,835,000	31
Pittsburgh Department of Parks and Recreation[a]	1998	9,864,000	28
Pittsburgh Department of Public Works[a]	1998	9,165,000	26
Boston Department of Community Centers[a]	1998–1999	13,712,000	25
Metropolitan District Commission (Boston portion only)[a]	1998	13,267,000	24
Tampa Sports Authority[a]	2000	3,900,000	14
Fairmount Park Commission (Philadelphia)[a]	1997–1998	18,752,000	13
Cleveland Lakefront State Park[a]	2000	5,000,000	10
Baltimore City Department of Public Works[a]	1997–1998	6,500,000	10
Cook County Forest Preserve District (Chicago portion only)[a]	1999	17,996,000	7
Gateway National Recreation Area (New York portion only)[a]	1999	16,878,000	2
Golden Gate National Recreation Area (San Francisco portion only)		N.A.	N.A.
Cleveland Metroparks (Cleveland portion only)		N.A.	N.A.

[a]Cities that have more than one park agency on the list.
[b]Includes $2,040,000 for Tower Grove Park, operated by the Tower Grove Park Commission.

Table 12. Park-Related Expenditure per Acre
(By Agency)

Agency	Acreage	Adjusted Budget[a]	Budget Year	Expenditure per Acre
Chicago Park District	7,329	$293,632,000	1998–1999	$40,064
Cleveland Department of Parks, Recreation, and Property	1,394	30,918,000	1998	22,179
San Francisco Recreation and Park Department	3,317	70,180,000	1998–1999	21,158
Boston Department of Parks and Recreation[b]	2,693	40,350,000	1998–1999	14,983
Seattle Department of Parks and Recreation	6,189	85,838,000	1998	13,869
Tampa Parks Department[c]	2,183	28,175,000	1999	12,907
Cincinnati Recreation Commission	2,560	30,889,000	1998	12,066
New York City Department of Parks and Recreation	28,126	305,812,000	1999–2000	10,873
Detroit Recreation Department	5,890	63,082,000	1998–1999	10,710
Cleveland Lakefront State Park	476	5,000,000	2000	10,504
Miami Parks and Recreation Department	1,291	12,988,000	1998–1999	10,060
Minneapolis Park and Recreation Board	5,694	54,919,000	1997–1998	9,645
Denver Parks and Recreation Department	5,643	51,358,000	1998	9,101
Los Angeles Department of Recreation and Parks	14,987	126,029,000	1998–1999	8,409
Atlanta Department of Parks, Recreation, and Cultural Affairs	3,122	25,250,000	1998	8,088
St. Louis Department of Parks, Recreation, and Forestry[d]	3,290	25,792,000	1998–1999	7,840
Pittsburgh Department of Parks and Recreation[e]	2,691	19,029,000	1998	7,071
Metropolitan District Commission (Boston portion only)	1,931	13,267,000	1998	6,871
Portland Parks and Recreation Department	9,659	65,260,000	1997–1998	6,756
Fairmount Park Commission (Philadelphia)[f]	10,364	69,007,000	1997–1998	6,658
Baltimore City Department of Recreation and Parks[g]	5,048	31,970,000	1999	6,333
Cook County Forest Preserve District (Chicago portion only)	3,687	17,996,000	1999	4,881
Kansas City, Missouri, Department of Parks, Recreation, and Boulevards	11,047	40,734,000	1998–1999	3,687
Houston Parks and Recreation Department	20,363	73,183,000	1998	3,594
Cincinnati Park Board	4,686	14,200,000	1998–1999	3,030
San Diego Park and Recreation Department	32,650	96,639,000	1998	2,960
Phoenix Parks, Recreation, and Library Department	34,901	80,304,000	1998–1999	2,301
Dallas Parks and Recreation Department	21,828	49,470,000	1998	2,266
Indianapolis Parks and Recreation Department	11,547	24,147,000	1999	2,091
Average, All Agencies				**$9,688**

[a]Includes both operating and capital expenses but excludes zoos, stadiums, museums, and aquariums.
[b]Includes budget of Boston Department of Community Centers.
[c]Includes budget of Tampa Recreation Department and Tampa Sports Authority.
[d]Includes acreage and budget of Tower Grove Park Commission.
[e]Includes park budget of Pittsburgh Department of Public Works.
[f]Includes acreage and budget of Philadelphia Department of Recreation.
[g]Includes park budget of Baltimore Department of Public Works.

Table 13. Comparison of Groundskeeping Expenses with Programming Expenses[a] (By Agency)

Agency	Budget Year	Grounds-keeping Expenses	Programming Expenses	Ratio of Groundskeeping to Programming Expenses
Atlanta Department of Parks, Recreation, and Cultural Affairs	1998	$10,232,000	$11,018,000	0.9
Baltimore City Department of Public Works	1997–1998	6,000,000	0	—
Baltimore City Department of Recreation and Parks	1999	4,708,000	16,176,000	0.3
Boston Department of Community Centers	1998–1999	540,000	11,210,000	0.0
Boston Department of Parks and Recreation	1998–1999	13,516,000	2,322,000	5.8
Chicago Park District	1998–1999	112,436,000	121,806,000	0.9
Cincinnati Park Board	1998–1999	6,700,000	2,200,000	3.0
Cincinnati Recreation Commission	1998	1,804,000	21,154,000	0.1
Cleveland Department of Parks, Recreation, and Property	1998	15,315,000	12,603,000	1.2
Cook County Forest Preserve District (Chicago)	1999	8,201,000	5,157,000	1.6
Dallas Parks and Recreation Department	1998	20,184,000	14,306,000	1.4
Denver Parks and Recreation Department	1998	25,328,000	13,405,000	1.9
Detroit Recreation Department	1998–1999	26,328,000	21,654,000	1.2
Houston Parks and Recreation Department	1998	29,758,000	24,526,000	1.2
Indianapolis Parks and Recreation Department	1999	10,031,000	10,716,000	0.9
Kansas City, Missouri, Department of Parks, Recreation, and Boulevards	1998–1999	16,551,000	9,315,000	1.8
Los Angeles Department of Recreation and Parks	1998–1999	58,721,000	36,683,000	1.6
Metropolitan District Commission (Boston)	1998	8,543,000	N.A.	N.A.
Miami Parks and Recreation Department	1998–1999	5,563,000	5,690,000	1.0
Minneapolis Park and Recreation Board	1997–1998	24,091,000	20,034,000	1.2
New York City Department of Parks and Recreation	1999–2000	140,685,000	26,070,000	5.4
Philadelphia Department of Recreation	1998	8,744,000	27,223,000	0.3
(Philadelphia) Fairmount Park Commission	1997–1998	9,665,000	906,000	10.7
Phoenix Parks, Recreation, and Library Department	1998–1999	34,480,000	32,912,000	1.0
Pittsburgh Department of Public Works	1998	6,335,000	0	—
Pittsburgh Department of Parks and Recreation	1998	0	9,864,000	—
Portland Parks and Recreation Department	1997–1998	25,613,000	13,877,000	1.8
San Diego Park and Recreation Department	1998	N.A.	N.A.	N.A.
San Francisco Recreation and Park Department	1998–1999	40,264,000	20,473,000	2.0
Seattle Department of Parks and Recreation	1998	37,196,000	19,478,000	1.9
St. Louis Department of Parks, Recreation, and Forestry	1998–1999	7,245,000	3,273,000	2.2
Tampa Parks Department	1999	12,973,000	0	—
Tampa Recreation Department	1997–1998	164,000	8,311,000	0.0
Average, All Agencies				1.9

[a]Agency administrative costs are prorated into groundskeeping and programming.

Table 14. Comparison of Operations Budget with Capital Budget (By Agency)

Agency	Budget Year	Operations Budget	Capital Budget	Ratio of Operations Budget to Capital Budget
Atlanta Department of Parks, Recreation, and Cultural Affairs	1998	$21,250,000	$4,000,000	5.3
Baltimore City Department of Public Works[a]	1997–1998	6,000,000	500,000	12.0
Baltimore City Department of Recreation and Parks	1999	20,884,000	4,586,000	4.6
Boston Department of Community Centers	1998–1999	11,750,000	1,962,000	6.0
Boston Department of Parks and Recreation	1998–1999	15,838,000	10,800,000	1.5
Chicago Park District	1998–1999	234,242,000	59,390,000	3.9
Cincinnati Park Board	1998–1999	8,900,000	5,300,000	1.7
Cincinnati Recreation Commission	1998	22,958,000	7,931,000	2.9
Cleveland Department of Parks, Recreation, and Property	1998	27,918,000	3,000,000	9.3
Cook County Forest Preserve District (Chicago portion only)	1999	13,358,000	4,638,000	2.9
Dallas Parks and Recreation Department	1998	34,490,000	14,980,000	2.3
Denver Parks and Recreation Department	1998	38,733,000	12,625,000	3.1
Detroit Recreation Department	1998–1999	47,982,000	15,100,000	3.2
Fairmount Park Commission (Philadelphia)	1997–1998	10,571,000	8,181,000	1.3
Houston Parks and Recreation Department	1998	54,284,000	18,899,000	2.9
Indianapolis Parks and Recreation Department	1999	20,747,000	3,400,000	6.1
Kansas City, Missouri, Department of Parks, Recreation, and Boulevards	1998–1999	25,866,000	14,868,000	1.7
Los Angeles Department of Recreation and Parks	1998–1999	95,404,000	30,625,000	3.1
Miami Parks and Recreation Department	1998–1999	11,253,000	1,735,000	6.5
Minneapolis Park and Recreation Board	1997–1998	44,125,000	10,794,000	4.1
New York City Department of Parks and Recreation	1999–2000	166,755,000	139,057,000	1.2
Philadelphia Department of Recreation	1998	35,967,000	14,288,000	2.5
Phoenix Parks, Recreation, and Library Department	1998–1999	67,392,000	12,912,000	5.2
Pittsburgh Department of Public Works[a]	1998	6,335,000	2,830,000	2.2
Pittsburgh Department of Parks and Recreation	1998	9,864,000	0	—
Portland Parks and Recreation Department	1997–1998	39,490,000	25,770,000	1.5
San Diego Park and Recreation Department	1998	80,463,000	16,176,000	5.0
San Francisco Recreation and Park Department	1998–1999	60,737,000	9,443,000	6.4
Seattle Department of Parks and Recreation	1998	56,674,000	29,164,000	1.9
St. Louis Department of Parks, Recreation, and Forestry	1998–1999	10,518,000	15,274,000	0.7
Tampa Parks Department	1999	12,973,000	2,467,000	5.3
Tampa Recreation Department	1997–1998	8,475,000	360,000	23.5
Average, All Agencies				4.5

[a]Includes only agency's park budget.

Table 15. Number of Employees
(By Agency)

Agency	Permanent Employees	Seasonal Employees
Atlanta Department of Parks, Recreation, and Cultural Affairs	215	59
Baltimore City Department of Public Works[a]	120	80
Baltimore City Department of Recreation and Parks[a]	291	531
Boston Department of Community Centers[a]	472	1,000
Boston Department of Parks and Recreation[a]	245	40
Chicago Park District	2,162	568
Cincinnati Park Board[a]	125	92
Cincinnati Recreation Commission[a]	255	900
Cleveland Department of Parks, Recreation, and Property	330	110
Dallas Parks and Recreation Department	900	400
Denver Parks and Recreation Department	859	1,430
Detroit Recreation Department	620	700
Houston Parks and Recreation Department	1,200	365
Indianapolis Parks and Recreation Department	206	400
Kansas City, Missouri, Department of Parks, Recreation, and Boulevards	720	200
Los Angeles Department of Recreation and Parks	1,807	N.A.
Miami Parks and Recreation Department	200	120
Minneapolis Park and Recreation Board	500	1,000
New York City Department of Parks and Recreation	2,160	3,000
(New York) Gateway National Recreation Area	200	450
Philadelphia Department of Recreation[a]	550	1,700
(Philadelphia) Fairmount Park Commission[a]	215	100
Phoenix Parks, Recreation, and Library Department	1,096	625
Pittsburgh Department of Public Works[a]	202	21
Pittsburgh Department of Parks and Recreation[a]	150	459
Portland Parks and Recreation Department	371	1,308
San Diego Park and Recreation Department	830	470
San Francisco Recreation and Park Department	680	355
Seattle Department of Parks and Recreation	910	600
St. Louis Department of Parks, Recreation, and Forestry	192	100
Tampa Parks Department[a]	305	0
Tampa Recreation Department[a]	182	350

[a]Cities that have more than one park agency on the list.

Table 16. Recreation Centers per 20,000 Residents (By City)

City	Population	Number of Recreation Centers	Number of Recreation Centers per 20,000 Residents
Minneapolis	359,000	50	2.8
Philadelphia	1,478,000	158	2.1
Atlanta	402,000	39	1.9
Chicago	2,722,000	260	1.9
Tampa	286,000	27	1.9
Cincinnati	346,000	30	1.7
Boston	558,000	43	1.5
Baltimore	675,000	47	1.4
Miami	365,000	25	1.4
Denver	497,000	29	1.2
Pittsburgh	350,000	19	1.1
Seattle	525,000	24	0.9
Dallas	1,053,000	44	0.8
San Diego	1,171,000	48	0.8
Cleveland	498,000	18	0.7
Los Angeles	3,554,000	127	0.7
Houston	1,744,000	55	0.6
Portland, Oregon	481,000	15	0.6
Detroit	1,000,000	31	0.6
St. Louis	352,000	10	0.6
Kansas City, Missouri	441,000	12	0.5
Phoenix	1,159,000	29	0.5
Indianapolis	747,000	18	0.5
San Francisco	735,000	17	0.5
New York	7,381,000	35	0.1
Average, All Cities			1.1

Table 17. Public Swimming Pools per 100,000 Residents (By City)

City	Population	Number of Pools	Number of Pools per 100,000 Residents
High-Density Population			
Philadelphia	1,478,000	85	5.8
Boston	558,000	32	5.7
Baltimore	675,000	24	3.6
Chicago	2,722,000	89	3.3
Miami	365,000	10	2.7
Los Angeles	3,554,000	58	1.6
San Francisco	735,000	9	1.2
New York	7,381,000	54	0.7
Average, High-Density Cities			3.1
Medium-Density Population			
Cincinnati	346,000	47	13.6
Pittsburgh	350,000	32	9.1
Cleveland	498,000	41	8.2
Portland, Oregon	481,000	16	3.3
St. Louis	352,000	8	2.3
Seattle	525,000	10	1.9
Detroit	1,000,000	14	1.4
Minneapolis	359,000	4	1.1
Average, Medium-Density Cities			5.1
Low-Density Population			
Dallas	1,053,000	63	6.0
Atlanta	402,000	23	5.7
Denver	497,000	26	5.2
Tampa	286,000	13	4.5
Kansas City, Missouri	441,000	19	4.3
Indianapolis	747,000	19	2.5
Houston	1,744,000	44	2.5
Phoenix	1,159,000	28	2.4
San Diego	1,171,000	11	0.9
Average, Low-Density Cities			3.8
Average, All Cities			4.0

Table 18. Tennis Courts per 10,000 Residents
(By City)

City	Population	Number of Tennis Courts	Number of Tennis Courts per 10,000 Residents
High-Density Population			
Chicago	2,722,000	703	2.6
San Francisco	735,000	153	2.1
Boston	558,000	100	1.8
Baltimore	675,000	110	1.6
Miami	365,000	51	1.4
Philadelphia	1,478,000	200	1.4
Los Angeles	3,554,000	299	0.8
New York	7,381,000	584	0.8
Average, High-Density Cities			1.6
Medium-Density Population			
Minneapolis	359,000	167	4.7
Pittsburgh	350,000	138	3.9
Cincinnati	346,000	125	3.6
Seattle	525,000	165	3.1
St. Louis	352,000	99	2.8
Cleveland	498,000	133	2.7
Portland, Oregon	481,000	122	2.5
Detroit	1,000,000	120	1.2
Average, Medium-Density Cities			3.1
Low-Density Population			
Atlanta	402,000	145	3.6
Denver	497,000	143	2.9
Tampa	286,000	92	2.7
Dallas	1,053,000	258	2.5
Kansas City, Missouri	441,000	107	2.4
Indianapolis	747,000	112	1.5
Houston	1,744,000	210	1.2
Phoenix	1,159,000	120	1.0
San Diego	1,171,000	108	0.9
Average, Low-Density Cities			2.1
Average, All Cities			2.2

Part III
Low-Density Cities

San Diego

WHEN IT CAME TO GIVING natural treasures to cities, somebody up there was partial to San Diego. The city is blessed with dramatic canyons, a series of coves and saltwater marshes, a grand harbor, 20 miles of sparkling coastline, and grasslands climbing up to snowcapped mountains in the distance—not to mention Pacific breezes and a balmy climate. Adding in human efforts—notably Balboa Park and an impressive program of open-space preservation—yields one of the more remarkable urban park systems in the nation. With 36,000 acres and still growing, San Diego's system is neck-and-neck with Phoenix's for second place (after New York) in total amount of "green" space, although much of San Diego's parkland is more accurately described as brown (parched canyons and grasslands) or blue (vast tracts of water, including the nation's largest urban underwater park).

Technically the oldest community in California—Europeans arrived in 1769—San Diego initially grew slowly and is, in fact, the fourth youngest of the cities discussed in this book, having reached a population of 100,000 only in 1924 (see figure 9 on page 172). (Despite possessing an unsurpassed natural harbor, San Diego was outmaneuvered in the late 1800s by Los Angeles, which landed federal subsidies, created the mighty Port of Los Angeles, and rose to its dominant position.) Being a late bloomer saved San Diego, however, because, unlike Los Angeles, most of San Diego's period of steep growth took place after the dawn of

James Blank, San Diego Convention and Visitors Bureau

With a multitude of natural attractions, San Diego barely needs parks. But it has them anyway—36,000 acres' worth, more than every other city except New York and Phoenix.

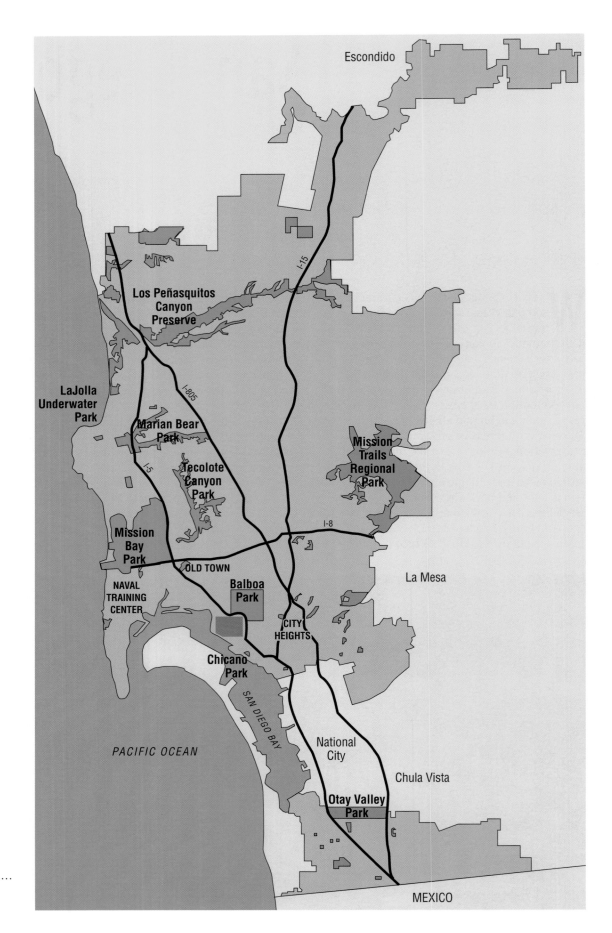

San Diego's network of parks and open space.

the environmental age, when people became aware of the need to conserve land and shape communities around natural formations. (Today, with one-third of the population and two-thirds of the land area of Los Angeles, San Diego has 20 percent more parkland and a bold vision to create much more.) Dominated by the presence of military bases and ships, San Diego is a rock-ribbed Republican town, whose conservatism is tempered by a Californian environmentalism.

San Diegans' love of green spaces started long before Earth Day, even before the establishment of Yosemite and Yellowstone National Parks. In 1868, a remarkable promoter and land developer from the East named Alonzo Horton persuaded the city leaders to set aside in perpetuity 1,400 acres of ravined land with a commanding view of the Pacific Ocean. Horton, who correctly saw that the city's future lay with its great harbor and not with its location along the intermittent San Diego River, made (and ultimately lost) a fortune in real estate, hotel development, and other ventures. But his lasting legacy is Balboa Park, the city's cultural center, the site of two world expositions, and the most visited tourist destination in San Diego. Though its size has been gradually whittled down, Balboa Park has played a pivotal role in the life of the city and is today its most beloved patch of green; and it really is green, thanks to a massive program of irrigation.

Horton created Balboa Park for financial gain as a means of increasing the value of his surrounding house lots. Soon after, the young city was the beneficiary of two other conservation leaders who helped set San Diego on a path notably different from many other Sunbelt destinations. The first was Kate Sessions, a young, entrepreneurial nurserywoman, who arranged with the city to use a portion of Balboa Park (then called City Park) rent-free, in return for which she agreed to donate and plant trees in the park and on city streets. Thus began the horticultural program that today places Balboa Park among the world's exotic natural showcases, with 350 species of trees (including 58 types of palms), 2,100 tropical plants, and 1,300 desert succulents. Sessions is revered as "the mother of Balboa Park." The other trailblazer was George Marston, "the father of Balboa Park," who, beginning in 1902, served on the Park Commission, hired the services of the superintendent of parks for New York City, and fought against park intrusions.

San Diego's love affair with Balboa has been both a blessing and a curse. Parts of Balboa are memorably lovely and reminiscent of New York's Central Park (it was partially designed by a protégé of Calvert Vaux and later by Frederick Law Olmsted's stepson). The park is well maintained and heavily used. But after serving as the site for two different world expositions, it also became the collecting ground for virtually every cultural and philanthropical idea ever hatched in the city. Today, Balboa Park contains 15 museums, an organ pavilion, a club, a swimming pool, a bicycle racing track, an archery range, two golf courses, 25 tennis courts, several ballfields, and a world famous zoo. It also contains a highway, nurseries, city operations yards, a 65-acre former dump, office buildings, public schools, gift shops, restaurants, two Scout camps, a huge U.S. Navy hospital, and a total of 7,000 parking spaces. Park historian Richard Amero calculated that only about 263 acres (out of 1,048) remain open parkland, free to the public. (The 40-year master plan for Balboa Park calls for construction of parking structures so that extensive surface lots can be de-paved, but most of the buildings and structures in the park are protected from demolition by historic designation.)

Most cities would be proud to have just one park as great as Balboa, but San Diego has three other large public land reserves, each strikingly different. Just north of downtown, in a former wetland that was dredged by the U.S. Army Corps of Engineers in the 1940s, lies Mission Bay Park, a 4,600-acre aquatic paradise for swimming, boating, windsurfing, waterskiing, and—along the shoreline—bicycling, shooting hoops, or enjoying a playground. To the east, inland,

City Profile for San Diego, California

City Population (1996)	1,171,000
City Area in Acres (1990)	207,360
City Population Density Level	5.6
County in Which City Is Located	San Diego County
County's Population (1996)	2,655,000
Metropolitan Area Population (1996)	2,655,000
City Relative Cost of Living (base = 100)	125.6
Number of Publicly Owned Vacant Lots	N.A.
Does the City Have a Developer Impact Fee for Parks?	Yes
Municipal Park Acres in City	32,650
National Park Acres in City	144
State Park Acres in City	1,814
County Park Acres in City	1,500
Total Park Acres in City	36,108

Lawn bowling is just one of the reasons that a walk through Balboa Park is endlessly surprising and memorable. Though the park has too many buildings and cars, it is nevertheless San Diegans' most beloved green space.

Brett Shoaf

lies the even larger Mission Trails Regional Park, eight square miles of unspoiled semiarid mountains and canyons crisscrossed by trails. And to the north, off the coast, lies La Jolla Underwater Park, 6,500 acres of a pristine marine environment for snorkeling, scuba diving, and exploring in glass-bottomed boats.

The San Diego Park and Recreation Department, the agency that oversees these varied riches, is adding parkland faster than any other agency in the country. Under Director Marcia McLatchy and her predecessors, San Diego almost tripled the size of its system between 1970 and 1999 (see figure 7). While laying impressive groundwork for the future, the growth has put financial strains on the agency and has left staffing extremely thin; Mission Bay Park, for instance, with 14 million visitors a year, has only two full-time rangers.

Determining whether or not the Park and Recreation Department is adequately funded is difficult. Because of its huge land base, the department spends only $2,960 per acre, less than the agencies in all but three cities described in this book (Phoenix, Dallas, and Indianapolis). The department also watches its pennies like a small nonprofit organization (even charging citizens for public documents that other agencies give away free). On the other hand, measured in dollars per resident, San Diego's $84 per resident is considerably above the average of the low-density cities.

The funding picture is more complex than it seems on the surface, however. Like every other

locality in California, San Diego was rocked in 1978 by the passage of Proposition 13, which halted any escalation of property taxes to pay for government services. As a consequence, the city was forced to design alternative financial structures. What has evolved is an elaborate layering of citywide and neighborhood assessments that operate like taxes but technically are not, and a contracting system that substitutes for what other cities accomplish using regular staff.

The most democratic levy is the Environmental Growth Fund, a citywide open-space assessment of about 30 cents per month that is tacked on to every gas and electric bill. This fund, which brings in about $8.8 million a year, has been used to buy large amounts of conservation land, including portions of Otay Valley, Mission Trails, Tecolote Canyon, and Marian Bear Parks.

Less equitable is a combination of laws and regulations that compels land developers to give money (or land) in proportion to the size of their new developments. This requirement is the principal reason for the continued growth of San Diego's park system, but it also means that almost all the new parkland is in the new, high-income north end, while there is a significant shortage of parkland in the already built-up, less-affluent areas of central and southern San Diego.

Least egalitarian, but economically elegant and efficient, is San Diego's program of Maintenance Assessment Districts, authorized by California's 1996 "Right to Vote on Taxes" Act, whereby every neighborhood can literally choose how much it wants to spend on its parks, streetscapes, and other community spaces. The community is charged extra for any project above the park department's uniform minimum level of service. For example, shrubs in street medians cost $0.02 per square foot per month for maintenance plus $0.01 per square foot per month for water; trees maintained in pits along the sidewalks cost $175 per tree per year; sweeping the center gutter of a street median costs about $0.03 per linear foot per month. Whatever the community wants is totaled up, prorated by the number of households, and then tacked on to each owner's property tax bill as an assessment. (In a further extension of market economics, the community can choose to contract either with the Park and Recreation Department or with a private landscaping company to do the work; bidding between the entities is lively, and the park department frequently wins.) No other big city in the country has taken park politics this far into the marketplace.

Theoretically, Maintenance Assessment Districts promote a microdemocracy, allowing pro-park neighborhoods to spend more than neighborhoods that have different priorities. In reality, it means that parks in high-income neighborhoods are immaculate and those in poor areas are not. In all, maintenance assessments brought in $10.3 million in 1998 (and

Figure 7. Growth of City Park Systems, 1970–1999

Agency	Acreage as of 1999	Acreage Added Since 1970	Percentage Growth
San Diego Park and Recreation Department	32,650	24,420	297%
Houston Parks and Recreation Department	20,363	14,781	265
Phoenix Parks, Recreation, and Library Department[a]	34,901	17,030	95
Seattle Department of Parks and Recreation	6,189	2,000	48
Dallas Parks and Recreation Department	21,828	6,924	46
Indianapolis Parks and Recreation Department[b]	11,547	2,994	35
Denver Parks and Recreation Department	5,643	1,391	33
Tampa Parks Department[c]	1,760	381	28
Cincinnati Park Board[c]	4,686	884	23
Portland Parks and Recreation Department[b]	9,659	1,578	20
New York City Department of Parks and Recreation[d]	28,126	4,202	18
Chicago Park District[d]	7,329	1,053	17
Baltimore City Department of Recreation and Parks[e]	5,048	707	16
Minneapolis Park and Recreation Board	5,694	307	6
Fairmount Park Commission (Philadelphia)	8,900	356	4
St. Louis Department of Parks, Recreation, and Forestry[f]	3,290	124	4
Boston Department of Parks and Recreation[g]	2,693	73	3
San Francisco Recreation and Park Department	3,317	88	3
Cincinnati Recreation Commission	2,560	N.A.	N.A.
Atlanta Department of Parks and Recreation	3,122	N.A.	N.A.
Kansas City, Missouri, Department of Parks, Recreation, and Boulevards	11,047	N.A.	N.A.
Pittsburgh Department of Parks and Recreation	2,691	N.A.	N.A.
Los Angeles Department of Recreation and Parks	14,987	N.A.	N.A.
Cleveland Department of Parks, Recreation, and Property	1,394	N.A.	N.A.
Miami Parks and Recreation Department	1,291	N.A.	N.A.
Detroit Recreation Department	5,890	N.A.	N.A.

[a]New acreage since 1964.
[b]New acreage since 1972.
[c]New acreage since 1975.
[d]New acreage since 1973.
[e]New acreage since 1978.
[f]New acreage since 1976.
[g]New acreage since 1982.

San Diego Park and Recreation Department

Address	202 C Street, MS 9B
Zip Code	92101
Telephone	(619) 236-6643
Fax	(619) 236-6219
Web Site	www.sannet.gov/park-and-recreation/general-info
Agency Acreage in City	32,650
Acreage as Percent of City	15.7%
Acres per 1,000 Residents	28.3
Number of Regional Parks	3
Number of Neighborhood Parks	80
Number of Recreation Centers	48
Number of Pools	11
Number of Golf Courses	9
Number of Tennis Courts	108
Number of Sports Fields	N.A.
Number of Marina Slips	0
Number of Beaches	21
Miles of Bikeways/Greenways	N.A.
Number of Skating Rinks	0
Number of Full-Time Employees	830
Number of Seasonal Employees	470
Number of Volunteers	N.A.

Adjusted Budget for Fiscal Year 1998

Revenue

General Funds	$45,942,000
Dedicated Taxes	26,416,000
Fees Retained by the Agency	5,692,000
Private Grants and Donations[a]	0
State and Federal Support	2,413,000
Capital Income	16,176,000
Total	$96,639,000

Expenditure

Grounds and Facilities Maintenance, and Recreational Programming and Activities[b]	$80,463,000
Capital Construction and Acquisition	16,176,000
Total	$96,639,000

Expenditure per Resident	**$84**

[a]Private grants are included with state and federal support.
[b]Agency was unable to separate figures; the combined figures are listed.

that figure is growing rapidly). The per-household, per-year average assessment is $64, but around the city it ranges between $3 and $340.

Well before Proposition 13, San Diego had decided to deeply entwine one of its big parks into the economy of the city. From the beginning, Mission Bay Park, the manmade park dredged from state tidelands and deeded to the city, has been operated as a public/private checkerboard. Four large hotels and resorts plus the Sea World Amusement Park have been built within the park and operate under long-term leases. The leases and a hotel occupancy tax directly provide the city with annual income of more than $20 million. In return, the parkland provides the hotels with a beautiful recreational attraction (and a justification for charging higher room rates). All in all, the arrangement has essentially privatized 425 acres, which could legally rise to 472 acres. (An environmentalist-led revolt in the late 1970s led to passage of a law capping the amount of commercial intrusion into Mission Bay's land area at 25 percent.) Public sentiment has shifted away from overdevelopment, but one unanticipated benefit of the arrangement is that the hotels' executives have become advocates for higher park appropriations, at least for the well-off tourists around Mission Bay.

Not that the San Diego Park and Recreation Department is not providing service to poorer communities. The agency's 48 recreation centers are distributed throughout the city, and each has an advisory council that provides support and programming assistance. In the low-income City Heights neighborhood, the department is part of an exciting multiagency project, seeded with a $5 million grant from Sol Price of Price Club/Costco, to create a revitalized urban village. At its center the village has a spanking new recreation center and pool, along with a library, outdoor performance stage, police station, gym, and vocational education center. Because land in the area is at a premium, the park department has signed an agreement with the neighboring school to use its fields after hours in return for grounds maintenance. The department hopes that the $29 million cluster of facilities will spur a rebirth of the community.

The City Heights pool is already a hit, with many users confiding that it is their first time swimming. In fact, because it turns out that many low-income San Diegans have never even been to the beach, the department has initiated a program to take them there. Using a San Diego Foundation grant acquired by the nonprofit support organization, Friends of Parks,

No park in the country is so deeply entwined in the economy of its city as Mission Bay Park. In return for leasing more than 400 acres of the watery park to four hotels and the Sea World Amusement Park, San Diego annually receives more than $20 million in revenue, not to mention staunch support for parks by the tourist industry.

in 1997 the department leased buses and gave low-income and disabled day campers such unprecedented treats as trips to Sea World, Disneyland, and Padres baseball games. (The funding lapsed in 1998 but picked back up again in 1999.) Other social and economic problems are not solved as easily, however. The city's many homeless persons are frequent users of the parks, and herding them out in the morning is one of the rangers' less-pleasant chores.

Citywide, park politics in San Diego are generally marked by civility, but one notable exception occurred in 1970, when the Hispanic community in southern San Diego rebelled against freeway construction and the lack of open space by occupying a small site until the city agreed to turn it into arts- and culture-oriented Chicano Park. Otherwise, politics are so placid that most of the organizations that support parks have opted not to challenge the city council's budgetary priorities but rather to raise funds privately to supplement the city's resources. (This situation may be changing, however, with the Friends of Parks and Recreation Foundation, an umbrella group, considering moving toward greater advocacy.)

San Diego continues to have ambitious plans for land acquisition, guided primarily by the philosophy of conservation. Under a new joint effort by the city and the county—called the Multiple Species Conservation Program— biologists have identified huge tracts of interconnected land that must be protected in order to save the 85 species of plants and animals that are endangered or threatened with extinction in San Diego County. (No other county in the United States has more imperiled creatures.) Under the plan, the city has agreed to acquire 17,000 more acres of parkland (which would bring its total to 52,000), partly through purchase and partly through regulatory agreements with developers. In 1998, voters agreed to a deal whereby developers of two large tracts in northern San Diego will preserve and donate 3,800 acres of open space in return for higher-density zoning (along with a so-called "no surprises" promise that construction may not be halted even if a new endangered species is found on the property).

Not all the excitement is in northern San Diego. Near Old Town, overlooking the San Diego River, the Pentagon plans to vacate the 500-acre San Diego Naval Training Center soon, and the city hopes to convert the site to housing plus a new 50-acre park. And, farther along the time horizon, San Diego Mayor Susan Golding has a grand vision of dredging a two-mile waterway connection—called the Bay-to-Bay Waterway—from San Diego Bay to Mission Bay and lining it with hotels, restaurants, and other attractions, following the model of the highly successful Riverwalk in San Antonio, Texas. Though not a park in the classic sense, the Bay-to-Bay Waterway could add another recreational jewel to a system that is already a treasure.

Denver

SPRAWL MAY BE GOBBLING up ranches and grassland along the entire Colorado Front Range from Fort Collins to Pueblo, but the city of Denver itself is adding publicly accessible open space. Under the leadership of Mayor Wellington Webb, Denver is using park creation as a tool to revitalize and spur growth in the most appropriate place: where the infrastructure already exists. Denver residents can happily take advantage of a plethora of recreational opportunities right in town. These include bicycling along the Highline Canal, kayaking on the South Platte River, strolling through a re-creation of Martha Washington's flower garden, paddle boating on Farrell Lake, rolling along a wheelchair nature trail through Overland Pond Educational Park, and sailing model boats in Vanderbilt Park. Meanwhile, Denver's Department of Parks and Recreation is busy upgrading an already excellent system to make it a national showcase for the 21st century.

When all is said and done—when the abandoned airport, a decommissioned military base, and a downtown rail yard are converted and added to the system—Denver's park system will surpass 7,000 acres. The system's size is not large (covering only 5.8 percent of the city's area, considerably less than the average of the low-density cities), but its impact is, because virtually every acre is developed, accessible,

Mark Upshaw, Denver Department of Parks and Recreation

For over 100 years, City Park has been Denver's largest and best-known gathering place. When the park appeared to deteriorate, Denverites rallied and formed the City Park Alliance to raise $10 million for renovations and to partially privatize some of the maintenance activities in the park.

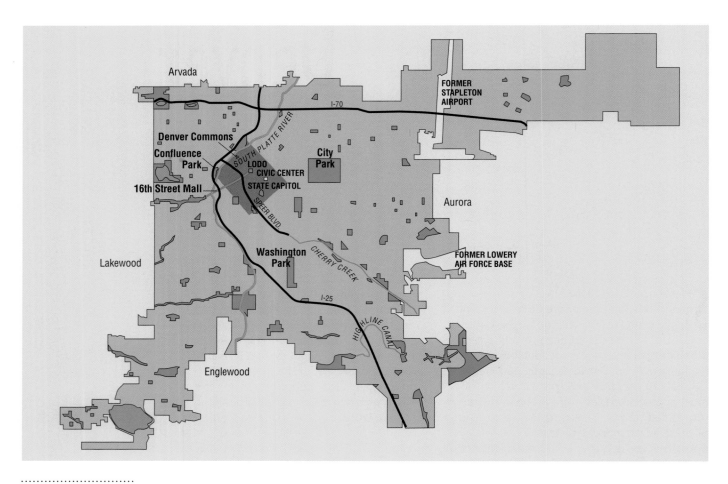

Denver's network of parks and open space.

attractive, and used. (For those yearning for wide open spaces, Denver's Parks and Recreation Department also owns a 14,000-acre reserve of mountain parks in outlying counties in the foothills of the Rockies.)

City Profile for Denver, Colorado

City Population (1996)	497,000
City Area in Acres (1990)	98,112
City Population Density Level	5.1
County in Which City Is Located	Denver
County's Population (1996)	497,000
Metropolitan Area Population (1996)	1,867,000
City Relative Cost of Living (base = 100)	107.9
Number of Publicly Owned Vacant Lots	N.A.
Does the City Have a Developer Impact Fee for Parks?	N.A.
Municipal Park Acres in City	5,643
National Park Acres in City	0
State Park Acres in City	0
County Park Acres in City	0
Total Park Acres in City	5,643

The most electrifying park development in Denver stemmed from the 1997 opening of the new Denver International Airport and the razing of Stapleton, the old airport on the city's east side. The master plan calls for housing, retail, and industry, in addition to 1,447 acres of green space. This effort (reputed to be the largest depaving project in U.S. history) is taking place on the heels of the 1994 closing of nearby Lowery Air Force Base, which is yielding another 201 acres for the Parks and Recreation Department. In both cases, the parkland will be multi-faceted, providing sports fields, golf courses, bike trails, riverine greenways, and natural areas (and even the city's first fenced, off-leash dog area, for which dog owners have lobbied for a long time). Aside from San Francisco, no big city in the country is recycling as much previously used land into parkland within its current boundaries.

What may be the city's most important new park is coming to life on a much smaller property downtown. Called the Denver Commons, the park is an ambitious effort to simultaneously reclaim Denver's historical roots, clean up a polluted rail yard, furnish green space in the heart of the city, and provide the seed for a growing downtown housing boom. The Commons is only 29 acres (three-fifths the size of Boston Common), but its location is ideal: a flat meadow between the South Platte River, Cherry Creek, refurbished Union Station, the new Coors Stadium, and the trendy LoDo (lower downtown) nightlife area. The Commons was designed in the Olmsted tradition, with open meadows, meandering walkways, native grasses, viewing platforms, and a meditation area. (The successful 13-year effort to create the Commons is in marked contrast to the defeat of a similar park proposal in Seattle, although, in fairness, assembling the Denver Commons involved only four landowners while Seattle's entailed hundreds.)

Begun in 1879 with the first land acquisition for City Park, Denver's system really began taking off in 1904 under Mayor Robert W. Speer. A Pennsylvania native who moved to Denver's dry air and sunshine because of tuberculosis, Speer had attended the great Chicago Columbian Exposition in 1893 and returned enchanted by the City Beautiful concept. A visionary and sometimes corrupt political boss, who was alternately loved and rejected by the voters, Mayor Speer brought to Denver many of the great Eastern city shapers of the day—Charles Robinson of New York, Edward Bennett of Chicago, and the parkway designer George Kessler, who made his name in Kansas City. By fits and starts, they created much of what defines Denver today: the Civic Center, many of the boulevards, and the streamside roadway now called Speer Boulevard. During his three terms, Mayor Speer dou-

bled Denver's park acreage, delighted Denverites by ordering the removal of all Keep off the Grass signs, created the City Forester's Office, and gave 110,000 shade tree seedlings to the citizenry.

As in many other cities, the next wave of park acquisition and building occurred during the Great Depression. George Cranmer, the "Robert Moses of the Rockies," never held the office of mayor but combined a penetrating vision, personal wealth, and the title of manager of improvements and parks with stealth, cunning, and a disdain for the democratic process; and he left an indelible mark on the system. Taking advantage of free land and a federally subsidized workforce, Cranmer acquired 30,000 tax-defaulted properties, built an army of 15,000

What was once a backwater of roadways, rail yards, and warehouses is being transformed into the Denver Commons and a series of other public and private attractions just steps from downtown. Among other spin-offs, the Commons is stimulating a revival in housing downtown.

Denver Parks and Recreation Department

Address	2300 Fifteenth Street
Zip Code	80202
Telephone	(303) 964-2500
Fax	(303) 964-2559
Web Site	www.denvergov.org/dephome.asp?depid=34
Agency Acreage in City[a]	5,643
Acreage as Percent of City	5.8%
Acres per 1,000 Residents	11.4
Number of Regional Parks	27
Number of Neighborhood Parks	208
Number of Recreation Centers	29
Number of Pools	26
Number of Golf Courses	8
Number of Tennis Courts	143
Number of Sports Fields	325
Number of Marina Slips	12
Number of Beaches	0
Miles of Bikeways/Greenways	145
Number of Skating Rinks	0
Number of Full-Time Employees	859
Number of Seasonal Employees	1,430
Number of Volunteers	5,700

Adjusted Budget for Fiscal Year 1998

Revenue

General Funds	$33,173,000
Dedicated Taxes	0
Fees Retained by the Agency	5,235,000
Private Grants and Donations	325,000
State and Federal Support	0
Capital Income	12,625,000
Total	$51,358,000

Expenditure

Grounds and Facilities Maintenance and Repair	$25,328,000
Recreational Programming and Activities	13,405,000
Capital Construction and Acquisition	12,625,000
Total	$51,358,000

Expenditure per Resident	**$103**

[a]Acreage includes Highline Canal Bikeway (110 acres), owned by the Denver Water Department but operated by the Parks and Recreation Department.; Bluff Lake Open Space (125 acres) within abandoned Stapleton Airport; and all park and open-space land within former Lowery Air Force Base except for Lowery Golf Course (350 acres), which is private.

New Deal laborers, and added nearly 800 acres to the system (including one, Mountain View Park, which was effectively an extension of his own frontyard). Unlike Speer, Cranmer loved views of the Rockies more than he loved trees; he prohibited the planting of trees in Mountain View and also had many boulevard trees cut down.

Cranmer's legacy continues to be felt throughout metropolitan Denver. In the 1980s, the land he had acquired along Cherry Creek and the South Platte became the seed properties for Denver's greenway system. Far outside the city limits, he bought Red Rocks Park, on the way to Loveland Pass, and turned it into arguably one of the most dramatic outdoor performance spaces in the nation. And, indulging his own passion for skiing, he went even further into the mountains to buy and develop the Winter Park Ski Area, which the city still owns.

The latest phase of Denver's park growth has been underway since the 1970s. When a catastrophic flood directed public attention to the long-ignored South Platte River, Mayor William McNichols responded by first building a flood-control reservoir upstream and then launching the South Platte River Greenway Committee to begin the arduous process of cleaning up the polluted waterway. The effort involved transforming many industrial and storage eyesores along the banks and opening it up to the public for land- and water-based recreation. Thirty years later, the land along the South Platte is one of the nation's great urban greenway successes with a continuous bike trail stringing together 15 separate parks, 10.5 miles of kayaking, seven wooden pedestrian bridges, the country's first permanent, manufactured, urban whitewater run, and a long list of sports and cultural facilities to replace the old tire dumps, junked car lots, and rubble fields.

In fact, the greenways along the South Platte River and Cherry Creek are gradually beginning to eclipse City Park and the Civic Center as the focal points of Denver's park system. For one thing, the greenways are like bracelets upon which the city can hang individual new charms —Confluence Park, the Commons, the relocated Children's Museum, and the newly announced skateboarding park. For another, the greenways are managed as quasi-public, quasi-private entities: the city owns and operates them, but private, nonprofit groups promote and support them. The Greenway Foundation—established in 1976 by former Colorado State Senator Joe Shoemaker and now run by his son Jeff—is responsible for the South Platte River Greenway.

Greenway Foundation

Cherry Creek offers a bit of Venice right in downtown Denver, thanks to the most innovative city park concept of the 1990s. Using inflatable minidams that raise the water level of the creek and specially designed shallow-draft punts from England, the city created "Punt the Creek," a recreational tourist attraction like none other in the country.

Over the years, the exuberant Shoemakers have raised $20 million from the Gates Family Foundation, the Denver Foundation, the Boettcher Foundation, Pepsi-Cola of Denver, and many others—to which the city and state added $40 million—for land acquisition, design, and construction. The Greenway Foundation also provides some supplemental maintenance besides that provided by the Parks and Recreation Department.

A strong union town, Denver has not embraced outsourcing like some other cities have, but the success of the public/private concept has led Denver Parks and Recreation to experiment. City Park is Denver's single largest park (450 acres) and also the location of an 18-hole golf course, the Museum of Natural History, the Gates Planetarium, and the Denver Zoo. With the deterioration of the surrounding neighborhood, however, park upkeep has suffered and use has declined. Following the model of New York City's Prospect Park, Denverites are launching the City Park Alliance to raise money and to partially privatize some of the maintenance needed in the park. Plans call for $10 million worth of renovations to roads, walkways, the fountain, and the statue of Martin Luther King, Jr., plus construction of a new golf clubhouse and creation of an environmental program.

All these disparate strands are coming together under Mayor Webb. Although fortunate to lead a citizenry already predisposed to envi-

ronmentalism, Webb is not riding on the voters' coattails. Under his leadership, Denver has become a trailblazer in the use of nonpolluting alternative fuels, and it was cited as one of the best cycling cities by *Bicycling* magazine. Webb is explicitly supportive of open space, naming parks and recreation as one of his three top priorities, along with education and public safety. "Our wonderful parks, parkways, and trails," he said, "are not only premier assets for our residents, but also critical factors in our long-term ability to compete economically for business development, tourism, and new residents."

When the city's contract with the Winter Park skiing concessionaire came up for renewal, the mayor bargained long and hard to improve the deal for Denver. Now, instead of an annual payment of only $7,000, the city receives nearly $2 million a year from the ski facility, and that money is earmarked for land acquisition and facility development. Webb also worked to get an unprecedented $6 million for the South Platte River Greenway from Great Outdoors Colorado, the state's environmental fund, which is derived from lottery profits. The city's 33 recreation centers serve more than 200,000 young people (and others) in a wide variety of programs annually.

Webb's enthusiasm for greenways is also raising the profile of the Highline Canal, a unique and beloved irrigation and recreation facility, whose history is intertwined with Denver's past. Built by hand in the 1880s, this meandering, tree-lined waterway descends not along a valley (as a stream would) but along a sloping, 71-mile-long ridge, allowing a series of headgates to distribute water to thousands of acres of formerly semiarid land on either side of the canal. Owned mostly by the Denver Water Board and still in operation, the Highline Canal has become the city's preeminent cycling and running path and is now maintained by the Parks and Recreation Department.

As a result of another unique program, Denverites are probably the only citizens in the country who know the names of their sister cities around the world. Every time Denver agrees to adopt a sister city, it names one of its parks in that city's honor, attempting, where possible, to choose a location that is ethnically suitable. Even the casual tourist is struck by the joint lesson in geography and sorority: Cuernavaca Park, Nairobi Park, Takayama Park, and Brest Park.

All together, Denver's efforts are starting to pay off. In the Washington Park neighborhood not far from downtown, soaring real estate values are attributed to proximity to the charming park. In addition, downtown housing is now booming after the conversion of old warehouses and lofts into apartments as well as the construction of new townhouses. While it's not all due to the Commons and Greenway projects—other factors include the LoDo revival, the new Coors Stadium, and the successful car-free 16th Street Mall—parks are playing a role in Denver's revitalization.

After a history of emulating ideas from the big cities of the East, Denver park leaders seem to be developing self-confidence and finding unique solutions from within. The Greenway Foundation is embarking on an unprecedented new recreational tourism experiment called "Punt the Creek," which involves raising the water level of minuscule Cherry Creek through a series of small inflatable dams and then offering rides on narrow, gondola-like vessels propelled by strong young people wielding poles. The venture is risky both technologically (the dams must be rapidly deflated in the event of a sudden rainstorm) and economically (the punts must be imported from England), but it is the kind of truly new idea that is putting Denver at the forefront of the nation's park movement.

The Denver Parks and Recreation Department is better funded than most, spending $103 per city resident (fifth highest of the big cities). And it's not due only to the city's strong economy. Even during the 1988 fiscal crisis, when every municipal employee was given five days of furlough and hundreds took early retirement (and dozens of high-maintenance flower beds were covered over with sod), Mayor Federico Peña made a special commitment to capital expenses for parks, saying, "This is a legacy we're leaving to future generations and we can't afford to squander it."

The pro-park culture runs so deep among the population that Denver does not seem to need much of a citizen advocacy presence. The city has an official advisory board and an unstaffed private fundraising group, The Parks People, which pulls in between $500,000 and $1 million a year to repair and refurbish parks and memorials. However, the pointed park advocacy found in San Francisco or Chicago is notably absent in Denver. "Many of us define our city by its parks and its environment," is how one Denverite put it. "Every politician and every city employee knows it. They don't need a lobby group to tell them." Perhaps this is why the Denver system shines.

Houston

LIKE TEXAS, HOUSTON IS BIG—really big. Houston's park acreage is so vast that just one of its parks—Cullen Park—could contain the entire park systems of Atlanta, Miami, Pittsburgh, and Tampa combined. At the same time, Houston *needs* lots of parkland, because the huge city exceeds the aggregate acreage of Baltimore, Boston, Cincinnati, Cleveland, Miami, Minneapolis, Pittsburgh, San Francisco, and St. Louis.

Cullen Park is the second largest city park in the country (after South Mountain Park in Phoenix). The park is also noteworthy, because it is larger than the rest of Houston's park system combined (see figure 8). Big is not necessarily synonymous with great, however, and most Houstonians have never been to Cullen Park nor, in fact, have even heard of it. Located on the far west side, an hour's drive or more for many residents (don't even ask how long it would take by bus or bicycle), Cullen consists of a minimally developed diked property, which, during periods of heavy rain, fills up with 10,000 acres of water.

Cullen is not a *bad* park. It is a new breed of park known as a multiobjective facility—a property put to more than one public use, in this case, flood control and recreation. The U.S. Army Corps of Engineers purchased the property, built the dike, and in 1945 created the Addicks Reservoir impoundment to reduce downstream, downtown flooding. In 1983, David Wolff, the creative chair of the Houston Parks Board, saw an opportunity to inexpensively reduce the embarrassingly severe deficit in Houston's parkland by leasing the property and making it available to the public. A grant from the Cullen Foundation paid for the development of sports fields, drainage systems, asphalt trails, restrooms, and picnic tables; another contribu-

tion paid for a new velodrome (bicycle racing track). Everything was designed to survive periods of standing water during the rainy season. (The park is closed when there is standing water.) The park will never have some things, such as trees, and for all its vast acreage, it does not do much for park-deficient neighborhoods in other parts of the city; but Cullen provides recreational opportunities where there would otherwise be nothing except barbed wire fences and Keep Out signs.

Fame may never come to Cullen Park, but Houston already has a nationally renowned

Featuring one of the most perfect running trails in the country, Memorial Park gets users from 4:30 a.m. to 11:00 p.m. Houston's challenge today is to acquire more parkland.

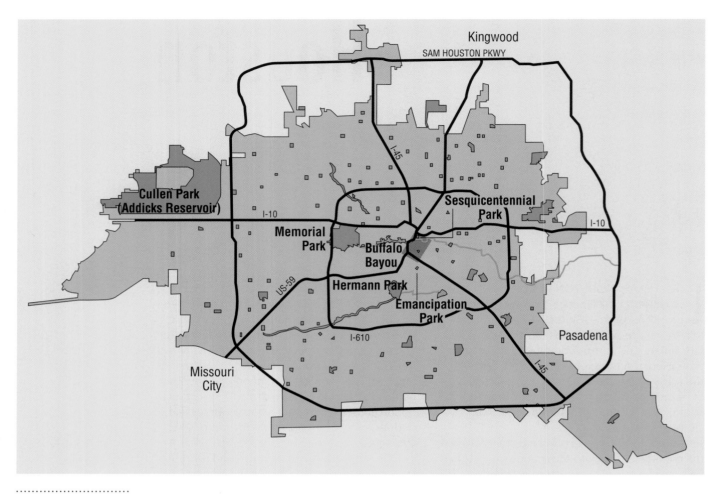

Kingwood
SAM HOUSTON PKWY

Cullen Park
(Addicks Reservoir)

I-10

Memorial
Park

Sesquicentennial
Park

I-10

Buffalo
Bayou

Hermann Park

Emancipation
Park

I-610

I-45

US-59

Pasadena

Missouri
City

Houston's network of
parks and open space.

facility in Hermann Park, a 445-acre oasis of
culture, zoology, horticulture, and recreation
about five miles from downtown. Donated in
1914 by industrialist, real estate investor, and

City Profile for Houston, Texas

City Population (1996)	1,744,000
City Area in Acres (1990)	345,536
City Population Density Level	5.0
County in Which City Is Located	Harris
County's Population (1996)	3,127,000
Metropolitan Area Population (1996)	3,792,000
City Relative Cost of Living (base = 100)	94.9
Number of Publicly Owned Vacant Lots	N.A.
Does the City Have a Developer Impact Fee for Parks?	No
Municipal Park Acres in City	20,363
National Park Acres in City	0
State Park Acres in City	0
County Park Acres in City	1,427
Total Park Acres in City	21,790

one-time city park commissioner George Hermann, and initially designed by prominent landscape architect George Kessler, Hermann Park
lies next to Rice University, the museum district,
several residential neighborhoods, and the huge
Texas Medical Complex (which was built on
land removed from the park in 1945). The park
includes the Miller Outdoor Theater, the Houston Zoo, the Garden Center, the Museum of
Natural Science, a famous equestrian statue
of Sam Houston, a reflection pool and a lake,
a nostalgic miniature railroad, and a golf course.
It hosts about six million visitors a year, a number sure to rise when the park's ambitious renovation is completed.

Like almost every older city park in the country, Hermann reached its heyday in the 1920s
and 1930s and began to lose some of its luster
shortly after World War II as a result of deferred
maintenance and unfortunate design decisions.
In Hermann Park's case, the problem was caused
by the relentless addition of buildings, extra
parking lots, new street alignments, many more
fences, channelized streams, and the like. Some
areas of the park suffered from neglect, others
from an excess of devotion and overuse. In re-

sponse, several fledgling efforts to protect the park were attempted, but it wasn't until 1990 that the various individual groups merged into Friends of Hermann Park, whose mission was to conduct a comprehensive analysis of the park's strengths and problems, make physical improvements, organize a political defense, and raise both capital and maintenance funds.

As with the Central Park Conservancy in New York, Forest Park Forever in St. Louis, and others, Friends of Hermann Park has demonstrated an impressive ability to raise money and get results. Between 1995 and 1999, Friends raised more than $13 million, an amount that the city matched almost equally. The renovations these funds will pay for include expanding the lake and building a boating facility; completing the reflection pool; planting trees and ground cover; rebuilding the outdoor theater; creating wetlands; replacing the golf clubhouse; replacing the huge, glaring, central parking area with multiple dispersed, smaller, shady lots; and increasing the number of park entrances from three to 14 to reduce congestion. The full cost for the effort will be $70 million. Amazingly, the first phase, which was expected to take a decade, was scheduled to be completed four years early.

Houston's other widely beloved green space is Memorial Park, the 1,431-acre arboreal heart of the posh River Oaks community and one of the engines that is helping to drive the city's new downtown housing boom. (In Houston, downtown refers to any place within Interstate 610, the inner loop, which, in most other cities, is big enough to be a perimeter beltway.) Once a World War I army camp, the land was assembled and sold to the city at cost by developer and philanthropist Will C. Hogg, the son of a famous governor, who is also remembered for giving away tens of thousands of crape myrtle trees to beautify the city. (When Hogg learned, to his dismay, that not one of his trees had found its way into the hands of African American Houstonians, he arranged a special giveaway in Emancipation Park, the park traditionally used by Houston's African Americans.)

Today, Memorial Park consists primarily of a large forest surrounding a golf course, a tennis center, and playing fields, plus the feature that generates most of the park's 4 million user-days each year: a three-mile running path. Reputedly the most heavily patronized trail in the nation, with an average of 10,000 users a day, this is the pathway that every trail designer in the country should study, with its nearly perfect combination of width (ranging from eight to 20 feet);

length (approximately three miles, allowing joggers of different capabilities to make one, two, or more circuits); surface material (decomposed granite); location (central and reachable by the masses); ambience (weaving under a cool, shady canopy of trees but in frequent sight of the wide open spaces of the landscaped golf course); and security (car-free but close to an automobile road just in case, plus lit at night). The trail has become so busy, and parking so tight, that the running day has stretched out from 4:30 a.m. to 11 p.m.

Friends of Hermann Park; Olin Partnership

The great basin of McGovern Lake was in George Kessler's original design for Hermann Park but was never completed. Now, under the park's $70 million renovation, the lake is being doubled in size and given three new islands, two of them for migrating birds. When finished, it will also host boating and fishing.

Friends of Hermann Park; Olin Partnership

Figure 8. Comparsion of Total Agency Acreage with Largest Park Acreage

Agency	Total Park Acreage	Largest Park	Largest Park Acreage	Largest Park as Percentage of Total Acreage
Houston Parks and Recreation Department	20,363	Cullen Park	10,534	52%
Portland Parks and Recreation Department	9,659	Forest Park	4,836	50
Fairmount Park Commission (Philadelphia)	8,900	Fairmount Park/Wissahickon Valley	4,167	· 47
Phoenix Parks, Recreation, and Library Department	34,901	South Mountain Preserve Park	16,238	47
Indianapolis Parks and Recreation Department	11,547	Eagle Creek Park	4,813	42
St. Louis Department of Parks, Recreation, and Forestry	3,290	Forest Park	1,293	39
Chicago Park District	7,329	Lakefront (7 contiguous parks)	2,879	39
Miami Parks and Recreation Department	1,291	Virginia Key	486	38
San Francisco Recreation and Park Department	3,317	Golden Gate Park	1,107	33
Cincinnati Park Board	4,686	Mount Airy Forest	1,472	31
Los Angeles Department of Recreation and Parks	14,987	Griffith Park	4,171	28
Metropolitan District Commission (Boston)	1,931	Stony Brook Reservation	482	25
Baltimore City Department of Recreation and Parks	5,048	Gwynns Falls/Leakin Park	1,100	22
Detroit Recreation Department	5,890	Rouge Park	1,200	20
Boston Department of Parks and Recreation	2,693	Franklin Park	510	19
Pittsburgh Department of Parks and Recreation	2,691	Frick Park	476	18
San Diego Park and Recreation Department	32,650	Mission Trails Park	5,760	18
Dallas Parks and Recreation Department	21,828	Trinity River Park	3,653	17
Kansas City, Missouri, Department of Parks, Recreation, and Boulevards	11,047	Swope Park	1,769	16
Minneapolis Park and Recreation Board	5,694	Wirth Park	743	13
New York City Department of Parks and Recreation	28,126	Pelham Bay Park	2,766	10
Cleveland Department of Parks, Recreation, and Property	1,394	Rockefeller Park	130	9
Seattle Department of Parks and Recreation	6,189	Discovery Park	512	8
Denver Parks and Recreation Department	5,643	City Park	450	8
Tampa Parks Department	1,760	Al Lopez Park	126	7
Atlanta Department of Parks, Recreation, and Cultural Affairs	3,122	Freedom Park	207	7
Average, All Cities				26%

The principal controversy in Memorial Park arises over the use of mountain bicycles. With fat, knobby tires and high-torque gearing, mountain bikes can traverse most types of terrain. They also attract young, hard-charging riders, who are more than a match for most trails, particularly in wet, poorly drained areas like Houston. The debate over mountain biking extends from Griffith Park in Los Angeles to Rock Creek Park in Washington, D.C., but Memorial Park is at the heart of it. Technically, off-road cycling is prohibited, but the rule is hard to enforce and widely violated. In response, the Memorial Park Advisory Board proposed a compromise: a network of sanctioned, marked forest bike

trails combined with stronger enforcement against violations elsewhere.

Even with Hermann, Cullen, and Memorial Parks, Houston is woefully short of parkland, particularly in low-income African American and Hispanic neighborhoods. The first effort to remedy the problem was the creation of a Green Ribbon Commission, which, under Mayor Kathy Whitmire in 1983, recommended a seven-year, $1 billion program of park improvements and land purchases. The timing was unfortunate—the proposal came just as Houston entered a prolonged period of severe economic recession—but the report did result in the "Parks to Standard" program, under which the city spent $151 million between 1984 and 1997 to refurbish parks and playgrounds and eliminate safety hazards, lead paint, and access impediments. (However, the most far-reaching recommendation of the commission—to merge the park systems of Houston and Harris County —was not implemented.)

Following a decade during which almost no new land was acquired and many facilities deteriorated, the city got back on its feet economically and moved into a second park phase. In 1998, under the leadership of Mayor Lee Brown and a newly hired veteran park director, Oliver Spellman, Jr., the Department of Parks and Recreation undertook an exhaustive study that resulted in a master plan calling for, among other things, the acquisition of 68 new parks (totaling at least 2,000 acres), the expansion of 16 existing parks, and the construction of 11 new recreation centers. Spellman's commitment to rational park planning has been hailed as a breath of fresh air for an agency that had been stagnating. The new director is also investigating the transfer of unused public properties to the department and, more fundamentally, broaching the concept of developers' setasides —a tool to create open space that New York City (Spellman's former hometown) has used for a long time but a radical concept in Houston, which does not even have zoning regulations.

Spellman hopes that another major park bond issue will be on the ballot in 2000, but meanwhile, Houston's Parks and Recreation Department also has the help of two private institutions—the Park People, a 1,200-member advocacy group that promotes land acquisition, tree planting, and tree preservation and also rewards ecologically oriented developers with its annual awards; and the Houston Parks Board, the organization that arranged for Cullen Park and many other properties. Under an unusual arrangement, the mayor appoints members of the Parks Board, even though the organization is technically a private, nonprofit group, thereby allowing wealthy donors to receive tax benefits and giving them the confidence that their gifts will not be diverted to other city priorities. One of the board's great successes occurred in the late 1980s, when a 570-acre, tax-defaulted property was picked up for a third of its value and paid for by the donated estate of an heiress of the Texaco fortune.

If Houston's parks are ever to evolve from individual properties into a coordinated system, the tool for their unification is likely to be the city's network of bayous. The bayous—natural and manufactured channels that carry off water

from the frequent torrential downpours in this swampy, flat city—are under the jurisdiction of the Harris County Flood Control District. For many years, they were designed only to manage flooding, and many were straightened and channelized to increase water flow. In the 1960s, however, environmentalists began extolling the ecological advantages of the bayous. The great showdown was the 20-year struggle over Buffalo Bayou, the famous waterway that begins as a trickle far to the west of Cullen Park, runs past Memorial Park and the heart of downtown, and culminates in the Houston Ship Canal, the busiest manufactured port in the world (and, for many years, the most polluted). Terry Hershey, a transplanted housewife from Fort Worth who formed the Buffalo Bayou Preservation Associa-

It took 20 years to save Buffalo Bayou from channelization and to begin molding it into Houston's premier linear park. Here Houstonians celebrate the opening of Sesquicentennial Park, a $22 million public/private partnership alongside the bayou in the heart of downtown.

Houston Parks and Recreation Department

Address	2999 South Wayside Drive
Zip Code	77023
Telephone	(713) 845-1000
Fax	(713) 942-7664
Web Site	www.ci.houston.tx.us
Agency Acreage in City	20,363
Acreage as Percent of City	5.9%
Acres per 1,000 Residents	12.0
Number of Regional Parks	7
Number of Neighborhood Parks	111
Number of Recreation Centers	55
Number of Pools	44
Number of Golf Courses	7
Number of Tennis Courts	210
Number of Sports Fields	305
Number of Marina Slips	0
Number of Beaches	0
Miles of Bikeways/Greenways	75
Number of Skating Rinks	0
Number of Full-Time Employees	1,200
Number of Seasonal Employees	365
Number of Volunteers	416

Adjusted Budget for Fiscal Year 1998

Revenue

General Funds	$45,594,000
Dedicated Taxes	0
Fees Retained by the Agency	6,485,000
Private Grants and Donations	863,800
State and Federal Support	4,811,000
Capital Income	18,899,000
Total	$76,652,800

Expenditure

Grounds and Facilities Maintenance and Repair	$29,758,000
Recreational Programming and Activities	24,526,000
Capital Construction and Acquisition	18,899,000
Total[a]	$73,183,000
Expenditure per Resident	$42

[a]Excludes the Houston Zoo.

tion, started the battle, which was not won until Houston's congressman at the time, George H. Bush, pushed a measure through Congress preventing the U.S. Army Corps of Engineers from proceeding with the project. Buffalo Bayou has been gaining ground as the premier linear park in the city ever since. (The latest charm to be added to this bracelet is Sesquicentennial Park, a $22 million public/private showpiece, 13 years in the making, in the heart of downtown.)

Houston is already a remarkably green city because of its lush vegetation and thick canopy of trees. What the city needs is publicly available open space, particularly in light of the recent boom in downtown infill development. The bayous could provide the space, but turning them into parks is not easy. For one thing, stripped of vegetation and sometimes paved, they are often unattractive and utilitarian backyard drainage facilities rather than landscaped and maintained frontyard parklands. Thus, when public trails are proposed, homeowners and community associations sometimes mount "not-in-my-backyard" opposition. In addition, for economic reasons, builders put up structures as close as possible to the channels and thereby squeeze out park use. In combating this outmoded mentality, ecologists have found an increasingly powerful partner in bicyclists. Bolstered by a 1991 change in federal transportation funding to allow money for nonmotorized travel, a small group of cyclists worked with the city to plan a 300-mile network of bicycle facilities, including 106 miles of off-street trails using bayous, abandoned railroad lines, and other available land. Funded with $31 million in federal money, the system will connect Hermann, Memorial, and other parks and serve both recreational and purposeful cyclists.

With a shortage of parkland and a system that needs millions of dollars in upgrades, Houstonians have a steep hill to climb before they can reach a great park system. The city is also hampered by the lack of any zoning laws that could be used to force developers to provide parks along with new housing. But the stars seem to be lining up, and a felicitous interplay of citizen activism, philanthropic backing, and governmental support could provide the political climate for great forward strides in the coming years.

Dallas

FOR MASSIVE AMOUNTS of sheer, raw parkland, one needs only to look at Dallas. With more than 21,000 acres, the Dallas Parks and Recreation Department has more land than all but three of the other big cities. The only problem is that much of the land can be described as a diamond in the rough, land waiting to be developed into a usable, coherent system. A large portion of the parkland lies along the vast floodplain of the Trinity River, the fickle waterway whose dangerous periodic flows have been tamed over the decades by a billion dollars' worth of channels, levies, and impoundments done by the U.S. Army Corps of Engineers. But the city may be on the verge of cutting some facets into its unpolished gemstone resource.

Of course, Dallas already has several historic and notable developed parks. Nationally, the most famous—or infamous—is three-acre Dealy Plaza, site of the assassination of President John F. Kennedy. Each year the park hosts hundreds of thousands of visitors. Among Texans, the most prominent park is 261-acre Fair Park, location of the 1936 Texas Centennial and currently home to the Cotton Bowl, several museums, the MCI Starplex, the Shakespeare Theater, the annual Texas State Fair, and a much beloved collection of art deco buildings.

Less well known statewide but most beloved locally is White Rock Lake Park and Greenbelt, which is made up of 2,956 acres of water, woods, paths, bike trails, sports fields, and an arboretum, and is the premier recreational destination on the city's north side. Created through impoundment by the city Water Department, White Rock Lake provided Dallas's water supply until siltation and decline in quality forced officials to go further for drinking water. In 1962, the lake and its shoreline were turned over to the Parks

and Recreation Department. Six years later, the department added the Greenbelt, an extension consisting of floodplain lands that had previously been used for grazing. Today, the Green-

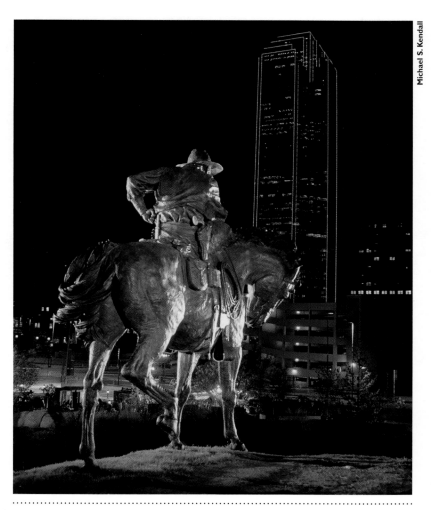

Pioneer Plaza was conceived by developer Trammell Crow as a larger-than-life memorial to Dallas's frontier heritage.

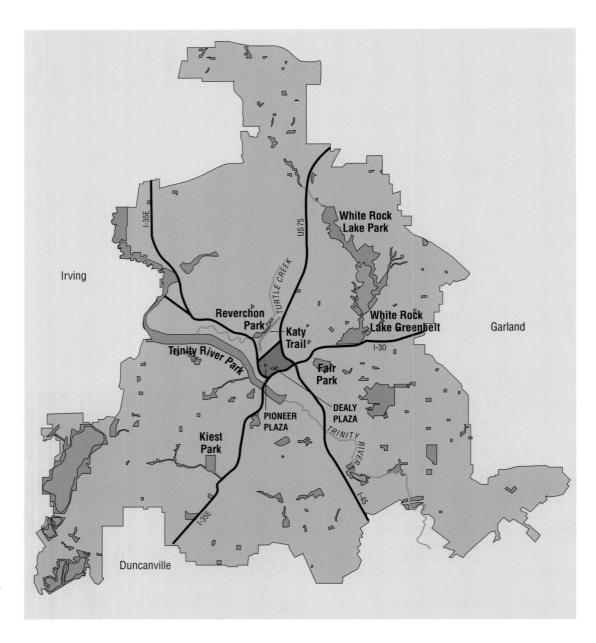

Dallas's network of parks
and open space.

belt is the most active trail in the city and is used by hordes of happy cyclists, runners, dog walkers, and others.

Possibly the loveliest green space in Dallas is 41-acre Reverchon Park. It is nestled between an old rail spur and the North Tollway but protected from noise and fumes by its steep topography. With Turtle Creek meandering down the center of the park, it is a nostalgic, romantic gem, a place for strolling couples, picnicking families, and children playing in the underbrush. Located directly on the north-south escarpment that divides flat east Texas from the hill country of west Texas, Reverchon's natural contours were embellished during the Great Depression by landscaping and stonework done by artisans of the federal Works Progress Administration.

Though Reverchon is in a state of perilous disrepair from years of neglect, it may finally be on the verge of salvation. When the city power-cleaned the stonework in late 1999, Reverchon looked so improved that residents far and wide took notice, with 450 showing up one weekend morning for a massive, enthusiastic cleanup. Recementing the stones, trimming underbrush, and solving some of the park's erosion problems are next on the city's agenda.

Even though virtually every city in the United States has experienced one or more economic downturns since 1980, Dallas's period of fiscal emergency was longer and more severe than most, and the park system was hit harder than many. Battered by the collapse of both the oil and the savings and loan industries, the Dallas recession lasted from 1985 until 1990, and the electorate responded by failing to pass a single capital bond measure between 1985 and 1995. The park department's annual appropriation dropped by $10 million and its staffing was reduced by 30 percent, with the largest cuts occurring in park maintenance. Irrigation was banned for a decade, except for critical plant resources, and this had disastrous consequences in arid north Texas. The park ranger/park police force, consisting of 70 members, was transferred to the Police Department and essentially eliminated. Ballfields received no maintenance until 1997. The lovely ornamental gardens of Kiest Park, the largest developed park in south Dallas, were abandoned. The Samuell Trust, which had been explicitly created to enhance the lands donated by a generous Dallas physician in the 1930s, was gradually relegated to pay for general maintenance. Care of parkway medians was transferred to the Streets Department. White Rock Lake's siltation intensified. The consequences of the economic downturn lingered even longer: as late as 1999, the Parks and Recreation Department did not have a users' map of the system to distribute to the public.

Paul Dyer, a native of Dallas, was hired to manage the Parks and Recreation Department through the blackest days of the period. Dyer had worked his way up through the department and reached the top post in 1992. Cautious, conscious of the numbers, and fiscally prudent, Dyer was just the man for that tough time. As the city's economy picked up, Dyer could begin to think about pursuing several more expansive visions, like extending the White Rock Lake Greenbelt to the Trinity River, constructing the Five-Mile Creek Trail, renovating Fair Park and the Dallas Zoo, and, most important, restoring hundreds of ballfields, playgrounds, and athletic facilities that had deteriorated as a result of lack of maintenance over the years.

Against this aspiration is the hard reality that Dallas spends a lot less on parks and recreation than other low-density cities—about two-thirds the average and $56 less per person, per year than Denver does. With the economy improving in the mid-1990s, however, park advocates—from the grass-roots level all the way up to the mayor's office—discovered that they could begin planning again, even if they had to find other sources of money.

The first dream to come true was hatched by Dallas mover and shaker Trammell Crow, a major national real estate developer with a soft spot for cattle. When Crow purchased a prime parcel in the heart of downtown and found himself next to an ugly parking lot owned by the Dallas Convention Center, he resolved to create a new park for the city, one that would celebrate Dallas's heritage of cattle drives. (Until the Civil War it was Dallas, not Fort Worth, from which the central Texas cattle drive began.) Crow persuaded the Convention Center to donate the $4 million property if he could match that value with private contributions for the development of the park. That's what Crow did: he brought in other contributors and hired stonemasons, horticulturists, and Texas sculptor Robert Summers.

The result is Pioneer Plaza, a commemoration of Dallas's frontier heritage, complete with a powerful sculpture of 40 oversized longhorn steers crossing a flowing stream, tended by three dramatic men: a cowboy, an African American cutter, and a Mexican vaquero bringing back a lost calf. The city's Fine Arts Commission rejected the design twice but was overruled by the city council, which clearly knew a crowd pleaser when it saw one. Pioneer Plaza became a raging success as soon as it was completed in 1999. (Later, deciding that he wanted to add 14 more steers to the sculpture, Crow solicited Dallas corporations to "buy" them for $50,000 each, though an initial concept of stamping corporate logos as cattle brands was dropped in favor of a more discreet acknowledgment on the cement underneath.) The site is operated under a loose partnership agreement, whereby the Parks and Recreation Department keeps it trimmed

City Profile for Dallas, Texas

City Population (1996)	1,053,000
City Area in Acres (1990)	218,880
City Population Density Level	4.8
County in Which City Is Located	Dallas County
County's Population (1996)	2,000,000
Metropolitan Area Population (1996)	3,048,000
City Relative Cost of Living (base = 100)	100.4
Number of Publicly Owned Vacant Lots	N.A.
Does the City Have a Developer Impact Fee for Parks?	N.A.
Municipal Park Acres in City	21,828
National Park Acres in City	0
State Park Acres in City	0
County Park Acres in City	0
Total Park Acres in City	21,828

and clean, the Dallas Trees and Parks Foundation issues permits for photo shoots involving the sculptures, and the Dallas Convention Center rents it out for special functions.

A few miles north is another new park, the Katy Trail, which, despite its small size (only 22 acres), is likely to have a civic impact far beyond its physical dimensions. Fashioned out of a track abandoned by the Missouri–Kansas–Texas Railroad and acquired as surplus property from the Dallas Area Rapid Transit Authority, the Katy Trail is the first urban rail trail in Texas. Though only three miles long, it is extremely well located, serving not only recreational users of Reverchon and Turtle Creek Parks but also purposeful cyclists between Southern Methodist University and downtown Dallas. If successful (it opened in 1999 after ten years of legal, political, and financial travails), the Katy Trail may provide the city's bicycling activists with the spark they need to develop a fully integrated on- and off-street network for two-wheel travel. The Katy Trail could also become a key segment in an ambitious multicounty trail network that

is being considered for development between the Trinity River and the Oklahoma border.

Much bigger than the Katy Trail is the Trinity River Corridor Project, which Mayor Ron Kirk brokered in 1996. At an estimated cost of over $1 billion, the project encompasses flood control, highway and bridge construction, and park development. The Trinity River project represented a difficult compromise between environmentalists and developers, but Dallas voters appreciated the end of a decades-long political logjam (and the fact that the federal government will pick up most of the tab) and, by the slimmest of margins, in 1998 authorized $246 million in bonds to get the enterprise moving.

The Trinity River Corridor Project is much more than a park, but it will allow Dallas to put some of its raw land to much more intensive recreational use. More important, it will provide a landscape-organizing principle that the city has been searching for ever since it failed to implement the ambitious park-and-parkway plan sketched out by landscape architect George Kessler in 1910. The plan envisions a network

Dallas Parks and Recreation Department

Address	1500 Marilla Street, New City Hall, Room 6-F North
Zip Code	75201
Telephone	(214) 670-4100
Fax	(214) 670-4098
Web Site	www.ci.dallas.tx.us/html/ park_and_recreation.html
Agency Acreage in City[a]	21,828
Acreage as Percent of City	10.0%
Acres per 1,000 Residents	21.3
Number of Regional Parks	26
Number of Neighborhood Parks	229
Number of Recreation Centers	44
Number of Pools	63
Number of Golf Courses	6
Number of Tennis Courts	258
Number of Sports Fields	408
Number of Marina Slips	0
Number of Beaches	0
Miles of Bikeways/Greenways	69
Number of Skating Rinks	0
Number of Full-Time Employees	900
Number of Seasonal Employees	400
Number of Volunteers	1,400

Adjusted Budget for Fiscal Year 1998

Revenue

General Funds	$31,483,000
Dedicated Taxes	0
Fees Retained by the Agency	1,156,000
Private Grants and Donations	301,000
State and Federal Support (noncapital)	1,550,000
Capital Income	14,980,000
Total	$49,470,000

Expenditure

Grounds and Facilities Maintenance and Repair	$20,184,000
Recreational Programming and Activities	14,306,000
Capital Construction and Acquisition	14,980,000
Total[b]	$49,470,000

Expenditure per Resident $47

[a]Acreage includes Joppa Preserve, owned by Dallas County but operated by Dallas City Parks and Recreation.
[b]Excludes the Dallas Zoo, the aquarium, and the Fair Park Museum.

Michael S. Kendall

Despite opposition from the city's Fine Arts Commission, Pioneer Plaza—including its 40 statues of longhorn steers—was approved by the city council and became an immediate signature space for the city.

of nonmotorized trails, both parallel and perpendicular to the river, in the downtown area. Upstream, material will be excavated from the floodplain to create a chain of lakes for both recreation and retention of periodic floodwaters. The Great Trinity Forest Park—2,000 acres of pristine bottomland hardwood forest in south Dallas—will be created downstream. The Trust for Public Land purchased the first 208 acres in 1997; $20 million is earmarked for additional acquisitions over the next ten years.

The project is gargantuan, as shown not only by its budget but also by a 23-year time line and a 1,100-member advisory committee. It is also still controversial, with environmentalists charging that the scheme's roadways pose unnecessary risks for the sake of development and that the plan does not respect the ecology of the Trinity River. Nevertheless, if the city's fractious political establishment can stick with the compromises that got the plan this far, the Trinity River Corridor Project could do for Dallas what the South Platte River Greenway has done for Denver.

Atlanta

IN 1998, ATLANTA DEDICATED Freedom Park, a swath of greenery linking the national memorials of two of the city's most famous sons—freedom fighters Jimmy Carter and Martin Luther King, Jr. The good news is that Freedom Park is now the largest park in the city. The bad news is that it consists of only 207 acres. The fact that the entire city has no public green space larger than one-third of a square mile is a commentary on how much further Atlanta needs to go if it is truly to become a world-class city.

Atlantans have a lot to be proud of—rolling terrain with a lovely canopy of tree cover, an assortment of good universities, the second busiest airport in the world, global corporate giants like Coca-Cola and CNN, a baseball powerhouse in the Braves, and, of course, their city's selection as the host for the centennial Olympic Games in 1996. Despite competition from Orlando, Charlotte, and other high-growth Sunbelt metropolises, Atlanta has maintained its status as the Queen City of the Deep South. Yet of all the low-population-density cities described in this book, Atlanta has the least amount of parkland per capita (7.8 acres per 1,000 persons). In parkland as a percentage of city area it's even worse: at 3.7 percent, Atlanta ranks lower than every other city studied in this book.

On paper, Atlanta is committed to improving its park statistics, and in 1993 a Green Ribbon

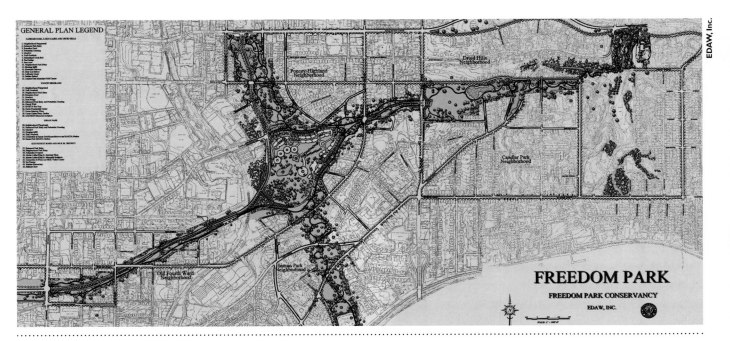

Atlanta's newest and largest park, Freedom Park, came into existence only after a 35-year struggle between community activists and Georgia's Department of Transportation. The park's unusual shape reflects its beginnings as two intersecting freeways.

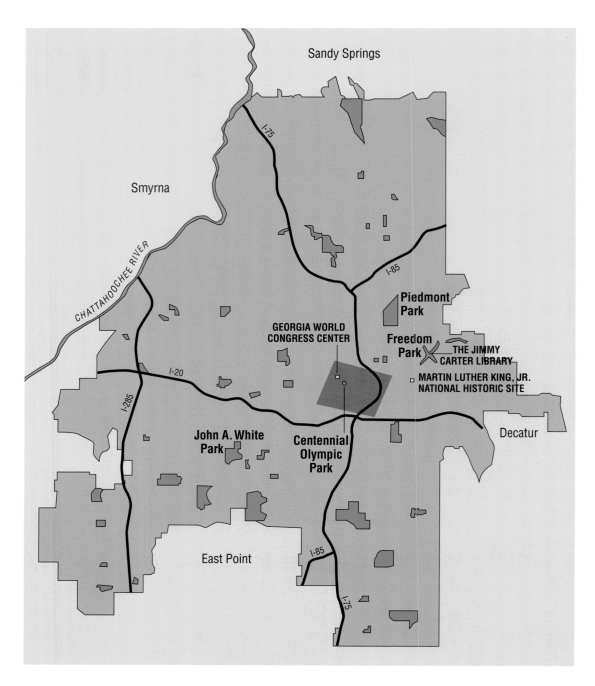

Atlanta's network of
parks and open space.

Commission set a goal of attaining 10.5 acres of parkland per 1,000 residents by the year 2000. However, because of the failure to identify a significant source of funding for capital improvements and land acquisition, that objective was not attained. (The city did follow up on the commission's report in 1994 with a $16 million park bond issue, but the money was allocated only for solving erosion and flooding problems, not for acquiring land.) Nevertheless, through a spate of recent developments—including the success of Freedom Park, the creation of a private conservancy for Piedmont Park, the emergence of a network of trails, and the aftermath

of the Olympic Games—Atlantans today have the best hope in decades for seeing some serious improvements in their park system.

Freedom Park was not planned as a park. The flattened swath through eight of Atlanta's most historic neighborhoods was originally to be paved as two intersecting freeways, one running east to Stone Mountain, the other north-south to relieve congestion on Interstate 75/85 downtown. The land was condemned, the Georgia Department of Transportation purchased it beginning in 1961, and 500 homes were torn down. The state had not expected the neighborhoods' tenacious, ten-year opposition, however. Under the banner of Citizens Against Unneeded Thoroughfares in Older Neighborhoods (CAUTION), the community finally persuaded then Governor Jimmy Carter to abandon the plan for the freeways in 1972. Ironically, the center of the property was later selected as the site of the Jimmy Carter Library and Museum, and eight years later, like the Night of the Living Dead, roadway plans were revived, this time for a "Presidential Parkway." Ten more years of battling ensued until Governor Zell Miller, fearing that the controversy would seriously mar the glory of the upcoming Olympic Games, fired the secretary of transportation and directed the two sides to reach a compromise. After 53 hours of negotiations, the result was an agreement for Freedom Park, a unique, cross-shaped park with the Carter Center, a major landscaped library and conference facility, in its center. Leased from the Department of Transportation for 99 years, Freedom Park is still far from developed, but the long-term vision includes trails, groves of trees, Olmstedian small meadows, and grand vistas. The first trail, the east-west route, which connects all the way to Stone Mountain, was completed in 1996; ground was broken for the second, the north-south trail, in fall 1999. The Department of Parks and Recreation maintains Freedom Park, but a new entity, the Freedom Park Conservancy, which also hopes to raise money for maintenance, is coordinating the park's design and management functions.

A few blocks to the northwest, at the same time that the CAUTION battle was waging, another group of neighbors was battling the city's Public Works Department over plans to build a sewage treatment plant in Piedmont Park. Piedmont, site of the Cotton States and International Exposition in 1895, had been purchased from the fabled Piedmont Driving Club and designed in 1912 by the sons of Frederick Law Olmsted. With its hilly topography, winding pathways, Lake Clara Meer, botanical garden, meadows and forests, popular arts and jazz festivals, Noguchi playscape, and much more, Piedmont Park is indisputably Atlanta's premier park. But Piedmont is a jewel whose facets have only been partially cut and shined, even after 100 years. Neither the Olmsted plan nor two others that followed were ever fully carried out (about one-third of Piedmont's acreage is still undeveloped), and by the early 1970s, misuse of the park was threatening to bring down the value of the surrounding community. The effort to bring Piedmont back from the brink began in 1976, when Commissioner Ted Mastroianni, recently brought in from New York City, recognized that excessive

car traffic in the park was precluding other potential uses, like running and cycling, and was keeping many visitors away. Taking a page from Central Park's book, the commissioner proposed closing the park to cars on weekends—a radical concept in car-oriented Atlanta—and a howl of protest erupted. But after seeing traffic projections that showed that the plan would have no significant impact on the neighborhood, Mayor Maynard Jackson agreed to test the idea.

Use of Piedmont Park went up almost immediately, while the crime rate went down. The experiment became permanent, and the closure was extended to seven days a week a few years later (making Piedmont today the most car-free major park in the country). In 1984, with their

Freedom Park—now Atlanta's largest park—is the location of the Carter Center. Jimmy Carter's involvement with the park goes back to 1972, when, as governor of Georgia, he shelved the plan to build the first highway on the site. Just south of Freedom Park lies the Martin Luther King, Jr., National Historic Site.

City Profile for Atlanta, Georgia

City Population (1996)	402,000
City Area in Acres (1990)	84,352
City Population Density Level	4.8
County in Which City Is Located	Fulton
County's Population (1996)	718,000
Metropolitan Area Population (1996)	3,541,000
City Relative Cost of Living (base = 100)	103.3
Number of Publicly Owned Vacant Lots	N.A.
Does the City Have a Developer Impact Fee for Parks?	Yes
Municipal Park Acres in City	3,122
National Park Acres in City	4
State Park Acres in City	21
County Park Acres in City	0
Total Park Acres in City	3,147

Atlanta Department of Parks, Recreation, and Cultural Affairs

Address	City Hall East, 8th Floor, 675 Ponce De Leon Avenue, NE
Zip Code	30308
Telephone	(404) 817-6744
Fax	(404) 817-6745
Web Site	www.ci.atlanta.ga.us
Agency Acreage in City	3,122
Acreage as Percent of City	3.7%
Acres per 1,000 Residents	7.8
Number of Regional Parks	7
Number of Neighborhood Parks	217
Number of Recreation Centers	39
Number of Pools	23
Number of Golf Courses	6
Number of Tennis Courts	145
Number of Sports Fields	71
Number of Marina Slips	0
Number of Beaches	0
Miles of Bikeways/Greenways	10
Number of Skating Rinks	0
Number of Full-Time Employees	215
Number of Seasonal Employees	59
Number of Volunteers	N.A.

Adjusted Budget for Fiscal Year 1998

Revenue

General Funds	$18,073,000
Dedicated Taxes	0
Fees Retained by the Agency	1,655,000
Private Grants and Donations	345,000
State and Federal Support	622,000
Capital Income	4,000,000
Total	$24,695,000

Expenditure

Grounds and Facilities Maintenance and Repair	$10,232,000
Recreational Programming and Activities	11,018,000
Capital Construction and Acquisition	4,000,000
Total[a]	$25,250,000

Expenditure per Resident	$63

[a]Budget numbers do not include the Bureau of Cultural Affairs.

park reclaimed, neighbors formed Friends of Piedmont Park to help the city keep the park clean and green. Five years later, recognizing that volunteer work would not suffice without some serious fundraising, the Friends metamorphosed into the Piedmont Park Conservancy and landed its first significant grant, $200,000 from Atlanta business owner Guy Milner, who had been impressed by the Central Park Conservancy's accomplishments when he stayed in New York for an extended period and jogged through Central Park.

Then the sewer crisis arose. As with most cities, Atlanta's wastewater system combines both sanitary sewage (the flow from residences and offices) with surface runoff (the flow from streets after rainstorms). Because cloudbursts often produce gigantic volumes of water in a short time, the city had numerous locations where overflowing sewer pipes could release excess stormwater into concrete trenches and then into streams flowing down to the Chattahoochee River. (Of course, because the sewer systems are combined, the released stormwater is inevitably polluted with household sewage.) One of those trenches ran through Piedmont Park for 65 years, and everyone knew that the immediate area smelled bad for a few days after every storm. Worse, the pollution downstream was beginning to affect the water quality of West Point Lake on the Chattahoochee River. Finally, in 1989, the Georgia legislature mandated primary treatment of all sewage overflows, and the city responded by proposing to build a treatment plant in Piedmont Park.

An age-old open sewer was one thing, but a brand new treatment plant was too much, and the park's neighbors mobilized. The Conservancy, caught between its commitment to the park's ecology and its fledgling effort to forge a political partnership with the city, could not lead the opposition. When the park site was defeated, however, the Conservancy proved its value by finding a suitable nearby location on some former railroad property. Today, Piedmont is marred by neither a treatment plant nor a sewer: the old swale was put into a pipe and covered over, and a pretty swath of grass was planted on top. (The campaign also inadvertently saved another park that had been programmed for a similar sewage plant. When neighbors of John A. White Park in a lower-income, African American community complained that they were not getting the same treatment as the rich folks around Piedmont Park, the city found a new location for that plant as well.)

Following the victory, the Conservancy worked with the city and the community to develop a master plan that called for limiting destructively large gatherings in the park (such as the Arts Festival, which attracted 100,000 people each year), in addition to raising $25 million to refurbish the park's visitor center, maintenance buildings, bathhouse, playgrounds, and other structures; to build water-purifying fountains in Lake Clara Meer; to redesign and widen paths and trails; and ultimately to develop the north end of the park with a new meadow and a healthy forest. With the support of major private funders—including the Woodruff Foundation, NationsBank, the Southern Company, and Georgia Pacific—by mid-1999, the Conservancy had accumulated $6.5 million.

In the 1990s, everything in Atlanta was played out as a backdrop to the Olympics and, in the final analysis, it appears that the Games may truly have a lasting effect on the way Atlantans think about and inhabit their city. Occurring just when exurban sprawl, highway gridlock, and unlawfully high regional air pollution were threatening to retard the region's phenomenal growth, the Olympic Games reintroduced downtown to suburbanites, who constitute eight out of every nine people in the area. (No other big city represents as small a proportion of its metropolitan region as Atlanta. See figure 6. Moreover, Atlanta is the only big city in the South that lost population between 1970 and 1990. See figure 5.) For one thing, amid predictions of impossible traffic in the city, every available old downtown office building, hotel, and warehouse was converted to housing and rented out. Each Olympic ticket included a free farecard for MARTA, Atlanta's beautiful but underused subway system, which impressed hundreds of thousands of first-time riders with its speed and advantages. After the Games ended, the downtown dormitories constructed for the 10,000 athletes were turned over to Georgia State University, thereby transforming the commuter-only institution into a 24-hour community. The impact of these changes was like a defibrillator for Atlanta's heart: the residential population in the central business district jumped from about 200 in 1993 to almost 7,000 in 1999 and helped propel the city back into a population growth mode in the 1990s.

The Olympics' great open-space legacy is 21-acre Centennial Olympic Park, a $65 million showpiece that is destined to become the principal focal point of the city's center. Heralded as the country's largest new downtown park since Pittsburgh created Point State Park in

EDAW, Inc.

EDAW, Inc.

1974, Centennial is located across from the colossal Georgia World Congress Center and near the new Georgia Dome football stadium. Collectively, the new facilities are expected to open up for development a large chunk of formerly derelict land on the west side of downtown, and already the Coca-Cola Company is considering building its new world headquarters nearby. Owned by the state, managed by the World Congress Center, and funded largely through private donations (including the individual purchase of 500,000 named paver bricks), the spare-no-expenses park has a high-tech Fountain of Rings with waters spilling out into a stream through the terrain, a six-acre great lawn, a court of flags, and an amphitheater amid a multilayered quilt theme that is sandblasted into granite paving blocks. Over the coming years, the park's young trees will grow and soften the initial image of a hardscape park.

A $65 million showpiece destined to become the focal point of center-city Atlanta, 21-acre Centennial Olympic Park is expected to spur development of the downtown's long-derelict west side. The largest downtown park built in the United States between 1974 and 2000, Centennial was partly funded by the sale of 500,000 named paver bricks.

The Atlanta Department of Parks, Recreation, and Cultural Affairs is a bit hard to find amid all the private sector and state agency activities. For one thing, the department is relatively poorly funded, with an adjusted budget of only $63 per resident in 1998, a figure that is substantially below the average of the cities profiled in this book. The agency's capital budget for acquisition and construction in 1998 was even more paltry: $4 million (although additional capital money was raised privately by the Piedmont Park Conservancy). The department is the beneficiary of the Park Improvement Fund, a property tax of $0.05 for every $100 of property valuation, but for many years half of the $3 million raised was not used for parks but to pay off the cost of the old baseball stadium (which was finally torn down and replaced in 1998). In theory, residents could vote for an open-space bond issue, or the city council could request permission from the state to increase its bonding authority, but no steps have been taken in either of these directions.

Another problem is that Atlanta's Parks and Recreation Department has no parks commission to provide guidance and the broad vision that most other cities receive from such a leadership body. In fact, the problem may go even deeper than that: some observers question whether most Atlantans have a civic commitment to enlarging their park system at all. The city's high crime rate and the burgeoning number of private, gated communities challenge many of Frederick Law Olmsted's rationales for parks—providing for the needs of the less-privileged, for instance, and democratizing urban spaces. At the same time, many Atlantans look at their city's famous tree cover and feel that they already have as much green as they need. (One observer said, "New York is a city that needs parks. Atlanta is a city within a park." However, with developers in metropolitan Atlanta cutting down 50 acres of forest per day, how long that statement will ring true remains a question.)

Although it is weak on land, the Department of Parks and Recreation is notable for some of its recreation programs, with higher-than-average numbers of swimming pools, tennis courts, golf courses, and recreation centers. The distribution of many of these facilities is quite uneven, however, and parts of southwest and northwest Atlanta are deficient in services.

Despite the city's modest vision for the future, at least two private-sector entities are able to imagine Atlanta with more parks and trails. One is the Woodruff Foundation (created by

Figure 9. Age of Major Cities

City	Year City Reached 100,000 Population	City Ranked by Age
New York	1811	1
Baltimore	1839	2
Boston	1842	3
Philadelphia	1843	4
Cincinnati	1848	5
St. Louis	1853	6
Chicago	1858	7
San Francisco	1865	8
Cleveland	1872	9
Pittsburgh	1873	10
Detroit	1876	11
Indianapolis	1885	12
Minneapolis	1885	12
Kansas City, Missouri	1886	14
Denver	1890	15
Los Angeles	1900	16
Portland, Oregon	1901	17
Seattle	1902	18
Atlanta	1902	18
Dallas	1912	20
Houston	1915	21
San Diego	1924	22
Miami	1928	23
Tampa	1938	24
Phoenix	1949	25

the former head of Coca-Cola), which is working with the Trust for Public Land, the Nature Conservancy, and others to protect and acquire land along the Chattahoochee River in order to create a continuous riverside greenway for environmental protection and recreation. Upstream from Atlanta, parts of the Chattahoochee valley are already wild and beautiful national recreation areas. The current effort, bolstered by a $25 million gift from Woodruff in 1999, seeks to extend that greenway the entire distance along the city's western boundary, converting the river from an almost ignored receptacle of wastewater and light industry to a gateway, perhaps the missing natural feature around which the city and its sprawling region can finally organize. (The effort got another boost in 1999, when environmentalists and the city settled a water pollution lawsuit with an agreement to spend up to $25 million on greenway acquisitions along the Chattahoochee and its tributary streams in an effort to prevent runoff from reaching the river. The effort began with a massive cleanup, which netted 550 tons of riverside trash, including tires, cars, and even parts of an airplane.)

At the other end of the spectrum is a "don't-take-no-for-an-answer" organization founded by Ed McBrayer, a transplanted Denverite who could not believe that Atlanta lacked the kind of bicycle trails, lanes, and routes that he was accustomed to using back home. Instead of cursing the darkness, McBrayer lit a candle, which became the Path Foundation, one of the nation's most successful trail advocacy organizations. In its first eight years of operation, the group raised $7 million in public and private funds to create a metropolitan trail network using donated land, abandoned railroads, the sides of roads, edges of golf courses, and existing parkland. As of 1999, ten miles of Path trails were within the city of Atlanta, with Freedom Park serving as "trail central" for the whole network. Moreover, McBrayer leaves nothing to the bureaucracy: even though the city owns the land, the Path Foundation builds and maintains the 12-foot-wide concrete trails.

Atlanta's park system has yet to earn bragging rights for the city. Compared with Seattle, which is the exact same age—both cities first attained a population of 100,000 in 1902 (see figure 9)—Atlanta has only one-third as much parkland. Through a string of recent successes, however, the city's activists have proven that almost anything is possible. If they can fashion the victories achieved by the private sector into a political climate that supports parks and park funding at city hall, Atlanta could take its rightful place as the quality-of-life leader of its sprawling region.

Phoenix

F ROM HIS OFFICE, Jim Colley, the director of the Phoenix Parks, Recreation, and Library Department, can do something that none of his colleagues around the country can match: he can physically see most of his park system. Not that the system is small. In fact, Colley administers more land than any other city park director does. In sprawling Phoenix, the people are down low and much of the parkland is up high, located in a ring of striking, craggy mountains. Meanwhile, in a downtown almost devoid of high rises, the view from Colley's dramatic 16th-floor City Hall office is almost unbroken.

Phoenix has the largest individual city park and the largest municipal park system in the nation. (The system falls to second place after New York only if urban national parks are added to the mix.) But Phoenix's numbers are not quite what they seem. For one thing, the size must be put in the context of this far-flung city. As a percentage of Phoenix's area, park and open-space acreage falls behind that of New York, San Francisco, San Diego, Minneapolis, Portland, Boston, and Cincinnati. Moreover, a tourist expecting a neighborhood playground on every corner or a large strolling park like San Francisco's Golden Gate Park would be disappointed. The city's giants, 16,000-acre South Mountain Preserve Park and 7,500-acre North Mountain Preserve Park, are largely undeveloped mountain wildlands that have few facilities beyond roads and hiking trails. Taking away the mountain preserves leaves a more modest 11,100 acres of traditional city parks (or 10.6 acres per 1,000 persons, a bit below average for low-density cities).

Nevertheless, the preserves are extraordinarily valuable and beloved. North Mountain

Papago Park's famous "Hole in Rock" attracts a continuous stream of climbers. In addition, Papago contains the Phoenix Zoo, the Desert Botanical Gardens, and one of the country's best golf courses.

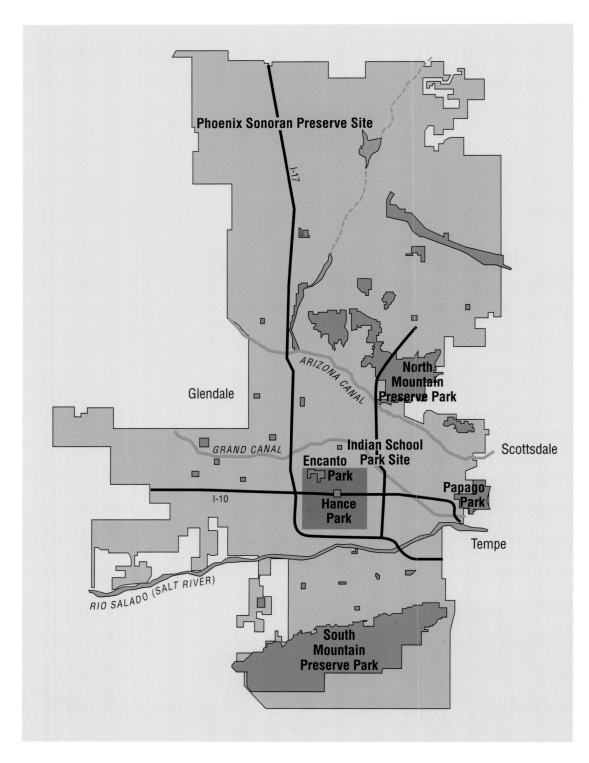

Phoenix's network of
parks and open space.

(formerly known as Squaw Peak), with half a million hikers a year, is reputed to be the most climbed peak in the United States. In addition, many visitors to Phoenix are treated to a night-time drive to the top of 2,690-foot South Mountain for a stunning view of the city lights that extend far into the desert. In almost any other locality, these areas would be state or national recreation areas, not city parks.

When it comes to building a city, Phoenix may have made more than its share of mistakes, but creating the mountain preserves was one of the great victories of environmental steward-ship over freewheeling development. The bulk of South Mountain Preserve Park was acquired in 1924 through the activism of equestrians and the political muscle of U.S. Senator Carl Hay-den. Although at that time the land was about eight miles outside the city limits, Phoenix had the foresight to purchase it from the federal government for the astonishing price of $17,000, or about $1.30 an acre. Soon after, when the Great Depression hit, the Civilian Conservation Corps laid out trails and constructed distinctive ramadas (stone picnic shelters) that survive to this day. (South Mountain's worst blemish, a forest of ugly transmission towers on its peak, came into existence later.)

Forty-six years later, in 1970, a different group of equestrians began to fear the loss of open space and the scarring of pristine ridgeline vistas caused by housing developments on the city's fast-growing north side. Taking the Phoenix City Council on a breakfast ride was powerful enough to set in motion a political process that established the 7,500-acre North Phoenix Mountain Preserve Park. By then, of course, Phoenix was a "real" city with "real" land prices and the second preserve ultimately cost about $70 million.

That kind of spending in a Republican city with a "less-is-more" attitude toward government shows the strength of the city's consciousness about open spaces. In fact, the Parks, Recreation, and Library Department[1] is such a major service provider that it is the fourth largest agency in the city. Besides overseeing 36,501 acres of parks and preserves, the department also operates more than 1,000 miles of parkways and bikeways and 29 recreation centers. Papago Park is famous not only for its unique red rock formations but also for the Phoenix Zoo, the Desert Botanical Gardens, and one of the country's best municipal golf courses. And all native Phoenicians have a warm spot in their hearts for lovely Encanto ("Enchanted") Park, a picturesque throwback to more innocent times, with its pedal boats, wooden bridges, children's train, duck pond, carousel, ballroom, and olive and date tree-lined walkways.

Jim Colley, the second longest serving of America's big-city park directors, with 20 years at the helm, oversees the system. A native of Alabama, who speaks with a southern drawl, Colley is a tireless and mesmerizing proselytizer for the importance of recreation, the benefits of parks, and the attractions of Phoenix. His efforts have paid off. Since 1964, Phoenix has doubled the size of its system, adding over 17,000 acres of parks and preserves, more than any other city except San Diego.

The mission of the Phoenix Parks, Recreation, and Library Department is not centered on land alone. In fact, Colley is as proud of his recreation program as his parks and, like former

City Profile for Phoenix, Arizona

City Population (1996)	1,159,000
City Area in Acres (1990)	268,736
City Population Density Level	4.3
County in Which City Is Located	Maricopa
County's Population (1996)	2,611,000
Metropolitan Area Population (1996)	2,747,000
City Relative Cost of Living (base = 100)	101.9
Number of Publicly Owned Vacant Lots	N.A.
Does the City Have a Developer Impact Fee for Parks?	N.A.
Municipal Park Acres in City	34,901
National Park Acres in City	0
State Park Acres in City	0
County Park Acres in City	1,600
Total Park Acres in City	36,501

Recreation Commissioner Mike DiBerardinis in Philadelphia, he has used youth programs to keep his agency central to the overall direction of the city. Parks and Recreation spends $1.3 million a year on after-school activities in over 100 schools. It manages a $3 million Youth-at-Risk Program (paid for mostly by the U.S. Department of Justice). The agency also runs a high-challenge outdoor adventure for mentally and physically disabled individuals and at-risk young people, called "River Rampage/River of Dreams." (Rejecting city attorneys' cautions, it scheduled its very first trip down the treacherous Colorado River.) Phoenix was one of the earliest big cities to agree to skateboarders' requests to build a skateboard park. Despite great skepticism, the $400,000 facility has been successful, is regularly toured by officials from other cities, and will soon be joined by two more skateboard parks. Because tattoos can represent a serious barrier for young people trying to get a job and begin a new life, the department facilitates tattoo removal from the face, neck, and hands of former gang members. Working with the American Society of Plastic and Reconstructive Surgeons, Parks and Recreation picks up the full tab for youngsters aged 13–19, charges only $25 for people aged 20–22, and works out a sliding fee scale for those above that age. (Since removing tattoos does not guarantee getting a job, the department also requires tattoo removal participants to attend workshops on job seeking, career planning, personal finance, teen pregnancy, and more.) In addition, the department seeks to build its own future workforce by offering a Recreation Intern Program to help youths learn jobs within the parks and recreation profession as well as at other agencies and nonprofit organizations. Interns are paid minimum wages and get classroom training plus practical experience.

The department's relationship with the police force is particularly close, and three recreation centers are kept open 24 hours a day to help the city enforce its teen curfew. If a young person is apprehended after midnight, the youth is brought to a center, not a police station. Before calling the parents, Recreation staff members conduct an interview to find out about disease, drugs, possible pregnancy, and abuse. Resistant to the police, many juveniles are happy to talk with Recreation staff. Because of that overwhelming success, the city put the whole Police Athletic League program into the Recreation Department.

Although Phoenix residents adamantly reject the comparison, their city is reminiscent of Los Angeles—not old Los Angeles with its narrow streets and tall palms, not glitzy Los Angeles with shimmering high rises in office parks, but valley Los Angeles with its arrow-straight, eight- and ten-lane avenues in mile-square grids, unending tracts of ranchette homes, and distant mountains flickering through the smog. In fact, Phoenix surpasses Los Angeles in rate of growth in the late 1900s (see figure 10) as well as in less-desirable ecological features: Phoenix has far lower population density, less public transit, and greater auto-dependency—perhaps greater auto-dependency than any big city in the United States.

Phoenix is very young, however, the youngest city described in this book, as measured by the year it first exceeded a population of 100,000 (see figure 9); and from the standpoint of parks, that youth may be a blessing. Phoenix came of age during and after the dawn of the ecological era and has had the opportunity to learn from the environmental mistakes of older locales. Even though the auto culture has stunted the city's urban design, the city is now determined to do things differently, to work more cooperatively with nature. For instance, 30-acre Hance Park is one of the largest city parks in the country to be constructed on a deck built over an interstate highway. The park added $91 million to the cost of building the Papago Freeway, but it came about because of pressure from the Central Village neighborhood, which refused to allow ten lanes of traffic to cut it off from downtown Phoenix. (Although not as well publicized as Seattle's famous Freeway Park, Hance Park is actually six times larger and much less affected by freeway noise.) Another environmentally conscious concept involves retooling the city's extensive network of water supply canals to provide interconnected recreation alongside them, thus doubling their value.

Today, the Phoenix Parks, Recreation, and Library Department is moving ahead on three new fronts, which, if successful, could help tame sprawl, preserve the desert ecology, and provide the city with a more urbane core. Furthest along is a plan to create a series of desert preserves on 20,000 acres on the city's far north side. Modeled after the mountain preserves, these will be minimally developed and minimally managed tracts designed not only to protect forever the desert that is Phoenix's primordial soul but also to do so in a biologically functional way, by keeping contiguous tracts large enough to sustain entire ecosystems. Designated the Phoenix Sonoran Preserve, the land may serve to establish the beginnings of a growth boundary on Phoenix's northern edge. Fortunately, although some of the land is privately owned, about three-quarters is in a state

Figure 10. Change in City Area, 1970–1990

City	Area in 1970 (In Acres)	Area in 1990 (In Acres)	Percentage Growth
Phoenix	158,656	268,736	41%
Denver	60,928	98,112	38
Portland, Oregon	57,024	79,808	29
Dallas	169,984	218,880	22
Tampa	54,080	69,568	22
Houston	277,696	345,536	20
Boston	29,440	30,976	5
Philadelphia	82,240	86,464	5
Miami	21,952	22,784	4
Baltimore	50,112	51,712	3
New York	191,808	197,696	3
San Francisco	29,056	29,888	3
San Diego	202,816	207,360	2
Chicago	142,464	145,408	2
Cleveland	48,576	49,280	1
Los Angeles	296,768	300,352	1
St. Louis	39,168	39,616	1
Pittsburgh	35,328	35,584	1
Detroit	88,320	88,768	1
Seattle	53,504	53,696	0
Atlanta	84,160	84,352	0
Minneapolis	35,264	35,156	–0
Cincinnati	49,984	49,408	–1
Kansas City, Missouri	202,432	199,360	–2
Indianapolis	242,816	231,488	–5

Phoenix Parks, Recreation, and Library Department

The main building of the venerable Phoenix Indian School will be preserved and renovated as a museum, while the rest of the 74-acre site will become Phoenix's newest park, complete with meandering paths, a pool, a pond, and a conservatory within a landscape symbolizing the Hopi Circle of Life.

land bank to benefit school systems, but it still needs to be purchased from the state. The full cost of acquisition of the land is estimated at $250 million.

The two other projects are located where parkland is much more scarce: in the urban core. One entails the creation of a new 74-acre historic, recreational, and passive park on the site of the old federal Phoenix Indian School, which educated thousands of American Indians from Arizona and throughout the nation between 1891 and 1990. Indian School Park, scheduled to open in 2000, will be a classic City Beautiful park with outdoor "rooms," meandering paths, a pool, a pond, a conservatory, three historic buildings, and a performance area within a large curved landscape symbolizing the Hopi Circle of Life. More than that, the $14 million park will educate residents and tourists alike about the 26 different American Indian tribes in the state.

The most exciting project is a huge, multi-agency plan to create a five-mile-long central-city greenway and park alongside the "former" Rio Salado—the river that spawned the city in 1867 but disappeared in 1922 as a result of the construction of a series of dams and irrigation canals. Except for rare periods of heavy rain, the Rio Salado (Salt River in English) has been bone dry for three-quarters of a century. Therefore, the city had turned its back on the unattractive gulch, leaving it a sociological barrier

between Phoenix's poorer near south side and the rest of the city.

As in Dallas, which is also planning to create a park out of its center-city waterway, the prime agency behind the Rio Salado project is the U.S. Army Corps of Engineers, the nation's primary financial resource when it comes to flood control. As in Dallas, many other interests are chipping in to join the ride, including

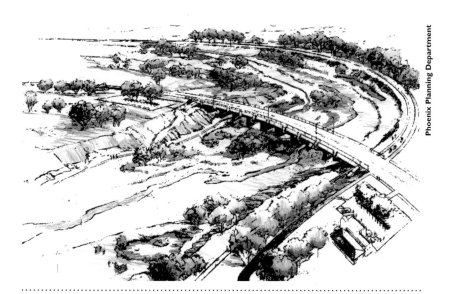

Phoenix Planning Department

The Rio Salado (Salt River) has been essentially dry since a diversion canal was built in 1922, but Phoenix has an ambitious plan to bring the river back to life, using treated, reclaimed water. The resulting initial five-mile greenway will provide 550 acres of wetlands, plus trails for hiking and bicycling.

Phoenix Parks, Recreation, and Library Department

Address	200 West Washington Street, 16th Floor
Zip Code	85003
Telephone	(602) 262-6862
Fax	(602) 495-3606
Web Site	www.ci.phoenix.az.us
Agency Acreage in City	34,901
Acreage as Percent of City	13.0%
Acres per 1,000 Residents	33.3
Number of Regional Parks	19
Number of Neighborhood Parks	99
Number of Recreation Centers	29
Number of Pools	28
Number of Golf Courses	5
Number of Tennis Courts	120
Number of Sports Fields	665
Number of Marina Slips	0
Number of Beaches	0
Miles of Bikeways/Greenways	79
Number of Skating Rinks	0
Number of Full-Time Employees	1,096
Number of Seasonal Employees	625
Number of Volunteers	22,588

Adjusted Budget for Fiscal Year 1998–1999

Revenue

General Funds	$64,061,000
Dedicated Tax	0
Fees (Golf Enterprise Fund)	4,822,000
Private Grants and Donations	15,000
State and Federal Support	689,000
Capital Income[a]	12,912,000
Total	$82,499,000

Expenditure

Grounds and Facilities[b]	$34,480,000
Recreational Programming and Activities	32,912,000
Capital Construction and Acquisition	12,912,000
Total	$80,304,000

Expenditure per Resident | $77

[a]Includes $2.166 million from developer fees.
[b]Includes $4.822 million from the Golf Enterprise Fund.

wildlife conservationists, recreationists, those seeking alternative methods to treat wastewater, and those seeking to revitalize the city's center. Unlike Dallas's Trinity River Corridor Project, however, Rio Salado will not include a highway; except for a few parking lots, this greenway is designed for pedestrians, bicyclists, and wildlife. The initial five-mile demonstration section will create 550 acres of semi-irrigated parkland along the river, using contaminated water from a formerly sealed well, which will first be partially treated and then allowed to percolate back into the ground for complete purification. Eventually Rio Salado will span the entire city, coursing 35 miles from east to west. Downstream, a companion project called Tres Rios will provide another 800 acres of wetlands (as well as education and recreation centers) through an innovative, land-based, wastewater tertiary treatment facility. Although the artificial wetlands, ponds, ledges, cascades, trails, and channels of Tres Rios will cost Phoenix and the four other participating cities $300 million over ten years, the project will actually save money by eliminating the need for a huge conventional sewage treatment plant. The design for Rio Salado has been funded, but construction money was not approved in 1998. Phoenix hopes to get approval in 2000.

Phoenix's economy is healthy, but even booming Phoenix could not afford the hundreds of millions of dollars that all the planned parks and open space will cost. Therefore, in 1999 Mayor Skip Rimsza proposed, and the voters overwhelmingly approved, the Phoenix Parks and Preserve Initiative, an increase of a tenth of a penny in the city's sales tax to be used to purchase land and to improve nine uncompleted regional parks (including Indian School Park). Projected to bring in $256 million over ten years, the bulk of the money will go toward expanding the Phoenix Sonoran Preserve. Although not enough for the full 20,000 acres, the amount is a start. Ideally, the additional value Phoenix's new parks bring to the city will generate the remaining funds needed to make America's biggest municipal park system even better.

Note

1. The library function of the department is beyond the scope of this book and has been eliminated from all statistics used to describe the department's budget and staffing.

Tampa

C AN GLORIOUS WEATHER and myriad views of sparkling water substitue for parks? For some Tampans the answer seems to be yes. Because of its God-given splendors of climate and geography Tampa does not *seem* to have a small amount of parkland. The hard facts tell a different story, however. With only 4.4 percent of the city devoted to parkland, Tampa scores 24th out of the 25 cities covered in this book (surpassing only Atlanta). When it comes to park acres per capita, it registers second to last of the low-density cities (again surpassing only Atlanta). In fact, when compared with another balmy city with magnificent views of the water —San Diego—Tampa has only about a third as much parkland per capita.

Of course, Tampa is not entirely without parks. The city has Lowry Park with its zoo, nature and jogging trails, ballfields, fishing dock, and community center; Copeland Park with its swimming pool, picnic areas, and tennis courts; and Picnic Island Park with its popular beach and view of St. Petersburg in the distance. Tampa also has beautifully landscaped

Tampa Downtown Partnership

Lykes Gaslight Square, the park that was never supposed to happen, has become downtown Tampa's instant focal space. Under the leadership of the Tampa Downtown Partnership, the whole community contributed to the greening of a temporarily vacant lot. Soon after, the square became so popular that the city bought it.

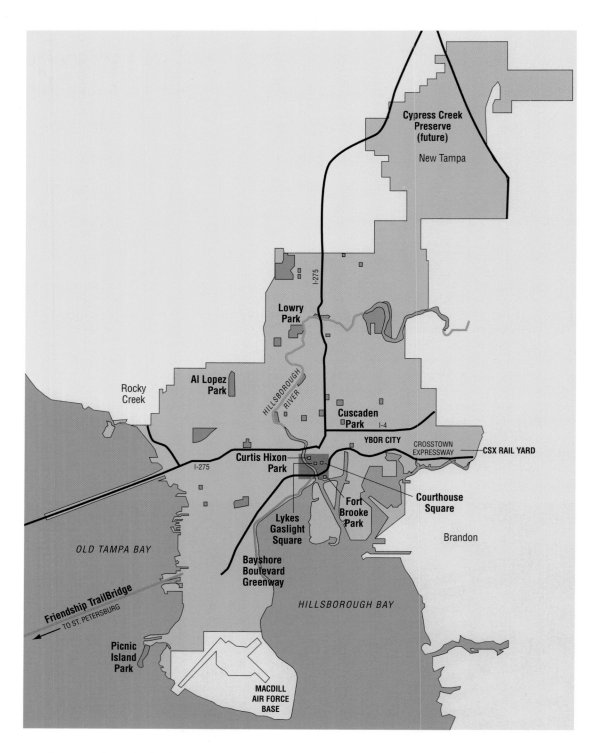

Tampa's network of parks and open space.

Bayshore Boulevard, which welcomes thousands of cyclists and skaters, offers captivatingly changing panoramas of the downtown skyline, and contains what is touted as "the world's longest continuous sidewalk" (a claim special enough to defy challenge). In addition, it has more than 160 other parks, 13 swimming pools, more than 200 landscaped boulevard medians, and a recreation program that emphasizes youth enrichment by offering super-vised after-school programs at playgrounds and all community centers.

Nevertheless, Tampa's park system shows gaping omissions and shortages. The Hillsborough River, for instance, has no greenway or bicycle trail, no significant walking promenade, and only occasional public access along its 30-plus miles (on both sides) within the city. Less than one-sixth of Tampa's 50-mile bayfront is publicly accessible. Ybor City, the historic heart of the Latino community and center of the old cigar industry, has only one significant open space, Cuscaden Park, where many famous Hispanic baseball players got their start. Both the African American and the Latino neighborhoods lost important park acreage to the construction of interstate highways in the 1960s.

Ultimately, simply too little parkland exists in Tampa. (The entire park system of Tampa could fit within Dallas's Trinity River Park, and no other city profiled in this book has a principal park as small as Tampa's. See figure 11.) Yet the demand and the use, especially among lower-income residents, is ever-present, and as a result, crowding is taking its toll. Al Lopez Park, for example, is so clogged that bicycling has been restricted. Because of the heavy wear, the park system as a whole needs an estimated $65 million in capital repair and improvements.

Even though Tampa has highly dedicated park professionals, it has a fragmented park and recreation structure, more so than any other city except Boston. The Tampa Parks Department, headed by veteran Director Ross Ferlita, owns the land and maintains the property. The Tampa Recreation Department, led by Joe Abrahamson, runs the pools and all the sports, crafts, and other programs. The Tampa Sports Authority, which also runs the city's football stadium, operates the golf courses. (To ensure accurate comparisons with other cities, the Tampa totals include the acreage and finances of the Sports Authority's golf courses—but not the stadium—as well as the Recreation Department's whole program and budget.) Relations between the agencies are cordial and supportive, but enough stories exist about communication problems and missed deadlines to give one pause. The split structure is not necessarily cast in stone, and (unlike in Philadelphia) some people do talk of a possible merger. An experimental first step is the planned relocation of the two departments into the same building as soon as an appropriate site can be found. Interestingly, while having three separate agencies may not lead to a large park system, the arrangement seems to do well financially: at $99 per resident, Tampa was second among the low-density cities studied in this book in its spending on parks and recreation in 1999.

Officially, Tampa denies that it has a shortage of parkland; the city relies on surrounding Hillsborough County parks to meet the acreage requirements set by the state of Florida. Under state rules, every Floridian must be within 30 miles or one hour's driving time of a regional park (defined as a park of at least 300 acres).

City Profile for Tampa, Florida

City Population (1996)	286,000
City Area in Acres (1990)	69,568
City Population Density Level	4.1
County in Which City Is Located	Hillsborough
County's Population (1996)	898,000
Metropolitan Area Population (1996)	2,199,000
City Relative Cost of Living (base = 100)	103.8
Number of Publicly Owned Vacant Lots	9,300
Does the City Have a Developer Impact Fee for Parks?	No
Municipal Park Acres in City	2,183
National Park Acres in City	0
State Park Acres in City	0
County Park Acres in City[a]	907
Total Park Acres in City	3,090

[a]Includes environmental lands slated to be turned over to Tampa.

Figure 11. Largest Municipal Park in Each City

City	Park Name	Acres	Year Created
Atlanta	Freedom Park	207	1998
Baltimore	Gwynns Falls/Leakin Park	1,100	1953
Boston	Franklin Park	510	1883
Chicago	Lincoln Park	1,212	1909
Cincinnati	Mount Airy Forest	1,472	1911
Cleveland	Rockefeller Park	130	1894
Dallas	Trinity River Park	3,653	1971
Denver	City Park	482	1879
Detroit	Rouge Park	1,200	1942
Houston	Cullen Park	10,534	1983
Indianapolis	Eagle Creek Park	4,813	1962
Kansas City, Missouri	Swope Park	1,769	1896
Los Angeles	Griffith Park	4,171	1896
Miami	Virginia Key	486	N.A.
Minneapolis	Wirth Park	743	1909
New York	Pelham Bay Park	2,766	1935
Philadelphia	Fairmount Park–Wissahickon Valley	4,167	1844
Phoenix	South Mountain Preserve Park	16,283	1924
Pittsburgh	Frick Park	456	1919
Portland, Oregon	Forest Park	4,836	1948
San Diego	Mission Trails Park	5,700	1989
San Francisco	Golden Gate Park	1,107	1870
Seattle	Discovery Park	513	1971
St. Louis	Forest Park	1,293	1876
Tampa	Al Lopez Park	126	1972
Median Size		**1,383**	

Tampa Parks Department

Address	7525 North Boulevard
Zip Code	33604
Telephone	(813) 931-2121
Fax	(813) 931-2120
Web Site	www.ci.tampa.fl.us
Agency Acreage in City[a]	1,760
Acreage as Percent of City	2.5%
Acres per 1,000 Residents	6.2
Number of Regional Parks	8
Number of Neighborhood Parks	79
Number of Recreation Centers	3
Number of Pools	0
Number of Golf Courses	0
Number of Tennis Courts	78
Number of Sports Fields	123
Number of Marina Slips	118
Number of Beaches	4
Miles of Bikeways/Greenways	9
Number of Skating Rinks	0
Number of Full-Time Employees	305
Number of Seasonal Employees	0
Number of Volunteers	5,000

Adjusted Budget for Fiscal Year 1999

Revenue

General Funds	$14,321,000
Dedicated Taxes	0
Fees Retained by the Agency	0
Private Grants and Donations	250,000
State and Federal Support	0
Capital Income	2,467,000
Total	$17,038,000

Expenditure

Grounds and Facilities Maintenance and Repair	$12,973,000
Recreational Programming and Activities	0
Capital Construction and Acquisition	2,467,000
Total[b]	$15,440,000

Expenditure per Resident	**$54**

[a]Does not include 902 acres of environmental lands purchased by Hillsborough County but not yet turned over to the city of Tampa.
[b]Excludes the department's Neighborhood Environmental Action Team (NEAT) program, which maintains vacant lots and removes street trash.

Although Tampa claims to have eight regional parks in its system, none comes close to meeting the state's acreage criterion. Therefore, the city uses approved regional parks in the 30,000-acre county system to meet the standard. However, this method of accounting ignores the reality that many older, younger, or low-income citizens do not have cars or otherwise cannot make much use of Hillsborough County parks.

Many Tampans, especially those who live in gated communities in the newer parts of town, do not notice the shortage of parks because they have their own private open spaces provided by developers. However, that does not solve the problem for the city's less-advantaged residents; in fact, it makes matters worse by significantly reducing the political constituency required for more community-wide park funding. Moreover, as the Parks Department's Ferlita and the Recreation Department's Abrahamson point out, developers do not typically provide the full spectrum of land and facilities the community needs. While golf courses as well as biking and walking trails are cost-effective amenities, developers shy away from providing soccer or baseball fields, tennis courts, and swimming pools—much less gyms, recreation centers, skating rinks, rowboat ponds, or the many other features that frequently make public park systems the heart of the community. In response, Ferlita and Abrahamson, together and with the city's Planning Department, have called for the imposition of an impact fee on all new development to pay for more parks and facilities. However, the city's Business and Community Services Department countered that plan, arguing that an impact fee would stifle growth and redevelopment in the city. The debate is profoundly relevant in a booming city that saw $4 billion in new construction between 1995 and 1999 alone.

The dispute over the value of parks has spilled over into the heart of downtown as well. On the one hand, there are those who are disappointed with Curtis Hixon Park, the $1.5 million makeover of the old convention center. Conceived as a top-of-the line gathering place for the city and designed by an environmental artist who installed walkways in the shape of leaves indigenous to central Florida (which, unfortunately, are visible only to a few executives looking down from their windows in high rises), the awkwardly located park is unable to generate activity on its own and is empty most of the time. Although the park has attracted crowds for a few major events, the expense of creating it and the antipathy it arouses did not strengthen

Tampa Recreation Department

Address	1420 North Tampa Street
Zip Code	33602
Telephone	(813) 274-8615
Fax	(813) 274-7429
Web Site	www.ci.tampa.fl.us
Agency Acreage in City	0
Number of Recreation Centers	24
Number of Pools	13
Number of Tennis Courts	14
Number of Sports Fields	44
Miles of Bikeways/Greenways	N.A.
Number of Skating Rinks	1
Number of Full-Time Employees	182
Number of Seasonal Employees	350
Number of Volunteers	N.A.

Adjusted Budget for Fiscal Year 1997–1998

Revenue

General Funds	$8,300,000
Dedicated Taxes	0
Fees Retained by the Agency	0
Private Grants and Donations	75,000
State and Federal Support	100,000
Capital Income	360,000
Total	$8,835,000

Expenditure

Grounds and Facilities Maintenance and Repair	$164,000
Recreational Programming and Activities	8,311,000
Capital Construction and Acquisition	360,000
Total	$8,835,000

Expenditure per Resident	$31

"somewhere" in a crowded and monotonous downtown cityscape.

The saga began in the late 1980s, when the locally based Lykes Brothers Company purchased a square block in the center of downtown with the intention of razing the buildings and constructing a new headquarters. But the endeavor was ill fated from the very beginning. First came an extraordinarily bruising battle with historical preservationists, then a fruitless tussle with the city over using the vacant property for a temporary parking lot, then delays in the company's construction plans. Finally, the Tampa Downtown Partnership, a business improvement organization with good ties to Tampa's Mayor Dick Greco as well as to the Lykes Company, offered to intercede on a temporary basis. Partnership Director James Cloar had once lived in Washington, D.C., where he cherished the urbanity provided by the capital's many green squares and circles. Under Cloar's leadership, the Tampa Downtown Partnership leased the property (for $1 a month), planned a modest passive park (helped by a $25,000 contribution from Lykes), and agreed to manage the site until the Lykes Company could begin construction.

It was the right space in the right place at the right time. Like an Amish barn raising, Lykes Gaslight Square miraculously came into being as a result of the whole community's involvement and generosity. People's Gas donated pedestrian-scale gas fixtures for the central walkways, and Tampa Electric donated high-level arc lights for the corners. Hillsborough County donated mature live oak trees (which the city planted at no cost), Tampa's Solid Waste Department furnished trash receptacles, and area companies and individuals contributed funds to purchase 20 handsome, specially designed benches for the park. Thanks to the outpouring, the final price tag was a minuscule $50,000, and immediately upon opening in June 1996, the small kernel of green space became an automatic hit, attracting not only lunchtime and after-work users but also a constant stream of pass-through walkers.

For a citizenry that normally equates any parcel of vacant land only with car parking, Lykes Square was a revelation. It was so "perfect" that Tampans soon were unable to imagine downtown without it, and only 17 months later the city purchased the land from Lykes Brothers (for $2.85 million). That was only the beginning, however. Mayor Greco's enthusiasm over the square's positive impact led to the purchase of a second open space nearby for Hillsbor-

the constituency needed to spark interest in developing downtown parks.

In diametric contrast is the new Lykes Gaslight Square, Tampa's most significant piece of downtown open space since railroad magnate Henry Plant built the gardens for his world famous Tampa Bay Hotel in 1891. Unlike Curtis Hixon Park, Lykes Square was never supposed to happen; when it did, it became downtown's well-used focal plaza almost immediately. Like Boston's Post Office Square, one-acre Lykes proves that size can be less important than location when it involves opening up a sense of

Gandy Bridge and Friendship Trail Corporation

Thousands turned out for the opening day celebration of Friendship Trail-Bridge, which runs from Tampa to St. Petersburg. Billed as "the world's longest over-the-water recreational trail," the 2.6-mile route is located on an abandoned auto bridge that a tenacious coalition of bicyclists saved from destruction. The retrofit was paid for with the same Florida transportation dollars that were originally earmarked for demolition costs.

ough County to develop into a new Courthouse Square. A few blocks south, directly on the Garrison Channel waterfront, the Trust for Public Land acquired a two-acre parcel that had been the site of historic Fort Brooke, once the most important military base in all of Florida. The site will be landscaped and revegetated and should become an important catalyst in the use and redevelopment of Tampa's east side downtown waterfront area.

At about the same time, a few miles to the west, a completely different effort sprang to life, one that is destined to have a long-term impact on Tampa's park and recreation system (as well as that of sister city St. Petersburg across the bay). After determining that 40-year-old, 2.6-mile-long Gandy Bridge was outmoded and unrepairable, the Florida Department of Transportation constructed a new causeway to St. Petersburg and announced that the middle two miles of Gandy Bridge would be demolished, leaving only fishing piers on either side. An ad hoc group of bicyclists from Tampa and St. Petersburg considered this a terrible waste and rose to save the bridge and renovate it. Under the banner of creating "the world's longest over-the-water recreational trail," the group proposed using the very $7 million that the state had budgeted for demolition. Despite the Transportation Department's opposition and numerous bureaucratic hurdles, the group's efforts were successful, and the old Gandy Bridge, renamed Friendship TrailBridge, opened in late 1999 as the centerpiece of an eventual 21-mile trail that will pump two-wheeled commuters

(as well as touring bicyclists and their dollars) into a downtown Tampa that had previously been less than hospitable to bikes. (As a state, Florida has the highest rate of bicyclist fatalities in the United States.) Although Tampa has had a plan for trails and greenways on paper for a long time, evolution of the projects has proceeded at a glacial pace. The hope is that the success of the Friendship TrailBridge will jumpstart efforts to develop the rest of the system.

Even though developed parkland may be scarce in Tampa, the city is increasing its inventory of natural preserves, thanks to Hillsborough County's aggressive land acquisition program, which is earmarked to preserve environmentally sensitive land. Begun in 1987, the Environmental Lands Acquisition and Protection Program (ELAPP) is funded through a countywide assessment of $0.25 per $100 of property valuation, generating $4 million to $5 million a year, which is supplemented by matching funds from the state. The popular program enabled the county to purchase a total of 30,000 acres through 1999 and has been extended by the voters through 2010. In the early years, Tampa residents complained that almost none of the purchased acreage was within the city, but ELAPP officials countered that the rules made brownfield (previously used land) purchases almost impossible. Following several compromises, by mid-1999, seven parcels totaling 218 acres had been purchased within the old city limits (as well as the 827-acre Cypress Creek Preserve wilderness in so-called New Tampa).

Tampa Sports Authority

Address	4201 Dale Mabry Highway North
Zip Code	33607
Telephone	(813) 673-4300
Agency Acreage in City	423
Acreage as Percent of City	0.6%
Acres per 1,000 Residents	1.5
Number of Golf Courses	3

Adjusted Budget for Fiscal Year 2000

Revenue

General Funds	$0
Dedicated Taxes	0
Fees Retained by the Agency	3,980,000
Private Grants and Donations	0
State and Federal Support	0
Capital Income	0
Total	$3,980,000

Expenditure

Grounds and Facilities Maintenance and Repair	$3,900,000
Recreational Programming and Activities	0
Capital Construction and Acquisition	0
Total[a]	$3,900,000

Expenditure per Resident	**$14**

[a]Excludes Raymond James Stadium and includes only the Sports Authority's three golf courses.

Tampa, the second youngest city in this book (see figure 9), is still growing rapidly. Unlike Miami, Tampa is not hemmed in by incorporated suburbs, and the city is aggressively annexing portions of Hillsborough County; the city's physical size increased by 22 percent from 1970 to 1990 (see figure 10). Although the growth is good for the city's tax base as well as for its ability to create more parkland and open space on the outskirts of town, the increase tends to direct attention and effort toward new development while obscuring the need to provide open space in older sections that are already built up.

Nevertheless, just east of the historic Ybor City neighborhood, one large tract holds a glimmer of park promise: a sprawling CSX Railroad yard. Although the rail yard has not been formally slated for abandonment, its use is declining, and it has the potential to provide the kind of large park parcel that Tampa has never had, similar to the one that Phoenix is developing out of the closed federal Indian School or the one Denver is creating from abandoned Stapleton Airport. If Tampa can recognize its need for parkland and muster the public/private partnership that first surfaced with Lykes Gaslight Square, the city might find itself with one of the most exciting new city park efforts in the United States.

Indianapolis

ONE OF THE MOST conservative big cities in the country is trying something new: Indianapolis hopes to become the greenway capital of the nation. "Round" parks may be fine for picnickers, boat rowers, and ballplayers, but skinny parks that go on forever are the rage among the Lycra crowd—bicyclists, skaters, runners, and walkers. From Boston to Seattle most cities have at least one river or abandoned railroad greenway open or in the works. But Indianapolis's blueprint is for a full 150-mile system, with the first 45 miles already open and used more than a million times a year.

Except for Monument Circle in the center of town and two military parade grounds mandated by the state, Indianapolis did not estab-

lish a single park until 1873, 48 years after it was founded. Civic-minded citizens made numerous attempts to donate land but were rebuffed by city leaders, who did not want to spend money to maintain it. The pattern continues into modern times. In 1957, when Josiah Lilly offered the extraordinary gift of 4,800 acres of forestland in northwest Marion County, Indianapolis refused the donation and steered him instead to Purdue University. Later, after a devastating flood, the intercession of the Flood Control Board, and the decision to construct a major dam on Eagle Creek, the land was finally transferred from Purdue to the city and today constitutes Eagle Creek Park, the largest urban park east of the Mississippi River and the city's most magnificent lake and forest resource, with

Indianapolis Greenways

Skiers enjoy a crisp solitude along the Falls Creek Greenway, as Indianapolis's trails become "whiteways" in the winter. The city is working toward an eventual 150-mile system of four-season trails.

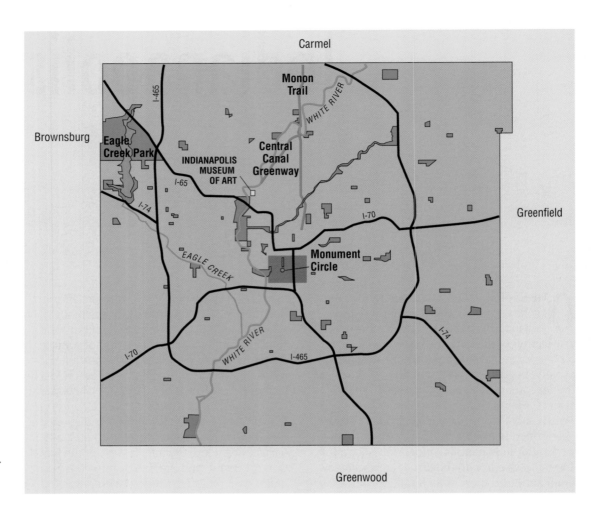

Carmel

Monon
Trail

Brownsburg

Eagle
Creek Park

INDIANAPOLIS
MUSEUM
OF ART

Central
Canal
Greenway

WHITE RIVER

Greenfield

I-465

I-65

I-74

I-70

EAGLE CREEK

Monument
Circle

WHITE RIVER

I-70

I-465

I-74

Greenwood

Indianapolis's network of
parks and open space.

a boat rental marina, a beach, ponds for study and for skating, several retreat houses, and even a magnificent beech tree on which Daniel Boone carved his name. (Nevertheless, the fiscal conservatives continued to rule: as a condition for accepting the park, the city mandated that Eagle Creek be financially self-sufficient and that no city revenues go toward its maintenance.)

To understand Indianapolis's parks, one must know a bit about the city's politics. Although Indianapolis is only two hours from Cincinnati and five hours from St. Louis, it bears much less resemblance to classic old towns of the heartland than to the sprawling newer cities of the South and West. Why? When the city merged with its surrounding Marion County suburbs into what is called "Unigov" in 1970, Indianapolis instantly became larger in physical spread than Dallas and less densely populated than Phoenix. (Indianapolis is the tenth most populous city in the country but the second least dense city profiled in this book.) Therefore, in most of the comparative charts, far-flung Indianapolis is measured not against its medium-density neighbors like Cleveland and Detroit but

against distant, low-density cities like Atlanta, Houston, and Tampa.

Indianapolis has another quirk. The city is home to the $15 billion Lilly Endowment, the second largest private foundation in the United States, one of whose mandates is to help improve the city. As Lilly's wealth has mushroomed (largely from profits from the sales of the antidepressant drug Prozac), the foundation and the city have developed an increasingly codependent relationship: (1) the city holds the line on taxes, (2) social and physical problems multiply, (3) private partners are brought into the mix to help solve the problems, (4) those partners turn to Lilly for financial support, and (5) with so much Lilly money in the system, there is no need to raise taxes. Until the 1990s, the environment was not one of Lilly's interest areas, but recently the foundation has started giving to the park system. Throughout the decade, the city's park department, known as IndyParks, along with several private park groups, received almost $19 million for the rehabilitation of playgrounds, a conservatory, and a sunken garden and for construction of family recreation centers and greenways, to name a few projects.

Aside from low taxes and its auto-racing speedway, Indianapolis's other claim to fame is that, under former Mayor Stephen Goldsmith, it became a leader in privatization (also known as outsourcing)—contracting out city services to the private sector. Goldsmith's first parks director, Leon Younger, was a similarly staunch advocate of privatization, as well as of market-based pricing of facilities and recreation services —setting fees by what the 80 percent of middle-class-or-better Americans can pay, rather than providing below-cost services to meet the needs of the 20 percent who cannot. (However, the department does have a fee differential between the wealthier and the poorer townships within the city.) Younger, who referred to himself as an agent of change, lasted only three years, but his impact on the agency continues to be felt in many ways: positively, through special partnerships with churches, community organizations, and corporations; and negatively, through diminished staffing, lower morale, and an ongoing debate over the agency's mission. In 1999, Indianapolis had the smallest full-service park and recreation budget, both per capita and per acre, of all the big cities. It found itself regularly outsourcing maintenance, design, and construction to a wide variety of private companies and nonprofit organizations. In fact, in 1998, Mayor Goldsmith did something that had never been done anywhere before: he contracted out the very directorship of the department. During the

Figure 12. Foundations That Have Invested $1 Million or More in Urban Parks (Listed Alphabetically)

Boston Foundation, Boston

Cleveland Foundation, Cleveland

Commonwealth Fund, New York

Danforth Foundation, St. Louis

Dayton–Hudson Foundation, Minneapolis

Geraldine Dodge Foundation, Morristown, New Jersey

Doris Duke Charitable Foundation, New York

Gates Foundation, Denver

Gund Foundation, Cleveland

Walter and Elise Haas Fund, San Francisco

J. M. Kaplan Fund, New York

Kresge Foundation, Troy, Michigan

Lilly Endowment, Indianapolis

MacArthur Foundation, Chicago

New York Community Trust, New York

William Penn Foundation, Philadelphia

San Francisco Foundation, San Francisco

Wallace–Reader's Digest Funds, New York

Woodruff Foundation, Atlanta

mayor's final year in office, the director of IndyParks was Jim Parham, the assistant director of the Eppley Institute for Parks and Public Lands in Bloomington, Indiana. Parham is an enthusiastic park advocate, who has years of experience at both the Indiana Department of Natural Resources and the National Park Service. However, no amount of zeal could compensate for the fact that his leadership was circumscribed by two six-month contracts. Morale at the agency, already down because of the departure of three previous directors since 1992, sank lower because of constant reorganization, extensive staff turnover, and a depletion of institutional memory (although Parham did institute a major study of what Indianapolitans want from their park system).

Had the city not embarked on the greenway crusade, its park system might be hard pressed to find a theme. IndyParks is significantly short on parkland, recreation centers, number of park units, and swimming pools. Moreover, surveys have shown that, with the exception of golf, Indianapolis residents do not support the concepts of privatizing park and recreation activities or charging market-rate fees—a fact Mayor Goldsmith belatedly recognized toward the end of his administration. The exception, golf, is a

City Profile for Indianapolis, Indiana

City Population (1996)	747,000
City Area in Acres (1990)	231,488
City Population Density Level	3.2
County in Which City Is Located	Marion (Unigov)
County's Population (1996)	815,000
Metropolitan Area Population (1996)	1,492,000
City Relative Cost of Living (base = 100)	96
Number of Publicly Owned Vacant Lots	1,000
Does the City Have a Developer Impact Fee for Parks?	N.A.
Municipal Park Acres in City	11,547
National Park Acres in City	0
State Park Acres in City	1,692
County Park Acres in City	0
Total Park Acres in City	13,239

Indianapolis Parks and Recreation Department

Address	200 East Washington Street, Suite 2301, CCB
Zip Code	46204
Telephone	(317) 327-7275
Fax	(317) 327-7033
Web Site	www.indygov.org/indyparks
Agency Acreage in City[a]	11,547
Acreage as Percent of City	5.0%
Acres per 1,000 Residents	15.4
Number of Regional Parks	6
Number of Neighborhood Parks	110
Number of Recreation Centers	18
Number of Pools	19
Number of Golf Courses	13
Number of Tennis Courts	112
Number of Sports Fields	158
Number of Marina Slips	2
Number of Beaches	1
Miles of Bikeways/Greenways	29
Number of Skating Rinks	2
Number of Full-Time Employees	206
Number of Seasonal Employees	400
Number of Volunteers	24,000

Adjusted Budget for Fiscal Year 1999

Revenue

General Funds	$16,718,000
Dedicated Taxes	0
Fees Retained by the Agency	3,951,000
Private Grants and Donations	33,000
State and Federal Support	45,000
Capital Income	3,400,000
Total	$24,147,000

Expenditure

Grounds and Facilities Maintenance and Repair	$10,031,000
Recreational Programming and Activities	10,716,000
Capital Construction and Acquisition	3,400,000
Total	$24,147,000

Expenditure per Resident	**$32**

[a]Excludes approximately 4,700 acres of greenways operated on flood channel land owned by the Public Works Department and other agencies.

true bright spot. IndyParks owns 13 golf courses (tied with Los Angeles for first place and covering 1,632 acres), and ever since 1993, management of the links has been contracted out to private companies. The city's golf program has been judged a stellar success: the quality of the courses and management of the turf have improved significantly, and users give the system a 95 percent approval rating. The triumph has spawned similar outsourcing experiments in Chicago, Cincinnati, New York, and elsewhere. (However, the labor unions point out that the program's costs have been borne by the new workers, who get lower wages and fewer benefits than their municipal predecessors.)

The city's 1994 Greenway Plan grew out of two failed industrial facilities—the Central Canal and the Monon Railroad. The canal, constructed in 1836 to provide inexpensive transportation of goods past the nonnavigable White River, was quickly eclipsed by railroads. It would have gone the way of most other canals if it had not been reconceptualized as a key link in the city's water supply. Even today, the Central Canal provides drinking water for six out of ten Indianapolitans. It also provides tens of thousands of recreation user-days on its packed gravel towpath and pastoral landscape. That number will escalate dramatically when IndyParks completes new bridge connections downtown, midtown, and uptown, and when the canal gets integrated into the city's growing network of purposeful transportation routes. A minor fly in the ointment is the growing number of dogs using the trail. Not only are their leashes potentially hazardous to cyclists, but their excrement is of concern to the water company that owns the canal. In response, IndyParks is considering putting up plastic bag dispensers along the trail and posting gentle messages for pet owners. The agency also signed a contract with Two Scoops, a firm whose existence was unimaginable a few years ago: for a payment of $12 a mile, the company cleans the trail of dog droppings three times a week.

On a brighter note, IndyParks is a partner in a new endeavor that combines recreation, conservation, and art. The Indianapolis Museum of Art, located on the best of several former Lilly family estates and only a stone's throw from the Central Canal, owns a lovely wooded peninsula and a small lake. However, because of unusual topography and the lack of a bridge, the nature preserve was inaccessible to art patrons, and the museum was unreachable by trail users. An imaginative deal and the help of the Indiana Historic Landmarks Foundation enabled Indy-

Parks and its partners to locate two surplus historic iron bridges in a rural county and to disassemble, move, renovate, repaint, rebuild, and equip them with wheelchair-accessible ramps. Soon, the weed-choked lakeshore will be transformed into experimental wetlands and prairies, a trail will be built around the lake, and a sculpture garden will be installed in the grassy clearing. By mid-2000, Indianapolis will have a true art and nature park that combines aesthetics with recreation.

The Central Canal Greenway has done more than promote fitness. In recent years, the lower portion, minutes from the state's Capitol downtown, has also shown its power as an economic development tool and today serves as a scenic anchor for the city's first new upscale housing development in the center of the city.

A mile or so east, the Monon Railroad project has been, if anything, an even greater success. Abandoned in 1987, the conveniently located north-south corridor was purchased under a federal mass transit grant and was first slated for use as a bus route. When neighborhood opposition defeated that plan, bicyclists gradually began beating the drum for a trail. Because neither the city nor Lilly initiated the project, the grass-roots effort was given no chance of success. The advocates slowly gained ground, however, pointing to extremely popular rail trails in surrounding Illinois, Michigan, Ohio, and elsewhere. Finally, as a result of the involvement of a determined former city-county council member named Ray Irvin, federal funding was obtained, and a few miles of the Monon corridor were constructed.

As soon as the first segment opened, wariness and opposition evaporated. Even skeptical neighbors became enthusiastic advocates, cutting gateways into the fences they had just built, and the rest of the route was finished quickly. In addition to prompting a boom in bike sales, the Monon has since become a lever for the redevelopment of the quaint but vulnerable Broad Ripple neighborhood.

Ray Irvin went on to become the project manager of IndyParks Greenways, where he proclaims his vision to anyone who will listen. Learning from the blue jay, which deposits her eggs in other birds' nests, Irvin hit upon a greenway creation scheme that essentially appropriates linear strips of unused land owned by other agencies—primarily the Department of Public Works, which has authority over all floodplains and floodchannels. By signing memorandums of understanding with the Public Works Department, Irvin amassed an astonishing 4,700 acres

of greenway land in only five years. Lawyers can debate about whether the system, based largely on handshakes and with almost no financial backing, is real or phantom, but every week thousands of happy cyclists, runners, and other trail users vouch for its positive impact on Indianapolis's park and recreation system.

Although Indianapolis's park program is angling for a gold star, it does not rate one quite yet. What the city needs most is strong, visionary leadership and commitment from the very top. The greenways program is poorly integrated into the overall park hierarchy and seems to be developing its own parallel structure of partnerships and a foundation. Operational spending is still below average, and staffing since 1990 has declined by 11 percent, even taking into account privatization. Although Mayor Goldsmith (who retired at the end of 1999) pointed proudly to the $80 million in capital construction that was invested during his two terms, that amount was a pittance compared with what the system needs and was less than the amount invested by smaller cities such as Boston, Denver, Portland, and Seattle.

Indianapolis may be in for some big changes in the 21st century. Despite Goldsmith's nation-

After more than a decade of political struggle, the abandoned Monon Railroad has become the Monon Trail, and even its former opponents are using it for everything from recreation to shopping and nonmotorized commuting.

wide glamor, his hand-picked successor was defeated in the November 1999 elections by Bart Peterson, a developer and the first Democrat to be elected mayor in the 30 years of Unigov's existence. The election was seen as a referendum on privatization, and Peterson immediately began a national search for a parks director.

Indianapolis has set forth compelling visions of interconnecting parkways twice before—first by John C. Olmsted in the 1880s, later refined by George Kessler in 1906—only to have plans falter for lack of funding and implementation. On the other hand, in the 1970s, Indianapolis set its sights on becoming the nation's center for amateur athletics, and within a quarter-century it had achieved that goal. If the city sets a similar goal for "regular" recreationists and users of open spaces, Indianapolis could accomplish its goal for parks and greenways as well.

Kansas City, Missouri

KANSAS CITY MAY LIE near the geographic center of the United States, but that by no means makes the city average. Far from being treeless and flat, as many people imagine, Kansas City has a hilly landscape that rises steeply from the Missouri River and then undulates irregularly, providing dramatic views, a set of intersecting stream valleys, and an attractive canvas for a network of boulevards and parkways. Trees are so ubiquitous that, even with the loss of 70,000 stately elms to blight and that many again to a catastrophic 1996 ice storm, the Department of Parks, Recreation, and Boulevards is still responsible for 540,000 of them. The city even has a theme unlike any other—fountains. Scores of fountains, both public and private, display water and sculpture

in parks, along streets, and in plazas throughout town. And in a country dominated by the design work of Frederick Law Olmsted and his sons, Kansas City is the preeminent showcase of America's other great landscape planner, George Kessler.

Kessler, who lived from 1862 to 1923, planned parks in Cincinnati, Dallas, Denver, Indianapolis, and elsewhere, with mixed results, but Kansas City is where his landscape genius was allowed to flower, because turn-of-the-century Kansas City was blessed with a small cadre of civic leaders who truly supported parks. Two of them in particular, August Meyer, a wealthy business owner who became chairman of the Park Board, and William Rockhill Nelson, the outspoken editor of the *Kansas City Star*, led the difficult,

Kansas City, Missouri, Department of Parks, Recreation, and Boulevards

The City of Fountains began its obsession modestly—by harnessing natural limestone springs to provide refreshment for animals. But after J. C. Nichols incorporated fountains into his Country Club Plaza development, the concept took hold in a big way. Today, Kansas City has scores of fountains, none as grand as this one named in honor of Nichols.

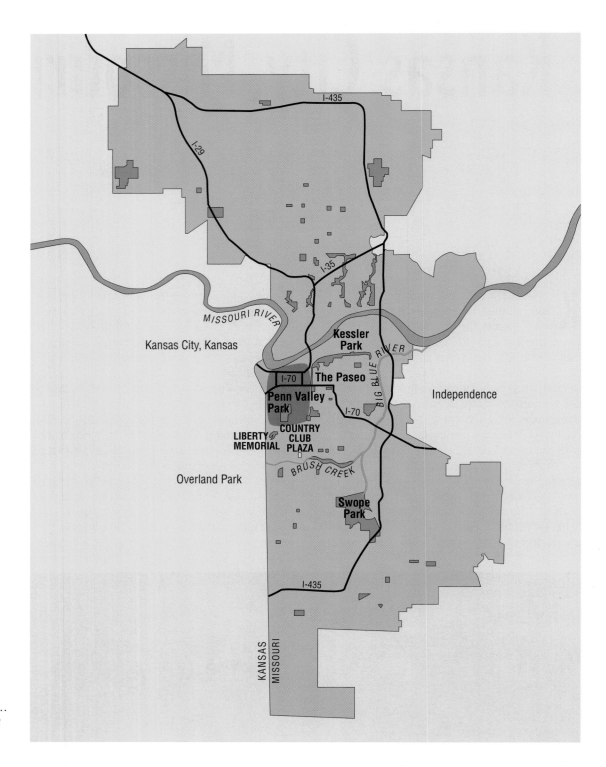

Kansas City's network of
parks and open space.

decades-long legislative and legal battles
against an almost equally shrewd group of anti-
tax agitators. In perhaps no other city at the
time did park politics play such a significant
role in general city politics. Between 1895 and
1915, while places like Indianapolis, Los Angeles, and Pittsburgh were rejecting park bonds
and sometimes even turning down land donations, Kansas City appropriated an astonishing

$15 million to build a parkway and open-space
system that was lauded around the country
and noticed by Europeans.

The key victory came in 1895 with the establishment of a semiautonomous park commission authorized to receive a portion of the property tax, including a higher amount from owners facing parks and boulevards. This arrangement, which lives on today through an annual

$1-per-linear-foot-per-year boulevard frontage fee, allows the city to reap a return from the value the parkways create. The craftily worded measure circumvented a previous defeat in the courts and enabled the board to sell bonds and repay them with the tax revenue, substantially speeding up the process of land acquisition. Perhaps the most amazing result of that victory came the following year, when Colonel Thomas Swope, a wealthy recluse and one of the stalwarts of the opposition, suddenly reversed his stance and donated his 1,334-acre property to the city. Today, his gift has been expanded to 1,769 acres and is known as Swope Park, the showcase of the city's park system. The 14th largest big-city park in the country, Swope Park is the home of the Kansas City Zoo, the Starlight Theater, an outstanding golf course, a nature center, stables, sports fields, and more.

Kessler was aware of Olmsted's ideas, but he had other influences too. Most memorable was a trip to Mexico City, where he was enormously impressed by the Paseo de la Reforma, which connects that city with Tepultepec Park. Because of the unrelenting pressure from anti-park forces, Kessler and Meyer saw the Paseo approach—a parkway solution—as a way to do more with less. Rather than expansive meadows and playing fields, their 1893 plan called for 100-foot-wide landscaped boulevards connecting the town's squares, high bluffs, and other notable public places. The boulevards followed shallow, curving valleys and other topographical elements and were attractively designed and planted (even serving as tree nurseries for later transplantation), but their primary role was to stimulate high-quality development. First and foremost was the Paseo, a broad boulevard leading south from downtown toward Swope Park. (Although today the area around the Paseo is suffering economically and the Paseo itself needs millions of dollars of repairs, a century later, it still boasts higher property values than do other streets in the vicinity.) Over time, as the city expanded, the boulevard system grid grew with it and now totals 124 miles.

On a per-capita basis, Kansas City has 30 acres of parkland for every 1,000 persons, more than every other big city except Phoenix. As a percentage of the area of the city, however, the number is less impressive—6.6 percent, somewhat below the average of the low-density cities. This anomaly is due to Kansas City's extraordinarily low population density, 2.2 persons per acre, by far the lowest of any city described in this book. (In contrast to Denver, which has roughly the same population, Kansas City residents are rattling around on twice as much land. Of course, greater Denver has its own sprawl but it is out in the suburbs.) Most Kansas Citians are pleased with their city's lack of density, attributing to it an easy-going quality of life, although Kansas City actually does have a downtown skyline and several built-up, walkable neighborhoods with an urban feel. The city also has a vast amount of land north of the Missouri River that was annexed for future development in the 1950s but never developed. (Ironically, economic and social forces pushed metropolitan population growth in the opposite direction, south and west into the state of Kansas.)

The city's park agency carries the complex name of Kansas City, Missouri, Department of Parks, Recreation, and Boulevards. (Kansas City, Kansas, is a separate, smaller city with its own park department and is not included in this book.) Relatively well funded, the department spends more than $90 per resident, per year on park and recreation programs—substantially above average for the low-density cities (where most residents have private yards). However, on a per-acre basis, the department is well below average, spending only about one-third as much as Denver or Minneapolis, the two cities with the most comparable park and boulevard systems.

As in Chicago and Minneapolis, the relative autonomy of the Kansas City Parks and Recreation Commission kept the department funded and shielded it from the occasional excesses of

City Profile for Kansas City, Missouri

City Population (1996)	441,000
City Area in Acres (1990)	199,360
City Population Density Level	2.2
County in Which City Is Located	Jackson
County's Population (1996)	646,000
Metropolitan Area Population (1996)	1,690,000
City Relative Cost of Living (base = 100)	98.2
Number of Publicly Owned Vacant Lots	N.A.
Does the City Have a Developer Impact Fee for Parks?	No
Municipal Park Acres in City	11,047
National Park Acres in City	0
State Park Acres in City	0
County Park Acres in City	2,282
Total Park Acres in City	13,329

Kansas City, Missouri, Department of Parks, Recreation, and Boulevards

The Liberty Memorial, the only U.S. monument to the veterans of World War I and a fixture of the Kansas City skyline, is now undergoing a $26 million renovation. Here, residents evaluate chalk paintings at the "Strada dell'Arte" festival.

the city government, although the department had its share of setbacks. One came in the early 1920s, when voters rejected Kessler's plan to buy land for a park at the confluence of the Big Blue River and the Missouri River. As a result, the land reverted to industry, and an opportunity for a great park on the Missouri River was lost for decades. Later, during the tenure of notorious "Boss" Pendergast, the commission was powerless to stop the mayor from using his own cement company to channelize Brush Creek. However, with only three park commissioners making all the decisions, a hodgepodge of private trust-fund money used to maintain and renovate the fountains and sculptures, and a tradition of long-tenured directors (there were only five between 1904 and 1999), the department gradually settled into an insulated complacency and a lower level of communication with the public. While the average Kansas Citian believed that the department was well funded, most parks and boulevards were noticeably deteriorating from insufficient maintenance. The striking Liberty Memorial downtown even had to be closed to the public, although a major public/private renovation hopes to return it to its original splendor in 2001. In 1999, public concern finally reached the mayoral campaign, with Kay Barnes calling for a greater focus on park maintenance and a halt to any further land acquisition. After her election, Mayor Barnes followed up by enlarging the

Park Commission and appointing five new members to broaden its constituency and increase its accountability.

Barnes's "back-to-the-core-mission" approach marked the return of a pendulum first swung by previous Mayor Emmanuel Cleaver and Park Commission President Ollie Gates, who sought to promote Kansas City's development with high-profile projects, such as an upgraded zoo, a jazz district, and a stellar greenway along Brush Creek. Unfortunately, most of the projects had been too expensive to complete at that time, leading one observer to charge the city with providing "half a Cadillac rather than a whole Chevy."

The Brush Creek project, despite its underfunding, is generating some true excitement in Kansas City. Passing through Country Club Plaza—the world famous Spanish-styled neighborhood with a shopping center and residential areas created by visionary developer J. C. Nichols in the early 1900s—the project has added a key parkway to what had already been Kansas City's signature location. While the city's premier natural feature is the mighty Missouri River, minuscule Brush Creek, which under natural conditions would dry up for much of the year, can claim to be the city's leading park engine of development in the 1990s.

As with so many similar tales, the story of Brush Creek began with a tragedy—a flood that killed 25 in 1977 and caused more than $60 million in property damage. In response, the U.S. Army Corps of Engineers proposed straightening and deepening the creek channel, but the Parks, Recreation, and Boulevards Department opposed the ugly concrete culvert. After years of wrangling between opposing hydrologists (a debate that was resolved only by constructing a 400-foot-long hydraulic test model of the creek), the Corps of Engineers agreed to build a much more attractive (and expensive) alternative that enabled stream water to be recirculated (thus keeping the creek flowing during the dry season) but also provided numerous ponds, storage basins, and other flood-fighting mechanisms for times of heavy rain. The stunning result spurred $750 million of new commercial and residential development along the Brush Creek corridor in the 1990s alone. Even better, because Brush Creek flows from west to east and traverses the city's racial and economic dividing line of Troost Avenue, a broad-based, dynamic group of corporate and neighborhood leaders known as the Brush Creek Community Partners arose to use the greenway as a way to break down psychological as well as physical barriers that have plagued Kansas City for years.

The Brush Creek corridor is also the site of many of the memorable fountains that have come to define the city's image. Initially created from natural limestone springs for the prosaic purpose of quenching the thirst of both people and horses and later fostered by Nichols in his new development, fountain mania began in earnest after World War II. Today, not only does the park department own and tend scores of fountains, but there are also support groups for fountains, bronze sculpture restoration, and more. (To deal with the challenge of ongoing upkeep, the department tightened its contribution rules to require that any donor provide 25 percent above the cost of the fountain and its installation as a permanent endowment to pay for its maintenance.)

The Brush Creek effort, as with at least one new boulevard effort across the Missouri River in the northern part of the city, is funded partly through tax-increment financing, a mechanism for using expected future tax receipts to pay for current infrastructure needs like roads, bridges, trails, and greenery. This device channels investment—although some critics contend that, because urban development is a zero-sum game, tax-increment financing and other such devices merely put money into one neighborhood by taking it out of others.

A similar issue may be afflicting Kansas City's entire boulevard system, which is gaining in length but, ironically, losing its special quality as time goes on. The city keeps extending the network out to subdivisions farther from the center, but at the same time, many of Kessler's innovative touches are being eliminated. The new boulevards no longer follow the terrain, no longer sport double rows of trees, do not provide recreational space for residents, and do not include the attractive, informal landscaping that

A 1977 flood that killed 25 persons led the city and the U.S. Army Corps of Engineers to rebuild Brush Creek to provide both storage basins (for spring deluges) and recirculating water (for late summer droughts), turning the fluctuating stream into a year-round park-and-trail amenity for midtown Kansas City. Developers responded with $750 million of new commercial and residential construction along the Brush Creek corridor in the 1990s alone.

Kansas City, Missouri, Department of Parks, Recreation, and Boulevards

Address	4600 East 63rd Street
Zip Code	64130
Telephone	(816) 871-5600
Fax	(816) 361-5607
Web Site	www.kcmo.org
Agency Acreage in City	11,047
Acreage as Percent of City	5.5%
Acres per 1,000 Residents	25.0
Number of Regional Parks	3
Number of Neighborhood Parks	118
Number of Recreation Centers	12
Number of Pools	19
Number of Golf Courses	4
Number of Tennis Courts	107
Number of Sports Fields	138
Number of Marina Slips	0
Number of Beaches	0
Miles of Bikeways/Greenways	22
Number of Skating Rinks	1
Number of Full-Time Employees	720
Number of Seasonal Employees	200
Number of Volunteers	1,927

Adjusted Budget for Fiscal Year 1998–1999

Revenue

General Funds	$14,565,000
Dedicated Taxes	6,267,000
Fees Retained by the Agency	5,203,000
Private Grants and Donations	124,000
State and Federal Support	1,300,000
Capital Income	13,275,000
Total	$40,734,000

Expenditure

Grounds and Facilities Maintenance and Repair	$16,551,000
Recreational Programming and Activities	9,315,000
Capital Construction and Acquisition	14,868,000
Total	$40,734,000

Expenditure per Resident	$92

made Kessler's work so appealing. Because the standards for modern road construction are based purely on the needs of automobiles, the boulevards are becoming increasingly indistinguishable from other streets with medians. Moreover, with new boulevard mileage opening up all the time, the system may be too large for the citizenry to sustain, particularly in a metropolitan area that is growing more slowly than most. Each new boulevard may actually undermine the very values that were sought with the previous boulevard closer to the center of town. Chicago's lakefront, New York's Central Park perimeter, and San Francisco's hilltops are all finite resources, which ensures that they will continue to be deemed desirable. Kansas City's promise of ever more mileage of green boulevards may help bring about the regular deterioration of older sections. In contrast, Denver has largely stopped adding to its boulevard network, thus locking in the value of what it already has.

If Kansas City wishes to maintain great parks *and* to reinvigorate the center of the city, it will have to use core resources—the downtown Missouri River and its dramatic bluffs—as the focal connection of the park and boulevard system, instead of providing every new subdivision with an attractive roadway for commuting. With parks, as with everything else, if it is not special, it will not be treated as something special.

Conclusion

THIS BOOK HAS GIVEN urban Americans the stories and statistics to help them work toward excellent city park systems. The data may still be a far cry from the reams of statistics that are available about shopping centers, highways, or housing developments—or even national parks, which have been better documented for years—but they represent a start, a snapshot.

Why are park data necessary? Why can't we just enjoy what we have? The answer is: accountability.

With numbers, politicians can be held accountable, park professionals can develop meaningful standards, taxpayers can know where their money goes, and urban dwellers can tally the benefits they receive from their green spaces. Trends become clearly visible, changes can be predicted and planned for, and officials can better define parks' usership and audience. Ultimately, a strong factual and numerical base is a source of power— political power—something that has been woefully lacking in most city park departments.

Ann States

Once dangerous and shunned, Atlanta's Piedmont Park is being revived through a partnership between the Piedmont Park Conservancy and Atlanta's Department of Parks and Recreation. The $25 million effort involves fixing old structures, improving the environment, and developing the never-completed northern third of the park. Similar partnerships are restoring parks in Houston, Pittsburgh, San Francisco, St. Louis, and elsewhere.

Without numbers, analyses are merely guesses, plans are merely hopes, and visions are merely empty dreams.

Part of the difficulty of understanding what is happening to our parks stems from a terminology problem: many different physical spaces are lumped together under the rubric of "parks." These include play lots, landscaped median strips, bucolic walking grounds, ballfields, forests, beaches, downtown sitting squares, golf courses, traffic circles, community gardens, wetlands, lakes, lagoons, linear trails, and flood control impoundments. Different facilities have different constituencies and require vastly different levels of maintenance, staffing, and construction. For example, a small, heavily programmed downtown brick plaza might be used a thousand times more than a huge, undeveloped wetland on the edge of a town. A lavishly flowered median that serves only to beautify a commuting boulevard might cost more to maintain than an inner-city ballfield complex.

Many city officials claim that they lack the money or staff to compile statistics about parks, but the truth is that many also do not believe in the value of maintaining rigorous information or of keeping score. Many fail to recognize that statistics on land use and economic benefits can be powerful tools in the annual budget battle. Many do not appreciate that parks and open spaces provide a critical framework for every city that's growing, reshaping, and redeveloping itself. For years, those in the park and recreation fields have not considered their work important enough to *warrant* generating all those numbers; and, in a kind of vicious cycle, it has been hard to show that parks and recreation really *are* important without the statistics to back up the claim.

This situation is finally changing. With cities bouncing back, city parks are assuming their highest level of importance in decades. A new generation of park professionals is brokering all kinds of deals with the private sector; and corporations, foundations, public interest groups, sports leagues, and others are again starting to funnel some serious money into park systems. At the same time, with heightened awareness and interest, advocacy groups, neighborhood associations, and park conservancies are demanding more from their elected officials, including more information on how land is being used and how park department money is being spent.

Putting together an accurate picture of park systems in big cities will take years of data collection and analysis. Nevertheless, even at this early point, there are instructive lessons.

Lesson #1: There's Nothing More Important Than a Vision

If scorekeeping and statistics provide a city with a picture of what *is*, having a vision allows a city to guide its parks to what *can be*. Just as a great park is more than a collection of leafy trees or stylized benches, a great park system is more than a collection of beautiful parks. What ties it all together is a compelling vision that unifies many diverse elements into a theme. It's the theme that people can build upon and that a city can market. A few cities had the compelling vision from the very start, such as colonial Philadelphia's five-square layout by William Penn or Kansas City's park-and-parkway design by George Kessler. Some cities—Boston with its Emerald Necklace, for example, or Phoenix with its mountain preserves—arrived at a vision later in their evolution. Others, like Detroit and Los Angeles, are still struggling to find an agreed-upon theme amid a multitude of disjointed concepts.

The power of a vision cannot be overstated. It provides an overall plan for urban design, a predictable framework for investors, and recognizable goals and benefits to the citizenry at large. The earlier a city develops a vision for its parks and open spaces, the easier and less expensive it is to implement the plan, before land uses are set, buildings constructed, waterways altered, and opportunities lost. Because cities are always evolving and changing, however, it is never too late for a community to develop a vision for its parks. Conversely, visions cannot be considered permanent. Many cities have had a strong guiding vision and then lost it, with grave results for the park network. The best system is the one that is designed according to an early vision and then maintained through a process that regularly revisits and refreshes that vision, as has occurred with the excellent park systems in Minneapolis and Seattle.

Deciding on a vision is not the responsibility of one particular office or agency. Visions must be thoughtful and feasible and must strike a chord with the general public, but they can originate anywhere. Some visions are hatched by a mayor, some by a park director, some come from a Green Ribbon commission, some from a private citizens' group or business association. The 1920s idea of grassy automobile parkways along many of New York City's shorelines was the dream of a single powerful agency director, Robert Moses; the 1990s concept of a de-channelized, park-lined Los Angeles River is being nurtured and pursued by scores of environmental groups and thousands of individuals. Ultimately, a vision's strength is based on the fact that it is larger and more powerful than any one person or institution and that it resonates with the public at large.

The vision can do something else. It can provide an opportunity to attract investment, leadership, and commitment through a planning process.

Formerly unfit for human contact, Denver's South Platte River was the beneficiary of a magnificent community vision and is now the centerpiece of the South Platte River Greenway, perhaps the nation's most successful reclaimed urban streamside park. After 30 years of steady progress, the Greenway is attracting millions of dollars worth of development along its edges.

Greenway Foundation

Greenway Foundation

Lesson #2: Moving from a Vision to Reality Requires a Plan

Having a plan allows the park department to gain a constituency, develop a power base, and make the vision a reality. With a plan, the agency becomes an active player in the city's complex, swirling politics. Without a plan, the department is merely a pawn in other players' games. Life always has surprises, but with a printed plan that is grounded in community participation, good things are more likely to happen. Without one, the unexpected crises and outrages—or just plain delays—will outnumber the successes.

Developers, politicians, road builders, and others tend to treat open space—and sometimes even developed parks—as temporarily vacant land that is available for the taking rather than as a permanent, valuable ecological resource. Houston's Memorial Park, for example, a large, forested area near downtown, has been the subject of scores of proposals by developers, each of which requires a time-consuming response by the Memorial Park Advisory Board. The Parks and Recreation Department finally decided to formulate a written park plan notifying developers that Memorial Park is an official reserved park, not an overlooked woodland awaiting bulldozers.

A plan allows two things to happen. First, it enables agency staff and private park advocates to reach consensus on their collective goals and objectives. This process alone often has wondrous results, greatly broadening the agency's scope into areas like services for youth and seniors, tourism, neighborhood development, violence prevention, literacy, and much more—areas that link the park plan to broader city goals and programs. A plan also allows the combined park community to claim a seat at the table with the other shapers of the city—developers, highway builders, port officials, housing advocates, retail promoters—and to negotiate the implementation of the plan. Although many park officials feel that they have neither the staff nor the time to develop a plan and that they will always be at the mercy of the unpredictable, entrepreneurial moment, this is demonstrably not the case. Denver's Commons, Seattle's Discovery Park, San Diego's Los Peñasquitos Park, Pittsburgh's Point State Park, and many others all came about through planning (even if it took many years for some plans to reach fruition). Conversely, the failure to create the Seattle Commons and the obliteration of a corner of San Diego's Balboa Park by Interstate 5 were partially the result of the absence of an inviolable park plan and the constituency that backs it.

The building of new downtown sports stadiums is a good example of a challenge faced by city parks. More than half the cities profiled in this book are building or have recently opened a downtown sports arena, and several are building two. Has this taxpayer-financed ballfield frenzy brought any benefit in terms of public parkland? In most cities, the answer is no. In a few, the facilities are actually taking away parkland or what was expected to be future parkland. However, planners with the Cincinnati Park Board were able to take a negative—two new stadiums proposed for the Ohio riverfront—and convert it into a positive, by creating a new park between the structures and directly in front of the central business district. Because the city had a plan for waterfront parks, advocates of green space had the clout to negotiate when the stadium concept suddenly gained political momentum. In the best of circumstances, the planners would have gotten all the riverfront land for a park, but they got second best. The nearly $1 billion appropriated for the stadiums will give the agency a $65 million park for free.

A plan is more than a pro forma document listing general goals of acres per 1,000, or acres per neighborhood, or other platitudes. Flexible and reviewed annually, the plan should guide the department's actions. It must have specific goals, deadlines, and budgetary figures associated with every activity. It should be clear about the roles of all the partners in the process and should reflect the community's input and involvement. (The planning process for St. Louis's Forest Park was so comprehensive that it enabled government and citizen leaders to agree to split the park's renovation price tag of $86 million down the middle, half from the private sector and half from the public.) Ideally, the plan should be adopted not only by the department or the parks commission but also by higher authorities—the mayor and the city council—thus ensuring conformity and a reality check with all the city's other plans and priorities.

Why does planning seem to be accorded a higher priority in some other urban fields like transportation, housing, and water supply than in parks? One explanation may be the availability of substantial federal funding in these other fields. (In programs that receive dollars from Washington, D.C., money does not flow until the federal bureaucracy sees a plan.) Perhaps park planning would be given a boost if the federal government were to offer matching grants to the cities; and perhaps the creation of such a federal program would be spurred if cities could demonstrate to their congressional representatives the existence of compelling plans. (This reality was borne out during the heyday of the Land and Water Conservation Fund program, when every state had to produce a Comprehensive Outdoor Recreation Plan in order to qualify.)

Lesson #3: Nothing Happens Without Leadership

A compelling long-term vision and a tight plan are powerful, but they need a human dynamo, a leader, to bring them to fruition. The leader can come from the public sector or the private sector; can be elected, appointed, or self-appointed. In many cases, the leader will be a committed mayor, someone like Thomas Swann in Baltimore in the 1860s, Tom Johnson in Cleveland in the 1890s, Robert Speer in Denver in the 1910s, or Richardson Dilworth in Philadelphia in the 1950s. Today, the great park advances seen in Boston, Chicago, Denver, and Pittsburgh can be attributed to the leadership shown by, respectively, Mayors Tom Menino, Richard M. Daley, Wellington Webb, and Tom Murphy.

In other cases, the leader might be an extraordinary park commissioner like Robert Moses in New York in the 1930s and 1940s,

Even the most compelling vision and best plan need a leader to make them happen. In Pittsburgh, the leader is the mayor himself, Tom Murphy, who is also an enthusiastic user of the trail system that he is helping to create.

Melissa Farlow

Frank McLaren in San Francisco from the 1890s through the 1930s, or Horace Cleveland in Minneapolis at the end of the 19th century. In recent times, the fast-growing park system of Phoenix and the impressively rejuvenating system of New York have been shrewdly guided and led by Jim Colley and Henry Stern, respectively.

Alternatively, the leadership can come from the private sector, as was demonstrated by business magnates John D. Rockefeller in Cleveland in the 1890s or A. Montgomery Ward in Chicago in the 1920s, by philanthropist George Hermann in Houston in the 1900s, or by newspaper publisher William Rockhill Nelson in Kansas City beginning in the 1880s. In today's world, the best private leadership often comes from a staffed membership group with a citywide mandate, like Chicago's Friends of the Parks, New York's Parks Council, or Seattle's Associated Recreation Councils. The next best source is often an umbrella organization that unifies many different advocacy groups for individual parks, like Friends of Philadelphia Parks or the Boston GreenSpace Alliance. Third best is a well-funded, staffed entity devoted entirely to a single park, such as Houston's Friends of Hermann Park or Atlanta's Piedmont Park Conservancy (or devoted to a concept, like Kansas City's Friends of Fountains). There is widespread agreement that New York's Central Park would never have been turned around without the leadership of Betsy Barlow Rogers and her remarkable creation, the Central Park Conservancy. Finally, in some cases, leadership can come from a philanthropic organization. Atlanta's Woodruff Foundation, Philadelphia's William Penn Foundation, St. Louis's Danforth Foundation, and Houston's Park Board (which sounds like a governing agency but actually operates like a foundation) have all recently played key leadership roles when other agencies might have failed to move to the forefront.

Effective leadership is so powerful that it can sometimes even turn a crisis into a solution. In Pittsburgh, after a slide collapsed and killed a young child, the brand new mayor, Tom Murphy, mobilized public outrage to support his commitment to spend $20 million to fix all the city's deteriorating playgrounds. In San Francisco, a huge arson fire in Golden Gate Park gave park advocates the opportunity to demand the removal of large encampments of often mentally unstable homeless persons from the world famous preserve. In Chicago, when a series of scathing *Sun-Times* exposés and editorials appeared about the malfeasance and incompetence of the Park District, park advocate leaders initiated a campaign that prompted the mayor to undertake a wholesale overhaul. Although other cities have experienced playground deaths, park fires, and newspaper crusades, most of these events have caused barely a ripple, because of the absence of a leader to convert the tragedies into blessings.

Lesson #4: Parks Have True Value That Can Be Measured in Dollars and Cents

Americans can be so indoctrinated by market economics that, for many of them, if something does not cost anything, it has little value. Because municipal parks have been mostly used for free, this attitude has subtly undermined the political movement to build and defend green space. In reality, urban parks have tremendous value—hard economic value—and cities that recognize the fact do better than those that do not.

Kansas City, Missouri, Department of Parks, Recreation, and Boulevards

Kansas City's parkway and boulevard system was originally conceived in the 1910s to add value to the city, and the success of the concept continues today. Residents facing such thoroughfares as Ward Parkway (pictured here) pay a yearly frontage fee to help cover the costs of maintenance; their reward is higher property appraisals.

Although the fiscal benefits generally do not show up at a turnstile or ticket booth, they are reflected in real estate value (such as in communities near Chicago's lakefront, Kansas City's boulevards, Houston's Memorial Park, and Atlanta's Piedmont Park), in associated retail and restaurant value (such as in neighborhoods surrounding New York's Bryant Park, Philadelphia's Rittenhouse Square, Boston's Common, and San Francisco's Union Square), and in tourism value (such as from cultural institutions and hotels at San Diego's Balboa and Mission Bay Parks and New York's Central Park). The calculations certainly total in the hundreds of millions or billions of dollars, even though the hard economic facts are inadequately documented, as is almost everything else involving city parks.

Interestingly, the economics may have been better recognized and understood at the beginning of the park building movement than they are today. In 1873, Frederick Law Olmsted demonstrated that the wards surrounding Central Park had increased in value so much that New York was receiving $4.4 million in excess property taxes alone. Similar calculations were used to convince the denizens of Denver, Kansas City, Minneapolis, and elsewhere that spending money on parks and boulevards would be fiscally advantageous. This message, lost for decades, is being heard again. Fiscal computations led to the creation of Post Office Square in Boston (paid for by profits from the parking garage under it), Denver Commons and Atlanta's Centennial Olympic Park (both of which are spurring development booms in neglected parts of downtown), and the Mississippi River Park on Minneapolis's Upper Harbor (part of the reestablishment of housing and seven-day-a-week retail near the center of the city). The benefits to tourism were perhaps less obvious in Olmsted's day, but they have risen to the forefront, as modern Americans travel and eat out more often and have more disposable income. Compelling parkside venues become attractive places to be, to be seen, to meet—and to spend money.

That's not all. For most of the past century, it was assumed that park and recreation departments should offer their services free or for the lowest possible price. After all, according to this logic, because everyone already pays for parks through taxes, it would be unreasonable to charge users twice. But in the 1980s, advocates of market economics began to question the axiom that free is better, even if free means lower quality. Noting the rapid increase in private health clubs, they pointed out that approximately 80 percent of city park users can afford to pay competitive rates for recreation facilities, so why not charge them a realistic price, arrange a subsidy for needy persons, and use the revenues to produce a higher-quality program and product?

Thus far, market pricing has gained greater acceptance in suburban park systems than in cities, but the philosophical impact of the concept has been undeniable. Most cities have revisited their fee structures to make sure that, at the very least, users are picking up all the costs of a program. The most price-aggressive agencies, like those in Portland and San Diego, have revamped their fee structures to take into account every expense, including electric bills arising from night ball games, the cost of security personnel at private park functions, and even the administrative cost of processing activity applications.

In lieu of a ledger sheet, park supporters in many cities fall back on the generalized claim that green space has an "incalculable" intrinsic value. In contrast, the New York City Department of Parks and Recreation decided to put a quantifiable number on the value. When the food concession in front of the Metropolitan Museum of Art in Central Park was opened to competitive bidding, the annual fee came to a staggering $200,000 for a single pushcart. Another company paid $730,000 a year for the exclusive privilege of selling T-shirts in Battery Park. And the U.S. Tennis Association paid $1.2 million to operate the National Tennis Center in Forest Hills. The city informed advertisers and promoters, who had routinely run roughshod over the park with photo shoots, concerts, and other events, that they would now have to pay for the privilege. In 1995, when the Walt Disney Company wanted to launch the movie *Pocahontas* with a splash, the department allowed the use of Central Park at a cost of $1 million. When BMW and United Artists wanted to unveil a new "James Bond" car in the park, they had to pay $600,000 and also donate a BMW for a park department raffle. When a dinner theater company erected a tent in a public park and put on private performances, it paid $160,000 and also undertook $20,000 worth of work on fences and shrubs in the park. Finally, in return for sponsoring the citywide chess tournament in a park, Simon and Schuster paid for chess instruction in all the recreation centers.

The commercialization of parks is a controversial issue and potentially a slippery slope. The practice has done a world of good for some parks but has led to some glaring inequities in others. Every city should have a citizen watchdog group (like the Neighborhood Open Space Coalition in New York) that constantly monitors the relationship between private and public interests in urban parks.

Park value does not need to be measured only by cash registers, however. In Philadelphia, Phoenix, Portland, and other cities, the recreation departments attempt to quantify the value they bring to the city and the general populace in such areas as crime reduction,

ParkWorks Cleveland

Students at Cleveland's George Washington Carver Elementary School hail ParkWorks Cleveland and area contributors at the first completed School Grounds as Community Parks project. The city's partnership with ParkWorks mirrors the increased public/private collaboration going on in city parks throughout the country.

youth skill improvement, and development of self-esteem through activities like sports leagues, midnight basketball, after-school programs, vocational training, activities for persons with disabilities, and more. Philadelphia's former mayor, Ed Rendell, thought so highly of his recreation department's rapport with young people that he turned over the city's gun-violence prevention program to that agency rather than to the police.

Lesson #5: To Find a Great Park Department, Look for an Entrepreneurial Attitude

For most of the 20th century, it was a given that, because they were government entities, park agencies should handle all their responsibilities internally. Thus, as park responsibilities grew, so did the size and scope of departmental operations. Ultimately, many park directors found themselves managing complicated empires that included everything from vehicle maintenance to golf marketing, to construction of boat marinas, to seniors' lunch programs, to land appraisal, to stadium food services, to trash removal from vacant lots— not to mention the more typical tree, horticulture, playground, and recreation responsibilities. For many agencies, it proved to be too much. Internal costs spiraled while productivity declined.

Around 1980, a few cities began experimenting with outsourcing some of the services previously handled by the government—soliciting private-sector companies to take over specific, clearly defined tasks for the agency. The movement began in Indianapolis and in several newer, less-unionized cities in the Southwest. It got a major shot in the arm when New York successfully outsourced its golf operations and Chicago privatized almost all of its multimillion-dollar nonpark operations—including parking under Grant Park, the marinas

Rick Friedman, Trust for Public Land

"Going tubing" takes on a different meaning on Cleanup Day on Boston's Neponset River. No park agency can handle all its cleanup needs using only paid staff; the best have aggressive volunteer programs that attract enthusiastic residents.

on Lake Michigan, the golf program, the Soldier Field football stadium, and vehicle maintenance. The Chicago experiment, part of Mayor Richard M. Daley's monumental housecleaning of the Park District, was credited with reviving an agency that had functioned poorly for decades.

Along with market pricing, privatization has provided a fundamental challenge to the way park and recreation departments have done business. Supporters praise the movement for increasing agency efficiency, eliminating unproductive jobs and employees, and improving services to the public. Critics charge that private companies are not really more efficient but win contracts only because they pay lower wages to their workers, give them fewer benefits, and lay them off at will. Many cities with strong unions have resisted the new policies, but all are aware that they can no longer operate in total disregard of the private marketplace's norms of prices, standards, and levels of efficiency. On the whole, reasonable outsourcing has been good for parks, because it forces agencies to figure out what is important, what they are good at, and what is better farmed out to others. Perhaps most indicative of the change in attitudes have been the cases when an agency throws open a particular task to a public bidding process and one of its own departments tightens its operation, then bids on and wins the contract.

Agency entrepreneurialism can take other forms as well. Most exciting is the broad range of public/private partnerships that have sprung up all over the country. Private organizations of every imaginable stripe have locked arms with governments to raise money, plant trees, bring in volunteers, organize cleanups, design advertising and publicity campaigns, change counterproductive uses of open spaces, design or build playgrounds, operate recreation programs, and more. In Indianapolis the partners include community churches; in Detroit, the Pistons basketball team; in San Francisco, the foundation community; in Dallas, the Trammell Crow Company; in Baltimore, the Trust for Public Land and the Parks and People Foundation; in Portland, the Nike Corporation; and in Philadelphia, the Pennsylvania Horticultural Society. The opportunities are endless, and the outcomes seem to almost uniformly exceed the sum of what has been put in; this was most dramatically demonstrated in New York, where partnerships with both the Central Park Conservancy and the Bryant Park Restoration Corporation resulted in turnabouts in parks that had been almost completely dysfunctional.

Every form of entrepreneurialism entails risks, none is free from controversy, and some have failed outright. The greatest challenge is to make sure that the needs of the parks and of the public remain paramount over the needs of special or wealthier groups. Nevertheless, the net benefit has proven so great that many cities have entered into partnerships or are actively considering them.

Lesson #6: To Find a Great Park System, Look for a Commitment to Improvement

One of the most erroneous myths about America's center cities is that they are "all built up" and do not have room for any more parkland. That would be true only if city parks were patches of untouched wilderness. But they're not. Parks are physically created just like every other structure in the city. In fact, if a city has room for one more building or one more auto storage lot, it has room for one more park. For this reason, among the older cities, the ones that are undergoing the greatest amount of redevelopment and reconstruction are the ones that are adding some of the largest amounts of parkland; among them are Chicago, Denver, New York, and Seattle. Even Baltimore and Cincinnati, whose rates of redevelopment are more modest, have picked up, respectively, 707 and 884 acres of parkland since 1970, increasing the size of their systems by 16 and 23 percent. The argument does not need to go further than New York, by far the most densely developed city in the country. The city has been steadily greening its shoreline and adding to its stock of community gardens, downtown plazas, and even forests and wetlands, as industry, government, and housing developers continually sell, buy, abandon, and rebuild properties throughout the city.

No city in the United States is "all built up." Even crowded Chicago has thousands of opportunities for creating parks and community gardens on underused or misused sites, many of which are already publicly owned.

Another myth is that park creation is entirely at the mercy of economic cycles. If the naysayers were correct, parks would *never* be developed, because the skeptics claim that economic booms make land too expensive and economic recessions dry up government coffers. In truth, neither of those factors need interfere with the task at hand. With the right leadership, economic depressions provide a good opportunity to acquire land (often through donation, tax default, or below-cost purchase), and expansions are a good time to develop the land into parks (often with the assistance of profitable corporations or well-heeled foundations).

The record demonstrates this point. The land for Central Park was acquired right after the Panic of 1857, and the nation's first period of widespread creation of city parks took place in the aftermath of the Panic of 1893, the worst American depression up to that time. It was following that panic that Griffith Park was donated to Los Angeles, Swope Park was given to Kansas City, Riverview Park was purchased by Pittsburgh (for $5), and much of

It is not true that city parks can be created only during economic boom times. The land for Swope Park in Kansas City, pictured here, was donated to the city following the Panic of 1893. Other major parks donated or acquired inexpensively after economic downturns include Griffith Park in Los Angeles, Riverview Park in Pittsburgh, and much of the Boston and Cleveland park systems.

Kansas City, Missouri, Department of Parks, Recreation, and Boulevards

the Boston and Cleveland systems were acquired. Forty years later, the Great Depression ushered in perhaps the crowning years of city parks in the United States. Because of the Works Progress Administration and the Civilian Conservation Corps, city officials in Chicago, Denver, Los Angeles, New York, Pittsburgh, and most other cities amassed large, no-cost teams of architects, designers, draftspersons, and stonemasons, plus vast armies of laborers. The efforts brought the cities' park systems up to a standard of construction, usability, cleanliness, and beauty unparalleled before or since. During the severe economic downturn of the late 1980s and early 1990s, many cities again increased their stock of tax-defaulted properties. Although few were turned into parks at the time, virtually every city currently has hundreds or thousands of acres of publicly owned vacant land awaiting the formulation of some kind of plan that could combine parks with other types of uses.

Conversely, many new city parks originated during strong economic times, most recently during the booms of the early 1980s and late 1990s. Developers were often eager to close deals, lots of cash was available and in circulation, and time was often more important than money. Moreover, throwing a gift of some parkland into the negotiation mix could sometimes grease the skids of government bureaucracy or sway public sentiment in favor of a controversial plan. Sesquicentennial Park in Houston, Lykes Gaslight Square in Tampa, the Bunker Hill Steps in Los Angeles, Pioneer Courthouse Square in Portland, Pioneer Plaza in Dallas, and Post Office Square in Boston are all small but critically important downtown open spaces that could have been created only during economic boom times.

The underlying message is continuous improvement. Continuous improvement does not mean hoping for the best, it means looking for opportunities. It means communication, advocacy, and hard work. Just as a canoe cannot be maneuvered through roiling rapids unless it is paddled faster than the speed of the current itself, so too must the park agency—and its private-sector park supporters—operate more dynamically than other city-shaping forces. By keeping their eyes on the prize—higher-quality, better-distributed parkland and open space in the city—supporters can continue to make unexpected and wonderful things happen, often by cooperating with other city agencies responsible for planning, community development, economic development, education, public works, or crime prevention. A commitment to continuous improvement does not mean that all decisions will fall into place easily; there are numerous tough issues that need to be resolved. Continuous improvement does mean, however, that new ideas and approaches will always be considered.

One tough issue for city parks involves cars. Most big cities have one or more large parks that are crisscrossed by roadways. The average American may equate cars with vitality, but the record shows that unimpeded automobile access exerts a deadening effect on parks by reducing other uses and promoting the proliferation of parking spaces. Conversely, banning or restricting cars can restore life to ailing parks. This lesson was most dramatically shown in New York, where strict auto restrictions in Central Park and Prospect Park coincided with the beginning of the upturn in both parks' fortunes. A few years later, in the mid-1970s, even tighter rules were set for Atlanta's Piedmont Park. Although Atlanta is much more auto-oriented than Manhattan (in fact, Atlanta did not even have a subway at the time), the experiment yielded similar results and has remained in effect for a quarter-century. Other significant parks that have benefited from auto bans or restrictions include Washington Park in Denver, Forest Park in Portland, Patterson Park in Baltimore, Seward Park in Seattle, and, on a limited basis, Griffith Park in Los Angeles (the rugged central portion of the park only) and Golden Gate Park in San Francisco (one road on Sundays only).

Although cleaner park air and water, less noise, and fewer injured animals are all advantages, the primary beneficiaries of bans on automobiles in parks are pedestrians, bicyclists, skaters, runners, and skiers. The dramatic 30-year rise of these sports in cities has paralleled the growth in the availability of trail and park roadway opportunities. In particular, bicycle advocacy organizations in Chicago; Denver; New York; Philadelphia; Seattle; Washington, D.C.; and elsewhere have moved to the forefront of campaigns to reduce the domination of parks by automobiles.

Despite the successes, the debate about the suitability of cars in city parks is still raging, particularly where prominent, pastoral central parks also house zoos, museums, theaters, and other cultural attractions. The disputes in Golden Gate Park in San Francisco, Forest Park in St. Louis, Balboa Park in San Diego, and Hermann Park in Houston are leading to agonizing appraisals of what is really important in cities and how multiple objectives can be achieved in limited, precious space.

The other, even thornier question is "Who are city parks being fixed up for?" If most of the residents surrounding a park are homeowners, then the local community usually throws itself into a renovation project with gusto. Such has been the case in scores of relatively affluent locations like Central Park and Riverside Park in New York, Washington Park in Denver, Piedmont Park in Atlanta, Commonwealth Avenue in Boston, the Chain of Lakes in Minneapolis, and Buffalo Bayou in Houston. If, however, most of the residents near a run-down park are lower-income renters, it is a different story. The residents may worry that a beautified park could raise property values and thus displace them through higher rents or turnover of property. If so, they may be highly conflicted by any pro-park campaign. Although it is not often articulated clearly or understood, this mixed commitment may be hampering park improvement efforts in many inner-city communities—particularly in rebounding cities with escalating housing prices, such as Boston, Chicago, Cincinnati, and San Francisco.

Consequently, it is imperative for park advocates to try to build bridges with housing providers, particularly those working in favor of homeownership rather than simply home rental. Homeowners of all economic levels gain from safe and attractive community parks; renters gain in the short term but may lose in the long term. Alternatively, by providing more housing near parks—thereby increasing density around the edge—it may be possible to use the law of supply and demand to hold down rent increases (and also get greater public value from the green space). Finally, it may be possible to institute some kind of rent protection for existing tenants in gentrifying neighborhoods in order to ensure that all residents will work collaboratively for the improvement of the neighborhood and its parks.

CITY PARKS are much more than meets the eye. Intricate urban organisms that take every bit as much thought and care as other municipal amenities, they are deeply entwined with such other municipal responsibilities as traffic flow, zoning, watershed protection, policing, festival promotion, trash pickup, and disposition of surplus property. Seemingly permanent, city parks actually change quite dramatically along with their neighborhoods.

Even though it may seem that city parks have been with us from time immemorial, the modern city park is really only a 150-year-old development, younger even than railroads, which date back to merely the presidency of Abraham Lincoln. It is this time scale, perhaps, that offers the greatest hope. We are only beginning to understand city parks and park systems. The facts and figures in this book are intended to help move that educational process forward, but much more remains to be learned.